BEA WebLogic Server™ 8 For Dummies®

W9-AZF-031

Common File Extensions

Extension	What It Is
.class	A CLASS file contains the output from compiling a JAVA file. CLASS files are often placed in JAR files.
.cmd/.bat	A Windows script file. Script files are discussed throughout the book.
.ear	An enterprise archive (EAR) file contains an enterprise web application. See Chapter 8 for more information on enterprise applications.
.html/.htm	A Hypertext Markup Language (HTML) file contains commands to define the display of a web page. See Chapter 5.
.jar	A Java Archive (JAR) file contains class files, which make up a Java program or modules. A JAR file can contain nearly any Java class but often contains EJBs. See Chapter 6 for more information on EJB.
.java	A Java file contains Java source code that will be compiled into a .class file.
.jsp	A Java Server Page (JSP) file contains Java code and HTML to be used to create a web page. See Chapter 5.
.sh	A shell (SH) file is one form of a UNIX script file. UNIX script files are often used instead of .cmd files.
.war	A web archive (WAR) file contains a web application. See Chapter 5.
.xml	An eXtensible Markup Language (XML) file in WebLogic contains configuration information.

Important WebLogic Configuration Files

Configuration File	What It Holds
web.xml	Configuration information for your web application. See Chapter 5.
application.xml	Configuration information for an enterprise application. See Chapter 8.
ejb-jar.xml	J2EE configuration information for an EJB. See Chapter 8.
weblogic-ejb-jar.xml	WebLogic-specific information for an EJB. See Chapter 6.
weblogic-cmp-rdbms-jar.xml	Database relationships for an entity EJB. See Chapter 7.
weblogic-jws-config.xml	Configuration information for web services. See Part III.

EJB Types

Type	What It Does
CMP entity bean	Accesses data. CMP entity beans use their container to manage this data access. See Chapter 7.
BMP entity bean	Accesses data. BMP entity beans use the bean to manage this data access. See Chapter 7.
Stateless session bean	A bean that makes methods available to the container. See Chapter 6.
Stateful session bean	Performs the operations of a session bean and also holds information about the current user. See Chapter 6.
Message-driven bean	Communicates using Java Message Service (JMS). See Chapter 15.

For Dummies: Bestselling Book Series for Beginners

BEA WebLogic Server™ 8 For Dummies®

Cheat Sheet

Commonly Used WebLogic Programs

Component	What It Does
Node Manager	Manages servers that make up a cluster. Node Manager is made up of several commands located in the WebLogic `bin` directory.
Domain Configuration Wizard	Sets up a domain. You must have a domain to add other WebLogic components. You can access the wizard from the WebLogic folder in the Start menu.
Administration Console	Configures your WebLogic server. You can access Administration Console from `http://localhost:7001/console`.
Resource Workshop	A GUI program that can be used to quickly create web services and EJBs. You can start Resource Workshop from the WebLogic folder under the Start menu.
Ant	Runs build scripts, usually named build.xml, provided with WebLogic. Ant is in the WebLogic `bin` directory and can be accessed by typing `ant` from the command line.
Install	Installs WebLogic. The installation program is in the root of your WebLogic CD-ROM or downloaded file.

Database Vendor Support Sites

Vendor	URL
Oracle	`http://www.oracle.com`
IBM DB2	`http://www.ibm.com/software/data/db2/`
MySQL	`http://www.mysql.org`
Microsoft SQL Server	`http://www.microsoft.com/sql`
Postgre	`http://www.postgresql.org`
Informix	`http://www.informix.com`

Useful Internet URLs

Site	URL
WebLogic Documentation	`http://www.weblogic.com`
BEA Software	`http://www.bea.com`
Java	`http://java.sun.com`
BEA Developer to Developer	`http://dev2dev.bea.com`

For Dummies: Bestselling Book Series for Beginners

BEA WebLogic
Server™ 8
FOR
DUMMIES®

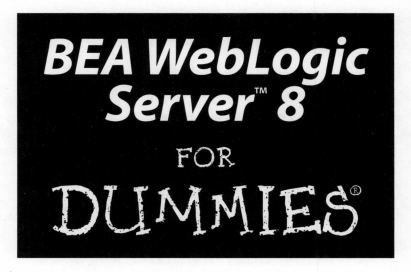

BEA WebLogic Server™ 8

FOR DUMMIES®

by Jeff Heaton

WILEY

Wiley Publishing, Inc.

BEA WebLogic Server™ 8 For Dummies®

Published by
Wiley Publishing, Inc.
909 Third Avenue
New York, NY 10022
www.wiley.com

About the Author

Jeff Heaton is the author of four books and more than two dozen articles, a college instructor, and a consultant. He teaches introductory and advanced Java at St. Louis Community College at Meramec. His specialty is in Internet, socket-level/spidering, and artificial intelligence programming. Many examples and tutorials can be found at his web site at http://www.jeffheaton.com. Jeff is a Sun Certified Java Programmer, a member of the IEEE, and holds a master's degree in Information Management from Washington University in St. Louis.

Dedication

This book is dedicated to my mother, Mary Heaton, for always supporting me in everything I do. I love you very much and am very grateful for all you have done for me over the years.

Author's Acknowledgments

There are many people who were helpful in the creation of this book.

I owe a great deal to Susan Pink for all her hard work editing this book and making sure that my ideas stayed on track and were easy to follow. I would also like to thank Allen Wyatt for helping construct the flow of many of the chapters in this book and adding additional material. Will Iverson did a great job as technical editor, making sure everything was just right and suggesting additional material as needed.

Everyone at Wiley was easy to work with, and I appreciate your support. I would like to thank Melody Layne for working out the initial details of this book and making it a reality. Melody was also helpful in getting information about version 8.1 of WebLogic.

Finally, I would like to thank everyone at the Studio B agency for helping with this and other book projects of mine. In particular, thanks to Laura Lewin for all your help and being my agent on this book.

Publisher's Acknowledgments

We're proud of this book; please send us your comments through our online registration form located at www.dummies.com/register/.

Some of the people who helped bring this book to market include the following:

Acquisitions, Editorial, and Media Development

Project Editor: Susan Pink

Acquisitions Editor: Melody Layne

Technical Development: Allen Wyatt, Discovery Computing Inc.

Technical Editor: Will Iverson

Editorial Manager: Carol Sheehan

Media Development Supervisor: Richard Graves

Editorial Assistant: Amanda Foxworth

Cartoons: Rich Tennant (www.the5thwave.com)

Production

Project Coordinator: Nancee Reeves

Layout and Graphics: Seth Conley, Kelly Emkow, Carrie Foster, Lauren Goddard, Tiffany Muth

Special Art:

Proofreaders: David Faust, Andy Hollandbeck, Angel Perez, Carl William Pierce, Charles Spencer, Brian Walls, TECHBOOKS Production Services

Indexer: TECHBOOKS Production Services

Special Help: Laura Bowman

Publishing and Editorial for Technology Dummies

Richard Swadley, Vice President and Executive Group Publisher

Andy Cummings, Vice President and Publisher

Mary C. Corder, Editorial Director

Publishing for Consumer Dummies

Diane Graves Steele, Vice President and Publisher

Joyce Pepple, Acquisitions Director

Composition Services

Gerry Fahey, Vice President of Production Services

Debbie Stailey, Director of Composition Services

Contents at a Glance

Table of Contents

Introduction

● ●

Welcome to *BEA WebLogic Server 8 For Dummies*. Whether you are an administrator, a developer, a manager, or all of the above, you will find something in this book to make your job easier.

WebLogic is the most widely used application server on the market today. You can use WebLogic in large or small projects and to develop both traditional client-server as well as web-based applications.

About This Book

This book gives you a broad understanding of BEA WebLogic Server. The main audience consists of developers and administrators, but anyone involved in a WebLogic project will benefit from reading this book. Managers can gain an overview of the components that make up their system. Quality assurance personnel can benefit from the same understanding.

For developers, this book shows quick examples to get you up and running in many of the technologies supported by WebLogic. Rather than give you extensive application examples, I focus on short, easy-to-follow examples than can become the starting point for something more complex. For administrators, I step you through many common WebLogic tasks and the configuration settings you should use.

Finally, everyone should have an understanding of how the components of a web application fit together and what WebLogic can do for your application. This book gives you that viewpoint too.

Conventions Used in This Book

Throughout this book, several typefaces are used. Here's a brief explanation:

- ✔ When an important term is introduced, it appears in *italics*.
- ✔ All URLs in the book appear in `computer font`. For example:

  `www.bea.com`

✔ The code examples appear in `computer font` as well. For instance:

```
int i=0;
```

✔ And when a variable or command appears in the text, it's in `computer font` too. For example: "The `JAVA_OPTIONS` variable allows you to pass additional parameters to the Java virtual machine."

✔ Directories appear in `computer font`. You'll see something like this: "You should switch to the `weblogic\bin` directory."

✔ Sometimes, you'll see *italic computer font*, such as

```
c:\weblogic\bin> install -name yourWebLogicServer
```

This means you should type everything as written, except you should replace *yourWebLogicServer* with — you guessed it — the name of your server.

✔ When you should choose menu options, each option is separated by an arrow, like this: Start⇨All Programs⇨Accessories⇨Command Prompt.

✔ Code listings contain complete Java source files or configuration files. A code listing always has a title, such as "Listing 1-1: Count to Ten."

✔ Code snippets are small sections of source code that do not make up a complete source file on their own.

What You Don't Have to Read

For Dummies books are designed so that you can read any chapter you like, in any order you want. This makes it easier to skip chapters that contain information you're already familiar with or simply don't need. In addition, if you

✔ Already have a WebLogic server up and running, you can skip Part I.

✔ Are familiar with EJB development or aren't planning to use EJBs, you can skip Part II.

✔ Are not using web services, you can skip Part III.

✔ Are developing a non-web application, you can skip Part IV.

✔ Are just starting out with WebLogic, don't concern yourself too much with clustering, security, and performance tuning. These Part V topics might be useful later, though.

✔ Just want to get started with WebLogic, Part VI (which contains many suggestions for using WebLogic) is not essential reading.

Foolish Assumptions

You should have at least a passing knowledge of the Java programming language, but you don't need to be an expert in Java. You should be familiar with the following concepts:

- ✔ Entering Java programs
- ✔ Compiling and executing Java programs
- ✔ Using classes, methods, and variables

You should also have a basic familiarity with the Internet, including the use of web browsers and downloading software from web sites.

You should also have some knowledge of SQL to understand how WebLogic accesses external data, which is stored in databases. It is not necessary for you to be an SQL expert, but you should be familiar with basic SELECT, INSERT, UPDATE, and DELETE statements.

How This Book Is Organized

BEA WebLogic Server 8 For Dummies has six parts. As you proceed through the book, each part increases in complexity. Each chapter covers a specific topic and provides code examples, explanations, and sample projects for you to complete. As you complete each chapter, you will have completed one or more projects that demonstrate the main ideas discussed in that chapter.

Part I: Installing and Configuring WebLogic

I begin by showing you how to install WebLogic. If you need no special options, installing WebLogic can be as easy as installing any other Windows application. If your installation has special needs, it can be a bit trickier. I show you a standard installation and describe the details of a more complex installation. After you find out how to install WebLogic, you discover how to customize it to meet your needs.

Part II: Understanding WebLogic Components

Creating web applications is perhaps the most common use for WebLogic. In Part II, you find out about some of the components that make up a web application. One of the primary components is Enterprise JavaBeans (EJB). I show you how to construct various types of EJBs and describe their differences.

Part III: Employing Web Services

Web services work much like any Java object that contains a set of reusable methods. The main difference is that a web service allows other programs to call these methods through the Internet. Web services are usually accessed using the simple object access protocol (SOAP), which means different systems can communicate. An object hosted on a Windows computer could be accessed by a Macintosh, for example. In this part, you create a web service using WebLogic. You also find out how to access your own web services and those provided by third parties.

Part IV: The Forgotten Services

A number of services run behind the scenes, so they're not noticed in a typical web application. These services take care of binding the entire application together and providing access to the underlying databases. For example, Java Database Connectivity (JDBC) allows your web application to access databases, Java Message Service (JMS) allows programs to exchange messages, and Java Naming and Directory Interface (JNDI) allows named resources to be located. In Part IV, you discover the ins and outs of all these "behind the scenes" services.

Part V: Big-Time, Heavy-Duty Server Configuration

After you develop your application and test it, you're ready for the big time. Part V shows you some of the more advanced configuration options available in WebLogic. For example, clustering allows you to use many different server computers as one large virtual server. A virtual server can be much more reliable and can process information faster than a single server. You also find out about different security issues and how to resolve them.

Part VI: The Part of Tens

In Part VI, you find out about ten best practices that are a result of my experience with WebLogic and web development in general. I also provide tips for administrators and general tips to heed before going live.

Icons Used in This Book

This icon signals a tip that I think you might find useful. These tips are provided to jumpstart your knowledge of WebLogic and save you from having to go through a lot of trial and error.

This icon lets you know that the information you're about to read is something that's often overlooked but should be remembered. For example, when you're setting a configuration option, doing so may have an unintended side effect. The remember icon will alert you to this.

Technical stuff is important, and you may find it interesting. But understanding something flagged with this icon is not necessary to accomplishing a job.

This icon means what it says. Pay attention to the common pitfalls or errors described. These warnings are issues that I have run into myself. By heeding these warnings, you can save yourself the time that I spent learning these issues.

Where to Go from Here

This book will give you a solid introduction to WebLogic. This will definitely get you up and running with a web application. However, entire books are dedicated to many of the topics that are covered here in a single chapter. In particular, you may want to check out books on some of these topics: EJB, JSP, JSTL, JMS, JDBC, and Java. You can find a lot of information about WebLogic on the web. Visit the WebLogic documentation site at http://e-docs.bea.com and the Sun site at http://java.sun.com.

Part I

Installing and Configuring WebLogic

The 5th Wave   By Rich Tennant

"One of the things you want to do before installing WebLogic Server, is fog the users to keep them calm during the procedure."

In this part . . .

Y ou begin by finding out exactly what an application server is. You look at the major components of an application server and how WebLogic implements them.

Installation is the first step in setting up your WebLogic-based application. You find out how to install WebLogic on a single machine. Then you look at installing WebLogic on many machines using a script. You also discover a variety of ways to start WebLogic Server.

Configuration is an important and ongoing part of setting up WebLogic Server. You need to configure WebLogic to initially set up your web application. Later, you need to monitor and adapt your server's configuration to the changing needs of your users. All these topics are covered in this part.

Chapter 1

Introducing Application Servers

● ●

In This Chapter

▶ Understanding the role of application servers

▶ Meeting the J2EE family of technologies

▶ Outlining the major features of WebLogic

● ●

*I*n the most general sense, a *server* is a program that provides information to a client that requests that information. Sometimes a server is a computer used to centralize resources so that they can be shared by a number of different users. For instance, file servers centralize file storage, database servers centralize data storage, and web servers centralize the distribution of web content. In a similar vein, an application server centralizes key programming tasks. Doing so has many advantages, as you will discover.

In this chapter, you find out about application servers, in particular BEA's WebLogic Server. In a recent Gartner study, BEA WebLogic Server had 34 percent of the application server market share — the largest market share of any single vendor. BEA Systems is at the forefront of market developments and support of new standards.

WebLogic is not the only application server on the market. WebLogic's main competitors are IBM's WebSphere and JBoss, an open-source application server released under the LGPL license. In addition to these two Java-based application servers, WebLogic faces non-Java competition, mainly from the growing Microsoft .NET family of products.

Application Server Basics

Enterprise JavaBeans (EJB) is a technology for developing, assembling, deploying, and managing distributed applications in an enterprise environment. This basically means that EJB provides a Java framework for executing objects residing on different machines over a distributed network. This is a powerful capability: It enables a user to harness the power of different machines transparently, in a single application.

A machine hosting and executing an EJB object is called an *EJB application server*. WebLogic, as an EJB application server, also acts as a container for EJBs. A *container* provides a management system for EJB objects. An efficient container removes the need for users and developers (to a certain extent) to be concerned about exactly how an object will be used. Put another way, an EJB application server provides APIs and interfaces, and an EJB is like a plug-in that provides business logic for a specific application. As a developer, you're writing modules (EJBs) that are dropped into the application server, which then loads and runs the EJBs when needed.

Servers work closely with clients. A *client* requests information from a server or requests that a server do something. The server, acting on the request, sends the requested information to the client or does what it is asked to do.

BEA WebLogic Server, as an EJB application server, interacts with clients in a similar manner. The machine that requests WebLogic to run an EJB program is the client. This client program can be a stand-alone Java program or another server. (Often web servers are the clients for the services of EJBs.) EJBs allow a busy web server to focus on what it was designed to do: serve web pages. The web server calls upon EJBs, which reside on an application server, to perform business-specific tasks, such as retrieving data from a database.

This division of labor is the key reason to use an application server. Dividing the task between the client and the application server results in three immediate advantages:

- ✔ Reliability
- ✔ Scalability
- ✔ Modularity

Achieving reliability through redundancy

You can run an application on your desktop machine only as long as your machine is operational. In other words, if your machine "hangs" (becomes locked) or the power goes off, you can't continue to work. Application servers, on the other hand, can offer a more reliable way of running an application through a concept called *redundancy*. This simply means that you add multiple servers, instruct them to act together as if they were a single server, and then allow clients to access them. If one of the servers becomes unavailable, the other servers pick up the slack and respond to the needs of the clients.

You can also work on an ailing server without disturbing the other servers. You are free to reboot the crashed application server without affecting the stability of the remaining application servers. Using multiple application servers in this way can increase the reliability of your application.

Making applications scalable

As more and more clients make requests of an application server, more and more demands are placed on that server. As the overall demands become greater, the capability of the server to quickly fulfill each individual request decreases. One solution to this problem is to add more horsepower to the machine used to run the application server — perhaps more memory, a faster hard drive, or even a faster CPU. A better solution, however, is to add another server, clustering it with the existing server. Now the deluge of client requests can be serviced by two machines acting as one. Need more power? Add a third, fourth, or fifth machine. This is the essence of *scalability*.

As requests for services come in from the clients, the cluster automatically dispatches these requests to the least busy of the application servers. This allows you to increase the capacity of your application by simply adding additional application servers rather than going through the costly process of upgrading a production server. As a bonus, the additional servers also increase the reliability of your system.

Improving modularity

Modularity has long been one of the chief design goals of computer programming. *Modular program design* breaks the program into smaller units, or modules, that are developed separately. Often these modules can be reused across several applications. Object oriented programming (OOP) was created to facilitate the creation of modular programs, among other design goals.

One of the most fundamental ways of making a program modular is to separate *presentation logic* — the part of the program that interacts with the user — from *business logic* — the part of the program that makes decisions and performs calculations. Presentation logic should be housed in the web server, because the web server is responsible for transmitting the HTML that will be presented to the user. Business logic should be housed in the application server so that it can be reused by any web pages that may need it. The same business logic is often needed across many web pages. For example, the business logic to update inventory would be reused on any page that affects inventory.

An application server enables this separation. Business logic is placed in EJBs. The application server executes the EJBs, and the results are sent to the presentation program running on the web server.

J2EE, Java's Approach to Application Servers

Java 2 Platform, Enterprise Edition (J2EE) contains additions to the Java environment that Sun Microsystems created to facilitate such enterprise concepts as application servers. Sun has defined a specific way in which to build application servers for Java. One advantage to this approach is that content you develop for WebLogic Server can be used also with other J2EE application servers. In other words, you can migrate the content to another J2EE application server, if needed.

J2EE is not just one technology, but rather a collection of technologies. Sun defines standards embodied as J2EE, which other vendors implement. For example, WebLogic implements the following J2EE components:

- JavaServer Pages (JSP)
- Enterprise JavaBeans (EJB)
- Java Transaction Service (JTS)
- Java Message Service (JMS)
- Java Naming and Directory Interface (JNDI)

In other chapters, you find out more about these components of J2EE. In this section, I briefly review the function of each of these to give you an overview of how they fit together.

JavaServer Pages

JavaServer Pages (JSP) allow you to embed Java code directly into HTML-like documents. JSP has access to nearly all the core features of the Java programming language, except you're returning only streams back to the user's browser. This allows you to construct complex applications using only JSP. However, just because you can construct complex JSP-based applications does not mean that you should. JSP is best restricted to presentation logic, with more complex business logic delegated to EJBs.

Enterprise JavaBeans

Enterprise JavaBeans (EJB) technology allows code to be executed on a remote system. This remote system is the application server. EJB is commonly used to isolate business logic from presentation logic, which usually consists of JSP. EJB coordinates access with the database and shields higher levels, such as JSP, from the need to directly access the database. In this way, if you were to change database servers or the format of your database, all code related to data access would be in one location.

Java Transaction Service

Java Transaction Service (JTS) is a transaction manager that allows requests to be segmented into transactions. These transactions succeed or fail as a whole. This prevents partial transactions from persisting if only a part of the transaction is successful.

Java Message Service

The *Java Message Service (JMS)* API was developed to allow Java applications to be message driven. A message-compatible EJB can receive and generate messages. These messages can contain any data needed by the program. Messaging is asynchronous, so considerable time can elapse before a response message is received, if at all. JMS also allows messages to be saved to a message store, such as a file or a database.

Java Naming and Directory Interface

Java Naming and Directory Interface (JNDI) is a standard extension to the Java platform that provides naming and directory information to Java programs. This allows EJB and other resources to have names that can be looked up by their client programs. JNDI is a high-level standard and can use any number of underlying name and directory services.

Enterprise applications

Enterprise applications tie many of the previously mentioned components together into one application. An enterprise application is most commonly made up of a web application and any EJB that may be used by that web application. The entire enterprise application is packaged as a single archive file, which can be easily deployed to a server such as WebLogic. This allows for easy packaging, distribution, and deployment of your enterprise applications.

Major Features of WebLogic Server

As mentioned, WebLogic is the most popular application server available for Java. WebLogic has gained this popularity due, in part, to a full set of features. In this section, you are introduced to some of these features. In other chapters, they are described in much greater detail.

Throughout this text, I refer to BEA's WebLogic Server product simply as *WebLogic*. BEA, however, uses the term *WebLogic* to refer to a family of products, including WebLogic Portal, WebLogic Integration, WebLogic Workshop, and WebLogic Express. The popularity of the core WebLogic Server product, however, has led to the shortening of the name to simply WebLogic in many circles.

Platform support

WebLogic can run on many platforms, including Windows and many flavors of UNIX. WebLogic is available also for many large mainframe computer systems, providing WebLogic with greater processing power and scalability. The extensive platform support of WebLogic allows you to mix and match technologies. For example, you might run WebLogic on a mainframe computer system, backing it up with a cluster of less expensive machines that run the same applications. Further, you can test your application on less expensive machines and run your production system on more expensive, higher-bandwidth hardware.

Web applications

Although WebLogic is most commonly thought of as an application server, it can also handle many web server functions. This means WebLogic could be used as an all-in-one solution. JavaServer Pages (JSP) is one of the most common forms of server-side Java programming. WebLogic includes the capability to execute JSP. You can to create web applications in WebLogic that make use of technologies such as JSP and custom tag libraries. Web applications are covered in Chapter 5.

EJB support

Perhaps the most basic feature of a Java-based application server is support for Enterprise JavaBeans (EJB). WebLogic includes extensive support for the five types of EJB:

- ✔ Stateless bean
- ✔ Stateful bean
- ✔ Message bean
- ✔ Container-managed persistence (CMP) entity bean
- ✔ Bean-managed persistence (BMP) entity bean

Additionally, WebLogic makes other important services available to these beans, such as database connection pooling and naming services. EJB support is discussed in Chapters 6 and 7.

Database connectivity

Databases are often the heart of any serious application. Because of this, WebLogic includes extensive support for relational databases. One of the most important features is *database connection pooling*. This allows WebLogic — instead of individual EJBs — to manage connections to the database.

Database connections are an expensive resource. Processor cycles and extensive network communication are required to open and close these connections, and this can slow down other operations. By using a database connection pool, WebLogic can reuse its pool of open database connections, freeing the application from the overhead of constantly creating and destroying database connections. Database connectivity is discussed more fully in Chapter 12.

Web services

Web services are a new technology that provides a more uniform way of accessing the components of an application. Web services allow your application to receive XML messages from other applications and respond to those requests using XML. This means other applications can make use of your application using only the HTTP protocol.

XML messages are sent and received using the Simple Object Access Protocol (SOAP), a W3C standard that specifies how web services should be accessed by their client programs. By supporting a standard protocol such as SOAP, many different systems can access the web services that you make available through WebLogic Server. Web services are discussed in Chapter 9. Accessing web services is discussed in Chapter 10.

One of the new features of WebLogic (as of Version 7) is WebLogic Workshop, which enables someone who is not familiar with J2EE to construct web services. WebLogic Workshop provides a number of tools and frameworks to make designing web services easier. WebLogic Workshop is discussed in Chapter 11.

Clustering

Clustering is the capability to chain together many individual application servers. These application servers are clones of each other, performing the same task. The clustering capabilities of WebLogic enable these servers to handle requests even though some of the application servers may fail. This greatly increases the reliability of your application.

Clustering also allows your web application to become very scalable. Because you now have many application servers handling requests from clients, you can handle a greater number of incoming requests. Clustering is discussed in more detail in Chapter 16.

Security

Security is a major concern in any application — and when your application is accessible through the Internet, the need for security increases. WebLogic can help you with three specific areas of security:

- **Securing your data transmissions.** Data transmissions are secured using SSL/HTTPS. This prevents a hacker from accessing data packets as they are transmitted between the browser and the web server.

- **Controlling access by users.** You may want to restrict some users from accessing the overall system and restrict other users from accessing only certain parts of the system. WebLogic provides features that allow you to define users and control exactly what they have access to.

- **Verifying administrators.** WebLogic's Administration Console enables you to easily configure your server remotely. Unfortunately, this also means that a hacker can configure your system remotely. WebLogic provides security to all configuration programs to limit access by unauthorized users. Security is discussed in Chapter 18.

Chapter 2

Installing WebLogic Server

· ·

· ·

*I*t makes sense that before you can use WebLogic, you must install it on the machine that you want to use as your Internet server. This chapter discusses the different ways that you can install the program on your system. Even if you inherited a server that already has WebLogic installed, you will probably want to at least skim this chapter so that you're aware of the different installation (and configuration) options available.

Installation Overview

Installing WebLogic is a straightforward process. WebLogic has several installation methods available, one of which should fit your needs:

✔ **GUI installation.** This is the most common method of installing WebLogic — and the easiest. The *graphical user interface* (GUI) allows you to see what's happening during the installation process.

✔ **Console installation.** If you're working with a so-called "headless" remote server, which allows only terminal connections, this installation method is for you.

✔ **Silent installation.** If you need to install WebLogic on a number of different systems, you can "script" the installation process to make it quicker and easier.

All three installation methods work on both Windows and UNIX systems. Which installation method should you choose? Unless restricted by the capabilities of the target system, the answer lies in your needs and your comfort level with your computer. Each installation method is covered in this chapter, so you can get a good idea of which method you should choose.

First, however, you should know the system requirements for WebLogic as well as how to get your hands on the software. It also doesn't hurt to know how WebLogic is licensed by BEA Systems. Read on for all the details!

System requirements

Before you can take a class at a local college, you must meet the prerequisites. To be successful in the class, you must fulfill the stated requirements. The same is true of WebLogic Server. The installation program will check that your system has met certain prerequisites before it attempts the installation. Those requirements are outlined in this section.

Essentially, you need a computer system that will function well under Windows NT Server 4; Windows 2000 Server; Windows 2000 Advanced Server; Sun Solaris 7, 8, or 9; HP-UX 11 or 11i; IBM AIX 4.3.3 or 5L; or several flavors of Linux. If your system will run one of these comfortably, you should have no problems running WebLogic.

You can find detailed information about which systems are certified to work with WebLogic at the following address:

```
http://e-docs.bea.com/
```

Hard-drive space requirements

If you install the complete WebLogic Server, approximately 525MB of disk space are required. This number includes 35MB for the JDK installation and 142MB for the examples. This is only the hard-drive space required for WebLogic itself. Your own application data will require additional space.

Hard-drive space requirements used to be considerably more important when hard drives cost more money than they do these days. It takes a considerable amount of trouble to move a system from one hard drive to a larger drive. Due to the low cost of hard drives today, it simply makes sense to go for one of the larger sizes available for your system.

It's likely that continuous operation of WebLogic Server will be important. Because of this, you should apply the same measures to WebLogic Server as you do to any other production server. For example, you may use a RAID array to provide redundant hard drives. This way, if one of your hard drives fails, your system will continue running while you replace the faulty hard drive. Plus, with a RAID array, your system does not go down during the replacement. The full scope of your system's redundancy and reliability capability is, in the end, driven by uptime needs and budget.

Memory requirements

Just as regular applications have memory requirements, so does WebLogic. However, the memory requirements for WebLogic are considerably higher than regular end-user applications that you may have installed. For WebLogic Server, 1GB of RAM is recommended. You can get by with less RAM, but it may degrade the performance of your server.

JDK requirements

WebLogic requires Java to be present. If you're using a Windows installation, a copy of Java Development Kit is bundled with your installation program.

Some UNIX distributions of WebLogic do not include a copy of JDK. Versions of the WebLogic installation program that *do* include JDK have a .bin extension. If you're trying to install from one of these distributions, you must make sure that the JDK BIN directory is in your path. If you don't have a copy of JDK already installed on your system, you should use a version of WebLogic that includes JDK.

Finding out whether Java is properly installed on your UNIX or Windows machine is easy. Simply enter the following command at the command prompt:

```
java -version
```

If Java is properly installed, you'll see the version information for your JDK. If Java isn't installed, you'll get an error. For more information about installing Java, refer to the online documentation provided with JDK that you downloaded.

Other requirements

Finally, if you're installing using the GUI installation program, you must have a color depth of at least 8 bits. Nearly any computer produced since 1997 will have a color depth of at least 8 bits and most likely higher. If you're using either of the other two installation methods, you don't need to worry about color.

Getting WebLogic

WebLogic is available on CD-ROM or from the BEA Systems web site. If you have WebLogic on CD-ROM, you save some time because you don't have to download a huge installation file. (CD-ROMs are available for purchase from any BEA Systems sales representative.) Most people download WebLogic from the BEA Systems web site. You can find the download here:

```
http://commerce.beasys.com/showallversions.jsp?family=WLS
```

The preceding URL is accurate as of this writing, but it may have changed by the time you read this book.

Registration is required of everyone who wants to download. After registering, you can proceed to the download area.

You can download WebLogic in two ways. The first is called the *net installer* and is similar to many net-aware installation programs. You essentially download a 20MB installation program and answer some questions; then the installation program downloads additional elements, as necessary.

The second download method is called the *package installer*. With this method, you download the entire stand-alone installation program, which varies in size depending on the version of WebLogic you want to download. (The size could be anywhere from 155MB to 275MB.) This option is great if you want to keep a copy of the installation program on CD (as a backup). If you plan on doing a silent installation, you must download the entire package installer. The silent installation mode is not supported by the net installer.

If you choose to use the net installer, the installation process is similar to downloading the package installer and using the GUI installation. Refer to the appropriate major sections, later in this chapter, for more information on each of the installation modes and how to use them.

Understanding licensing

To use WebLogic Server, you must have a valid license. When you first install WebLogic, an evaluation license is created and is valid for 90 days. This evaluation version works just like a real license, except that you're limited to 20 concurrent connections. After this evaluation period is up, you must purchase a real WebLogic license.

You can choose from two different licenses:

- Development license
- Production license

A development license, which costs less than the production license, allows only 15 concurrent connections at a time. A production license has no connection limit.

The development license allows you to create several development servers, potentially one for each of your developers, to create your system before you place it into production. This spares you the prohibitive cost of buying a production license for each developer.

If you have licenses for older versions of WebLogic, you must purchase new license files. Contact BEA software to see whether upgrade pricing is available.

Using the GUI Mode Installer

The easiest way to install WebLogic is to use the GUI mode installer. This program uses a graphical user interface to guide you through the installation process. Here's how to do an installation using the GUI mode installer:

1. **If you obtained WebLogic as a CD-ROM product, insert the CD-ROM in your CD-ROM drive. If you obtained WebLogic from the web, double-click the installer that you downloaded.**

    The installer program begins, and you see the Welcome screen shown in Figure 2-1.

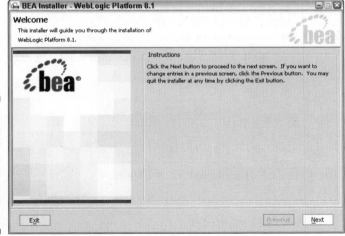

Figure 2-1: The Welcome screen for the WebLogic GUI installation.

2. **Click Next.**

    A license agreement appears.

3. **Assuming you agree to all the fine print, choose the Yes option and click Next.**

The screen shown in Figure 2-2 appears. The BEA home directory is where the common programs used by all BEA software are stored. The default home directory on Windows is `c:\bea`.

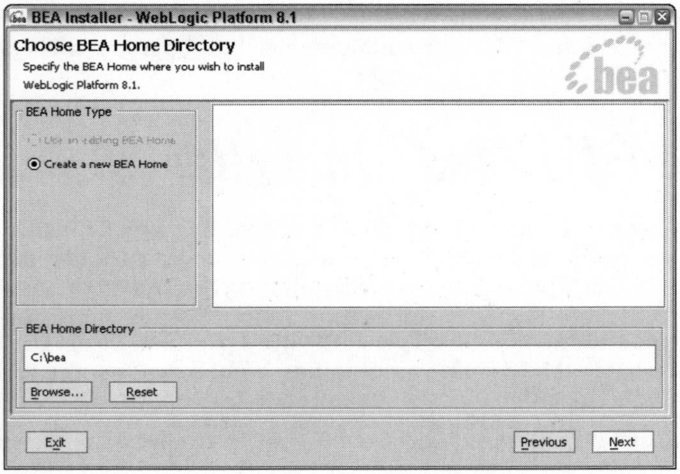

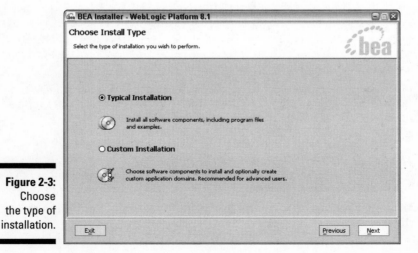

Figure 2-2:
Specify a
BEA home
directory.

4. **Use the default directory or choose a new directory.**

   If you want a new directory, click Browse and select the directory or type a new directory path in the text box just above the Browse button.

5. **When you're satisfied with the home directory, click Next.**

   The screen shown in Figure 2-3 appears.

Figure 2-3:
Choose
the type of
installation.

6. **Choose the type of installation you want and then click Next.**

   Usually, you'll want to perform a typical installation. If you choose Typical Installation, skip to Step 8. You might choose Custom Installation if you don't want certain WebLogic components installed for security or space considerations.

7. **If you choose Custom Installation, specify what you want to install, as shown in Figure 2-4, and then click Next.**

   By default, all components are installed. If you don't need a certain component installed, clear the check box beside its name.

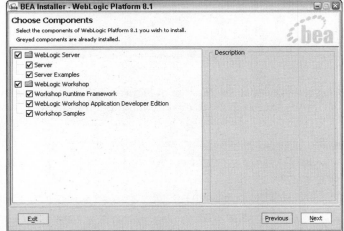

Figure 2-4:
You can specify which components to install.

8. **Specify a directory for WebLogic, as shown in Figure 2-5.**

   In Steps 4 and 5, you created a BEA home directory. This step creates a directory for WebLogic itself. This product directory is usually a subdirectory of the BEA home directory. The product directory will contain all files needed by your application.

   As in Steps 3 and 4, you can use the default directory, you can use the Browse button to select a different directory, or you can simply type a new directory path in the text box.

9. **When you're satisfied with the product directory, click Next.**

   The installation begins. In the installer's title bar and in the lower-right corner, you can see progress indicators. When the indicators reach 100%, the installation is complete, and you see a *Congratulations* message, as shown in Figure 2-6.

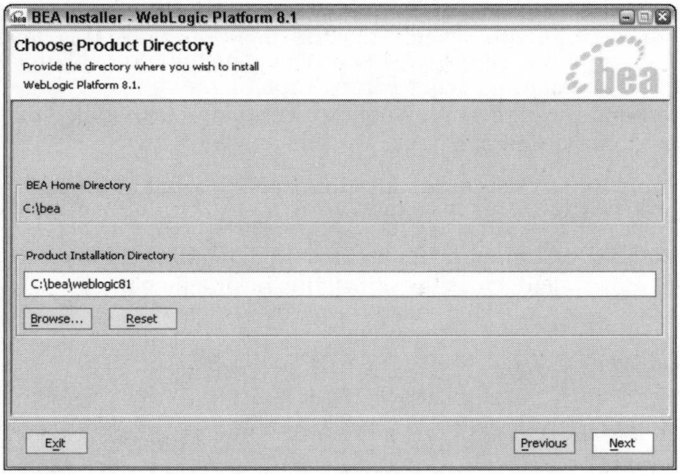

Figure 2-5:
Choose a
directory for
installing
WebLogic.

Note the option shown at the bottom of Figure 2-6. This option allows you to install XML Spy, which is an XML development environment.

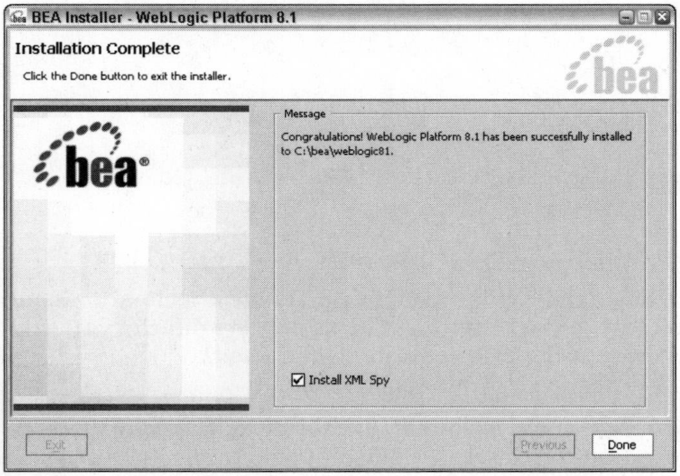

Figure 2-6:
Congrat-
ulations.
You've
installed
WebLogic.

Using Configuration Wizard

In this section, you use Configuration Wizard to create a server. After installing WebLogic, Configuration Wizard is accessible right away.

Throughout this process, you'll see references to a *domain*. Although a domain can contain multiple web servers, the examples in this chapter assume that your domain has only one server. For more on domains, see Chapter 4.

To create a domain, follow these steps.

1. **Choose Start⇨BEA WebLogic Platform 8.1⇨Configuration Wizard.**

   Configuration Wizard starts and the screen shown in Figure 2-7 appears.

2. **Select the Create a new WebLogic configuration option, and then Click Next.**

   In this example, you create a server. To modify an existing server, you would choose the Add to an existing WebLogic configuration option.

3. **Select a template and type a name for your domain. Click Next.**

   To follow along with the example, select the Basic WebLogic Server Domain template.

4. **Choose Express as your configuration type.**

   This is the most common option. (You might choose Customized if you want to create a clustered environment, which is covered in Chapter 16.)

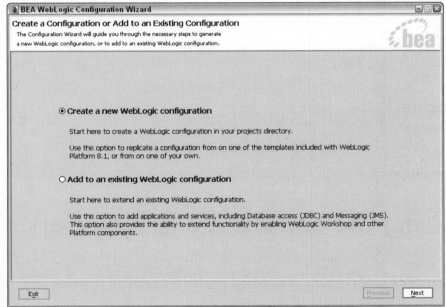

Figure 2-7: BEA Configuration Wizard.

5. Create the administrative user.

To create the administrative user, type a user name and a password. Ideally, the password should be something that's not found in the dictionary and should consist of both letters and numbers.

Make sure that you remember the user name and password because you'll need them to change configuration settings on your server.

6. Click Next.

The screen shown in Figure 2-8 appears.

7. Review your settings, and then click Create.

In a few moments, your domain is created.

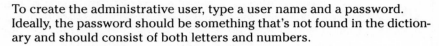

Figure 2-8:
Server
summary.

Using the Console Mode Installer

The console mode installer does not use a graphical interface, and many people think it's harder to use than the GUI installer. You can use the console mode installer in Windows or UNIX. If you're using a UNIX system that doesn't have access to a GUI, you must use the console mode installer.

Two types of console mode installers are available, and which type BEA Systems provides depends on the version of the operating system you're using. If you have UNIX, the extension of your installer can be .bin or .jar. For Windows, it's .exe. The following sections describe how to install under UNIX and Windows operating systems.

Installing under UNIX

If your system uses UNIX, your installer could have a .bin or a .jar file name extension. If your installer has the .bin extension, that means the installer includes Java Development Kit (JDK), as described earlier. Installation files ending in .jar do not include JDK.

Installing with a .bin file

If you have an installer file that ends in .bin, how you install the file depends on whether you downloaded the installation file from the Internet or have it available on CD.

To install your .bin file if you have it available on a CD, follow these steps:

1. **Log on to the system as the user who will run WebLogic Server.**

2. **Open a command-line shell.**

3. **Insert the WebLogic CD in the CD-ROM drive.**

4. **Change to the** weblogic_platform801 **directory on the CD.**

5. **Invoke the following command:**

   ```
   ./filename.bin -mode=console
   ```

   where filename.bin **is the name of the installer.**

   The installation program installs WebLogic.

If you downloaded the .bin file, the steps are slightly different:

1. **Log on to the system as the user who will run WebLogic Server.**

2. **Open a command-line shell.**

3. **Go to the directory where you downloaded WebLogic and invoke the following two commands:**

   ```
   chmod a+x filename.bin
   ./filename.bin -mode=console
   ```

   where filename.bin **is the name of the installer.**

   The installation program installs WebLogic.

Installing with a .jar file

If you have an installer file that ends in .bin, follow these steps:

1. **Log on to the system as the user who will run WebLogic Server.**

2. **Open a command-line shell.**

3. **Include the `bin` directory of your JDK at the beginning of the PATH variable:**

```
PATH=javapath/bin:$PATH
export PATH
```

   where `javapath` is the full path to your JDK directory.

4. **Change to the directory that contains the .jar file.**

5. **Do one of the following:**

   • If you're using JDK 1.3.1_03 or higher, type the following:

   ```
   java -jar filename.jar -mode=console
   ```

   where `filename.jar` is the name of the installer.

   • If you're using the AIX version of UNIX, type the following:

   ```
   java -classpath filename.jar
        com.bea.installer.BEAInstallController
   ```

   where `filename.jar` is the name of the installer.

   The installation program installs WebLogic.

Installing under Windows

If you have an install file that uses the .exe file extension, WebLogic assumes that you already have Java installed and set up in your system path. How you install the file depends on whether you downloaded the installation file from the Internet or have it available on CD.

If you're installing from a CD-ROM, follow these steps:

1. **Log on to the system as the user who will run WebLogic Server.**

2. **Open a command-prompt window.**

   To do so, choose Start⇨All Programs⇨Accessories⇨Command Prompt.

3. **Go to the** `weblogic_platform801` **directory on the CD-ROM.**

   If you obtained WebLogic from the Web, go to the directory where you downloaded WebLogic.

4. **Invoke the following command:**

   ```
   net_platform801_3in32.exe -mode=console
   ```

   The installation program installs WebLogic.

If you downloaded WebLogic from the web, follow these steps instead:

1. **Log on to the system as the user who will run WebLogic Server.**

2. **Open a command-prompt window.**

3. **Go to the directory where you downloaded WebLogic.**

4. **Invoke the following command:**

   ```
   filename -mode=console
   ```

   where `filename` **is the name of the file that you downloaded.**

Using the Silent Mode Installer

Silent mode installation works much like the GUI installation program. The main difference is that the silent mode installer gets all its input from a file, whereas the GUI installer gets all its input from the user. Silent installation can be used under Windows and UNIX.

Silent installation is valuable when you must perform the same installation on many different computers.

Using the silent mode installer involves two main steps:

1. **Create an installer properties file.**

2. **Use the installer properties file to invoke the installer.**

You perform Step 1 once and then repeat Step 2 on every computer on which you want to install the server.

In this section, you see how to carry out these two steps. I begin by showing you how to create an installer properties file, sometimes referred to as a *template file*.

Creating a template file

To install using the silent method, you must create a template file. The template file contains all the setting information that you would normally provide to the GUI installation utility. These settings are all expressed inside XML tags. Make sure that you do not modify the structure of the XML tags.

Follow these steps to create a template file:

1. **Obtain a template file from the following location:**

   ```
   http://e-docs.bea.com/wls/docs81/install/instsil.
        html#1042712
   ```

   An example template file is also shown later in this chapter.

2. **Save the contents of the template file to a file named silent.xml. Place this file in the directory containing the WebLogic Server installation program.**

3. **Modify your template file so that the settings make sense for your needs.**

   See Table 2-1 for a list of settings.

Table 2-1	Mandatory Silent Mode Installation Properties
Property	*What It Is*
BEAHOME	The BEA home directory. This directory holds common files used by multiple BEA products, such as the license file.
RUN_DOMAIN_WIZARD	Specifies whether Configuration Wizard should be run. If True, the wizard is run; if False, it is not. If you choose to run Configuration Wizard, you must specify the data values used by the wizard, as detailed in Table 2-2.
USER_INSTALL_DIR	The directory into which you will install WebLogic.

Only a few properties need to be set in the template file; these are shown in Table 2-1. If you choose to control Configuration Wizard with the template file (by setting RUN_DOMAIN_WIZARD to True), the number of properties you need to set suddenly becomes much larger. The Configuration Wizard properties you can set in the template file are detailed in Table 2-2.

Table 2-2	Configuration Wizard Properties
Property	*What It Is*
ADMIN_HOST_NAME_OR_IP	The Administration Server name or IP address.
ADMIN_LISTEN_PORT	The port at which the Administration Server listens.
C_domainName	The beginning of a domain name specification. One or more of these attributes can be specified to create domains. (On UNIX systems, do not include spaces in the domain name.)
C_password	The password to be used with the administrative user for this server. The password must contain at least 8 characters but no more than 20. Do not use spaces or XML reserved characters such as <, >, {, or }.
C_serverListenAddress	The DNS name or system IP for the server.
C_serverListenPort=	Used to specify the server listen port. Most web servers use port 80. WebLogic uses port 7001 by default.
C_serverName	Used to specify the server name for the specified domain. Do not include spaces in the server name.
C_serverSSLListenPort=	Used to specify the SSL server listen port, which is used for HTTPS connections. Most web servers use port 443. WebLogic uses port 7002 by default.
C_username	A user name to start the server and access Administration Console. Do not use spaces or XML reserved characters such as <, >, {, or }.
ClusterMCAddr	The multicast IP address that Administration Server uses to communicate with clustered servers. WebLogic uses 237.0.0.1 by default.
ClusterName	Name of the cluster (if any) to create. Do not include spaces in the cluster name.
ClusterPort	The multicast port that Administration Server uses to communicate with clustered servers. WebLogic uses port 7777 by default.

(continued)

Table 2-2 *(continued)*

Property	What It Is
`clusterServers data group`	If the `SERVER-RUN-AS` parameter is set to Admin Server with Clustered Managed Server(s), specifies the configuration of the cluster. For each server in the cluster, you must specify the following three items: `clusterServerRegName` (the name of the server as registered with Administration Server), `clusterServerHostIP` (the DNS name or IP address of the machine), and `clusterServer ListenPort` (the server listening port).
`DB_EMAIL_ADDRESS`	The e-mail sending address used by WebLogic Integration.
`DB_EMAIL_HOST`	The default e-mail server used by WebLogic Integration.
`domain.directory`	The full path to the domain directory. On UNIX systems, do not include spaces in path names.
`INSTALL_NT_SERVICE`	Used to specify whether the server should be installed as a service when installing on a Windows system. Possible values are `yes` and `no`.
`INSTALL_WINDOWS_ STARTUP_MENU`	Used on a Windows system to specify whether a WebLogic option should be installed on the Windows Start menu. Possible values are `yes` and `no` (the default).
`MANAGED_SERVER_ REGISTERED_NAME_ IN_ADMIN`	The machine or server name as registered with Administration Server.
`managedServers data group`	If the `SERVER-RUN-AS` parameter is set to Admin Server with Managed Server(s), specifies the configuration of the managed servers in the domain. For each managed server, you must specify four items: `managedServerRegName` (the name of the server as registered with Administration Server), `managedServerHostIP` (the DNS name or IP address of the machine), `managedServer ListenPort` (the server listening port), and `managedServerSSLListenPort` (the secure listening port).
`selectedJar`	The full path and file name of the template JAR file to be used by Configuration Wizard to create the domain and configure the server.

Property	What It Is
SERVER-RUN-AS	Determines the server configuration created by Configuration Wizard. Possible settings are Single Server, Admin Server with Managed Server(s), Admin Server with Clustered Managed Server(s), and Managed Server (with owning Admin Server configuration).

To specify a setting for a property, you use the property name and value as an XML tag. For example, the following sets a value for the USER_INSTALL_DIR property:

```
<data-value name="USER_INSTALL_DIR" value="C:\bea\weblogic81"
        />
```

Using the property types shown in Table 2-1, you can create a properties file that the installer will use. An example of a Windows silent.xml file is shown in Listing 2-1.

Listing 2-1:   Silent Install Properties File

```
<?xml version="1.0" encoding="UTF-8"?>
<domain-template-descriptor>
<input-fields>
  <data-value name="BEAHOME"              value="C:\bea" />
  <data-value name="USER_INSTALL_DIR"     value="C:\bea\weblogic81" />
  <data-value name="RUN_DOMAIN_WIZARD"    value="false" />
  <data-value name="domain.directory"     value="C:\bea\user_domains\mydomain" />
  <data-value name="C_domainName"         value="mydomain" />
  <data-value name="C_serverName"         value="myserver" />
  <data-value name="C_username"           value="system" />
  <data-value name="C_password"           value="weblogic" />
  <data-value name="C_serverListenAddress" value="" />
  <data-value name="C_serverListenPort" value="7001" />
  <data-value name="C_serverSSLListenPort" value="7002" />
  <data-value name="ClusterName"          value="mycluster" />
  <data-value name="ClusterPort"          value="7777" />
  <data-value name="selectedJar"
            value="C:\bea\weblogic81\common\templates\domains\wls.jar" />
  <data-value name="INSTALL_NT_SERVICE" value="no" />
  <data-value name="INSTALL_WINDOWS_STARTUP_MENU" value="no" />
  <data-value name="DB_EMAIL_HOST"        value="myserver" />
  <data-value name="DB_EMAIL_ADDRESS"     value="name@bea.com" />
</input-fields>
</domain-template-descriptor>
```

Invoking the silent mode installation program

Now that you've created a properties file to be used as a template for your installation, you're ready to invoke the silent installer program and perform the actual installation. You can perform the silent installation once or many times. (The silent mode was designed to be used when you want to perform the same installation more than once.)

The instructions for how to start the silent mode installation program are slightly different between UNIX and Windows. The next two sections explain invoking the silent mode installer in both UNIX and Windows.

If you're using the silent mode installation under Windows, follow these steps:

1. **Log on to the Windows system with an account that has administrator rights.**

2. **Open a command-prompt window.**

3. **If you're installing from a CD-ROM, go to the CD-ROM directory. If you obtained WebLogic from the web, go to the directory where you downloaded WebLogic.**

4. **Invoke the following command:**

```
filename.exe -f fullpath\silent.xml
```

   where *filename*.exe **is the name of the installer and** *fullpath* **is the path to your installer properties file.**

   The installation program installs WebLogic.

If you're using the silent mode installation under UNIX, follow these steps:

1. **Log on to the UNIX system as the target user.**

2. **Open a command-prompt window.**

3. **If you're installing from a CD-ROM, go to the CD-ROM directory. If you obtained WebLogic from the web, go to the directory where you downloaded WebLogic.**

4. **Invoke the following command:**

```
sh filename.bin -f fullpath/silent.xml
```

   where *filename.bin* **is the name of the installer and** *fullpath* **is the path to your installer properties file.**

   The installation program installs WebLogic.

Chapter 3

Gentlemen, Start Your WebLogic Engines

· ·

· ·

*Y*ou normally don't think much about starting application programs. You simply click the appropriate icon and the application starts. If you want, starting WebLogic can be this simple. However, WebLogic also offers several other ways to start the server: from a script and from the Windows Start menu.

Writing a WebLogic Startup Script

One of the most common ways to start WebLogic Server is by using a startup script. A *startup script* is nothing more than an ordered list of commands that would normally be issued at the Windows or UNIX command prompt. Starting WebLogic Server from an existing startup script has several advantages:

- ✔ There is no need to enter the admin ID and password each time.
- ✔ Other related commands, such as mapping network drives, can automatically be performed as part of the script.
- ✔ The script can be started easily by other automated processes.

However, using a custom startup script has some potential disadvantages, such as the following:

✔ If the admin password is embedded in the script, the script is less secure than the supplied script.

✔ It takes time to properly create a startup script.

✔ A user must be logged on to the server to run the startup script.

You begin finding out about startup scripts by examining the standard startup script that WebLogic creates for new server instances.

The standard startup script

Fortunately, you do not need to build your startup script from scratch. Every time that you create a new server instance, as described in Chapter 4, a standard startup script is created for you. You can modify this script as you see fit. The standard startup script is named startWebLogic.cmd if you're running Windows and startWebLogic.sh if you're running UNIX. The contents of the Windows and UNIX startup scripts are similar. Listing 3-1 shows an example of the standard startup script generated by WebLogic for the Windows operating system.

Listing 3-1: Typical Windows WebLogic Startup Script

```
echo off
SETLOCAL

@rem Set SERVER_NAME to the name of the server you want to
@rem start.
set SERVER_NAME=myserver

@rem Set WLS_USER equal to your system username and
@rem WLS_PW equal to your system password for no username
@rem and password prompt during server startup. Both are
@rem required to bypass the start prompt. This is not
@rem recommended for a production environment.
set WLS_USER=
set WLS_PW=

@rem Set Production Mode. When this is set to true,
@rem the server starts in production mode. When
@rem set to false, the server starts in development
@rem mode. If it is not set, it will default to false.
set STARTMODE=

@rem Set JAVA_OPTIONS to the java flags you want to pass to
@rem the vm. i.e.:
@rem set JAVA_OPTIONS=-Dweblogic.attribute=value
@rem                  -Djava.attribute=value
```

```
set JAVA_OPTIONS=-
          Dweblogic.security.SSL.trustedCAKeyStore=C:\bea\
          weblogic81\server\lib\cacerts

@rem Set JAVA_VM to the java virtual machine you want to run.
@rem For instance:
@rem set JAVA_VM=-server
set JAVA_VM=

@rem Set MEM_ARGS to the memory args you want to pass to
@rem java. For instance:
@rem set MEM_ARGS=-Xms32m -Xmx200m
set MEM_ARGS=

@rem Call Weblogic Server
call "C:\bea\weblogic81\server\bin\startWLS.cmd"

ENDLOCAL
```

The startup script is not too difficult to understand. Lines that begin with @rem are remarks, or comments, added so you can understand what the different command lines do. The lines that do not begin with @rem are interpreted by WebLogic and are used to start the server.

Through the startup script, you set environment variables that control the launch and runtime operation of WebLogic Server. To create a customized startup script, you begin by modifying these variables in the standard script. I show you how to do this in the next section.

If additional commands must be executed before the server starts, simply modify the script to include the commands. A script is executed line by line, so make sure that the commands appear in the script file before the end, where the startWLS.cmd file is invoked. (This is the script command to start WebLogic Server.)

Constructing your own startup script

In the preceding section, you saw that WebLogic creates a standard script that you can modify. In this section, you find out how to set the various environment variables in the script. The first step in modifying a startup script is to load it into a text editor. A startup script doesn't require a special program for editing; it is nothing but a plain text file. In Windows, you can do your editing in a program such as Notepad. In UNIX, you can use a program such as vi or pico. However, you're not limited to using these programs; any text editor will suffice.

If you're not familiar with the UNIX environment, you will probably find the vi editor confusing. The pico editor more closely resembles Windows Notepad. To use the pico editor from UNIX, you type the `pico` command followed by the name of the file you're editing. For example, the following command edits the web.xml file using pico as your editor:

```
pico web.xml
```

Now that the startup script is opened, you can make your desired changes. Table 3-1 lists some of the environment variables you can modify.

Table 3-1	WebLogic Environment Variables
Variable Name	*What It Is*
JAVA_OPTIONS	The Java command-line options for running the server.
JAVA_VM	The Java argument specifying the VM to run such as `-server` or `-client` (hotspot is deprecated).
MEM_ARGS	The variable to override the standard memory arguments passed to Java.
STARTMODE	The operating mode for the server. Specify True for production mode servers and False for development mode.
WLS_PW	The WebLogic user password used to start the server.
WLS_USER	The WebLogic user ID used to start the server.

Usually, you will not want to change the default virtual machine that Java is using. Java achieves performance gains by compiling Java instructions into the native instruction set of the computer. If you specify the `-classic` option for JAVA_VM, no compiling is used. If you specify the `-server` or `-client` option, a compiler optimized for server or client operations, respectively, is used. There's no reason to ever run WebLogic using the `-client` option.

In Table 3-1, look at the STARTMODE variable and the mention of development and production modes. When you want to know whether something is working properly, use development mode because it helps you track down problems. Production mode reports fewer errors and generally runs faster.

A side effect of development mode is that you'll need to clear the logs more often and pay more attention to your server. Production mode also preloads more of the server, so if you're restarting the server frequently, you'll want to use development mode.

You can also specify the user ID and password when staring the server. To specify the user information, you should use the WLS_PW and WLS_USER variables. This will prevent WebLogic from prompting you each time it starts. The JAVA_OPTIONS variable allows you to pass additional parameters to the Java virtual machine. The MEM_ARGS variable allows you to request additional memory. The format for MEM_ARGS follows:

```
MEM_ARGS=-Xms128m -Xmx512m
```

This command specifies 128MB of initial memory size and 512MB as the maximum memory size.

If you get out-of-memory errors in WebLogic, you should adjust the MEM_ARGS variable.

Now that you have seen how to start WebLogic Server using a startup script, I will now show you how you can easily start WebLogic Server from the Windows Start menu.

Starting WebLogic from the Windows Start Menu

You use the Windows Start menu to start most Windows applications. When you choose to start WebLogic from the Start menu, a default script is created for you and a shortcut to that script is placed in the Start menu.

Starting WebLogic Server from the Start menu has a few immediate advantages. Perhaps the biggest advantage is that this method is simple. Another benefit is that if you've defined several different instances of your server, you can see them all in a single place. All WebLogic Server instances are started by choosing Start⇨BEA WebLogic Platform 8.1⇨User Projects.

To start WebLogic from the Start menu, you must specify — when you configure your server — that you want to use the Start menu. For more information on setting up WebLogic Server instances, refer to Chapter 4.

Starting WebLogic from the Start menu also has a few disadvantages. For example, you can't use the Start menu to automatically start the server when the computer boots. (For this reason, using the Start menu is considered a manual method of starting WebLogic Server.) A related drawback is that a user must be logged on to the system before the server can be started.

Starting WebLogic Server Automatically

So far, you've read about two methods of starting WebLogic Server: through a startup script and from the Windows Start menu. Both methods require you to be logged on to the system to start WebLogic Server. When you're using WebLogic Server in a production environment, you normally want the server to start automatically as part of the overall machine booting process. After all, it could be that this machine's only purpose is to run WebLogic Server. In this section, I describe two methods you can use to automatically start WebLogic Server at machine startup, without any manual intervention on your part.

The first automated method works only on the Windows platform. You can configure WebLogic to run as a Windows service. Windows *services* run in the background, out of the direct reach of users who may be logged on to the system. Additionally, services can be configured to start when the machine is first started.

The second automated method that can be used works only on the UNIX platform. UNIX programs that run in the background, independent of the current user, are called *daemons.* By configuring WebLogic to run as a UNIX daemon, your server starts automatically and is not directly affected by users logging on to and off the system.

Running WebLogic Server by one of these automated means makes server startup, shutdown, and error handling less obvious to system users, so these methods are more suitable for a production environment. When you're still developing your application and will likely be starting and stopping your server often, you'll find that using the Start menu or a startup script is much more convenient than running either a UNIX daemon or a Windows service.

Configuring WebLogic as a Windows service

The most common way to start WebLogic Server in a Windows production environment is as a Windows service. In this section, you find out how to configure WebLogic Server to run as a Windows service, as well as how to start and stop a Windows service. Starting WebLogic Server as a Windows service has several advantages:

- Your WebLogic service starts automatically when Windows loads.
- No user needs to be logged on for WebLogic Server to be running.
- WebLogic Server can be stopped and restarted by any program designed to work with Windows services.
- WebLogic Server runs out of direct reach of the current user.

The only drawback to running WebLogic Server as a Windows service is that debugging server applications can be more difficult because the current user doesn't have direct access to the running server. (This is why you should run WebLogic Server as a service only on a production machine, not on a development machine.)

Next, you configure WebLogic Server as a Windows service. You see how to do this for a new WebLogic Server instance as well as an existing WebLogic Server instance. Finally, you see how to remove WebLogic as a service.

Configuring a new WebLogic Server instance

Configuring a WebLogic Server instance to run as a Window service is easy. When you first configure a server instance using Domain Configuration Wizard (see Chapter 4), you are given the option of making this server a Windows service. If you select the option to install your server instance as a service, your WebLogic Server will be running in the background the next time you reboot the machine.

To configure WebLogic Server to run as a service, you must be a Windows user with administrative privileges.

Configuring an existing WebLogic Server instance

If you have an existing WebLogic Server instance that you'd like to configure to run as a Windows service, you must run a command-line utility. Follow these steps:

1. **Open a command-prompt window.**

   To do so, choose Start➪All Programs➪Accessories➪Command Prompt.

2. **Switch to the** weblogic\bin **directory.**

3. **Run the install command, specifying the name of the WebLogic Server instance that you would like to configure as a service.**

   For example:

   ```
   c:\weblogic\bin> install -name yourWebLogicServer
   ```

To configure a WebLogic Server instance to run as a service, you must be logged on to Windows using an account that has administrative privileges. Replace *yourWebLogicServer* with the name of your server.

Removing a WebLogic Server instance

Configuring a WebLogic Server instance as a Windows service doesn't have to be a one-way operation. If you ever need to turn off the instance, so that it doesn't operate as a service, follow these steps:

1. **Open a command-prompt window.**

   Choose Start➪All Programs➪Accessories➪Command Prompt.

2. **Switch to the** `weblogic\bin` **directory.**

3. **Run the** `remove` **command, specifying the name of the WebLogic Server instance that you want to remove.**

   For example:

   ```
   c:\weblogic\bin> remove -name yourWebLogicServer
   ```

To change how a service operates, you must be logged on to Windows using an account that has administrative privileges. Replace *yourWebLogicServer* with the name of your server.

Starting and stopping your service

If you're already familiar with how to manage Windows services, you'll find that WebLogic service administration is similar. To start or stop your WebLogic service, you use the Services applet from the Control Panel, which is shown in Figure 3-1.

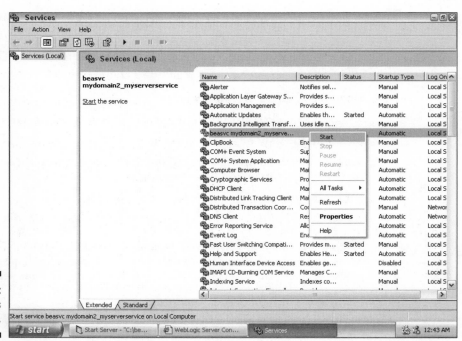

Figure 3-1:
Windows
services.

The following steps show you how to start and stop your service:

1. **Choose Start⇨Control Panel.**

2. **Click the Administrative Tools icon.**

3. **Double-click the Services icon.**

   A listing of all services configured on this system is displayed. All WebLogic services begin with *beasvc*.

4. **Right-click your WebLogic service.**

   A menu appears that allows you to start or stop your service.

 The Properties menu option allows you to configure the start type for your service, which determines whether the service should be started automatically when Windows starts. The default setting for this option is Automatic Startup When Windows Starts.

Running WebLogic as a UNIX daemon

If you want your WebLogic Server to start automatically under UNIX, you must configure the server to run as a UNIX daemon. A UNIX *daemon* process, like a Windows service, is a program that runs in the background.

Starting WebLogic Server as a daemon has the following advantages:

- ✔ This startup method is compatible with the UNIX operating system.
- ✔ Your WebLogic service starts automatically when UNIX loads.
- ✔ No user needs to be logged on for WebLogic Server to be running.
- ✔ Your WebLogic service starts and stops in a way that is consistent with other UNIX daemon processes.
- ✔ WebLogic Server runs out of direct reach of the current user.

The last advantage in the list, however, can also be a disadvantage. Having direct access to the running server can be helpful when debugging the server.

To set up your WebLogic Server instance to run as a daemon, do this:

1. **Change to the superuser by issuing the** su **command and entering the root password.**

   To set up WebLogic Server to run as a daemon, you must have root access.

2. **Create a daemon script.**

    This script will start and stop your WebLogic Server instance by calling the startup script that you created earlier in the chapter. Listing 3-2 shows an example daemon script; note that you need to supply the complete path to your own script. The name of this script should reflect the server instance it was associated with. For this example, I assume that you named it `myserver`.

3. **Place this script in the `/etc/rc.d/init.d/` directory.**

4. **Add a symbolic link to this script from the appropriate run levels.**

    This will cause your script to be executed both when the machine is starting up and shutting down. Inside `/etc/rc.d/rc5.d/` and `/etc/rc.d/rc3.d/`, you must place a symbolic link using the `ln -s` command. You must start the name of your link with an `S`, which means startup. The command you would use for the name `myserver` follows:

    ```
    ln -s /etc/rc.d/init.d/myserver /etc/rc.d/rc5.d/Smyserver
    ```

5. **Create a kill script.**

    This is accomplished by placing a link, which starts with `K`, in the `/etc/rc.d/rc6.d` and `/etc/rc.d/rc0.d` directories. You would use a command such as

    ```
    ln -s /etc/rc.d/init.d/myserver /etc/rc.d/rc5.d/Kmyserver
    ```

    The preceding directory structure was taken from Red Hat Linux. Other UNIX implementations may vary.

Listing 3-2: Sample Daemon Script

```
#!/bin/sh

#see how we were called

case "$1" in
  start)
# ... enter the complete path to your startup script here
  ;;
  stop)
# ... enter the complete path to your shutdown script here
  ;;

esac

exit 0
```

Now that you have created the appropriate links, your server should start in the background the next time you start the machine.

Chapter 4

Configuring and Administering WebLogic

- -

- -

*C*onfiguration and administration are two important topics when dealing with an application server such as WebLogic. In other chapters, you find out how to perform tasks that are usually carried out while you're developing a web application. Configuration and administration, however, are ongoing, day-to-day operations.

Common configuration tasks for WebLogic include adding users, defining network channels, defining access points, setting up security, and creating server instances. Administration involves checking the health of your server and ensuring that everything is properly configured. In this chapter, you find out how to perform all these tasks.

Domains are an important WebLogic feature. The next section describes domains as well as other logical structures in WebLogic.

Understanding Domains, Clusters, Servers, and Machines

When configuring or administering WebLogic, you're working at one of the following four levels:

- ✓ **Domain.** A collection of servers and clusters. The domain is the highest administrative level in WebLogic.
- ✓ **Cluster.** A collection of servers that acts like one server.
- ✓ **Server.** An instance of WebLogic running on a machine.
- ✓ **Machine.** An individual computer that may be running one or more servers.

It is important that you understand these levels so that you understand the scope of any changes you may make.

A *machine* is the physical hardware on which you run WebLogic. When you install WebLogic, you install it on a machine. A *server* is defined by an installation, or *instance,* of WebLogic. Most times, a one-to-one ratio exists between machines and servers (in other words, one machine has one WebLogic Server installed on it), but you could install multiple servers on a single machine, if you needed to. You should always remember the distinction that WebLogic makes between servers (which are virtual or logical) and machines (which are physical).

A *cluster* is a group of servers that acts as one single server. The two main reasons for using a cluster are reliability and scalability. A cluster can be more reliable than a single server. If a single server goes down, your web application is no longer available to your users. If you have more than one server running in a cluster, however, one server can go down without taking the entire web application down with it.

A cluster can also make your web application more scaleable. Rather than buying bigger and more expensive machines to house your system, you can simply add additional services. As new requests come in from users, the cluster will assign each individual request out to one of the servers in the cluster. To learn more about clusters, refer to Chapter 18.

A *domain* is the highest administrative level in WebLogic. It is simply a number of clusters and servers grouped together for administrative purposes. You will likely use more than one domain if you have a large number of servers and clusters. For most applications, a single domain will suffice.

Do not confuse a WebLogic domain with an Internet domain name. There is no connection between the two.

Using Administration Console

Most of your configuration activities will take place at the server level, inside Administration Console. Administration Console allows you to configure one server at a time. You access Administration Console through a web browser, just like you do your actual web site. Because of this, you must make sure that your web server is started before trying to use Administration Console to configure it.

Because Administration Console is accessed through a web browser, you can easily configure your server from anywhere on the Internet.

Logging on to Administration Console

Before you can administer a server, you need to know how to access and log on to Administration Console. Follow these steps:

1. **Make sure that WebLogic Server is running.**

   See Chapter 3 if you need a refresher on how to start your server.

2. **Start your favorite web browser.**

3. **In the browser, type the URL of your server's Administration Console.**

   If you're running the browser and the server on the same computer, use `http://localhost:7001/console/` for the URL. If you're running the browser and the server on different computers, use `http://computername:7001/console/`, where *computername* is the name of the computer running WebLogic Server. The WebLogic login screen appears, as shown in Figure 4-1.

   Note: If you didn't install WebLogic using the default settings and WebLogic listens to a different port than 7001, you must replace `7001` with the port number you specified during installation.

4. **Type your username and password.**

   If you're trying to administer one of the sample servers provided by WebLogic, your username is `installadministrator` and the password is `installadministrator`.

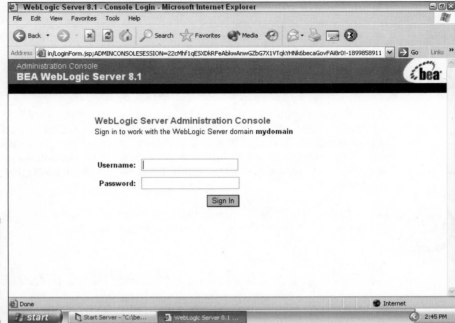

Figure 4-1:
Logging
on to
Admini-
stration
Console.

Because Administration Console enables you to configure your server from anywhere on the Internet, make sure that you secure it by using a username and password that are not easily guessed. It's always a good idea to have a password that is not in the dictionary. A password with more than eight characters that includes numerals is ideal.

5. Click Sign In.

Administration Console appears, as shown in Figure 4-2.

Using Administration Console

Now that you're logged on to Administration Console, you're ready to configure your server. Administration Console is divided into two major sections, similar to many other Windows tools, such as Windows Explorer. On the left side of the screen is a hierarchical depiction of the major configuration areas, with each configuration area displayed as a folder. If a folder has a plus sign to its left, you can click it to show more detail. (To hide the details, click the minus sign to the left of the folder.)

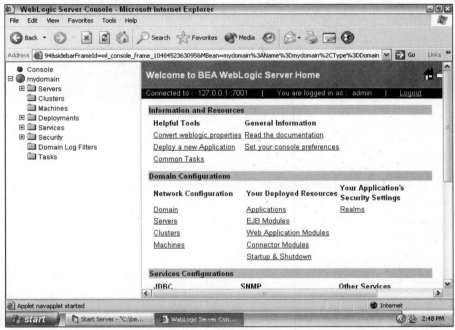

Figure 4-2:
Viewing
Administration
Console.

The right side of the screen contains information and options related to whatever you selected on the left side of the screen.

Administration Console offers a wide range of choices, which at first glance can be overwhelming. Fortunately, you need to concern yourself only with configuration areas corresponding to the parts of WebLogic that you're using.

Table 4-1 summarizes the configuration areas supported by Administration Console. Also listed is the chapter to turn to for more information on each of these areas, with two exceptions: Domain Log Filters and Tasks, which are explained next. The Domain Log Filters configuration area is similar to corresponding features in a regular web server. It allows you to specify the type of information that should be maintained in the log files for the domain. The Tasks item is basically a way to review the most recent actions taken in Administration Console. When you click this item, WebLogic displays the completed tasks in the right portion of the screen. You can then click one of the tasks listed and see a description of what the task involved and when the task was completed.

Table 4-1	Major WebLogic Configuration Areas	
Configuration Area	*What It Does*	*See*
Servers	Configures the servers that you have set up.	Chapter 5
Clusters	Creates and manages clusters. From this area, you can assign servers to clusters.	Chapter 16
Machines	Configures machines using Node Manager.	Chapter 4
Network Channels	Creates and configures network channels that allow users to connect to your server in a variety of ways.	Chapter 4
Deployments	Configures and deploys your EJBs.	Chapter 6
Services	Configures a variety of tools such as JDBC, JCOM, JMS, and JTA.	Chapter 12 (JDBC); Chapter 15 (JMS); Chapter 14 (JTA)
Security	Maintains and manages the security of your site.	Chapter 18
Domain Log Filters	Allows you to select which server log entries are passed to the domain log. You usually keep the default settings.	
Tasks	Displays a list of tasks that were recently carried out by WebLogic administrators.	

Defining Network Channels

Network channels establish a connection between WebLogic Server and the outside world. By using network channels, WebLogic can support a variety of protocols. This means that you don't need to be aware of the differences between these protocols when you create your web application. Instead, you create your application to be compatible with WebLogic and leave the protocol infrastructure to the network channels.

After your web application is ready, you simply make it available over whatever protocols you want. If you want to add additional protocol support later, you just add additional network channels.

Network channels allow you to specify how TCP/IP ports on a computer are connected to the services provided by WebLogic. Each network channel defines the following attributes about a connection to WebLogic Server:

- ✔ The protocol (for example, HTTP, HTTPS, T3, T3S, or COM)
- ✔ The TCP/IP port to listen on
- ✔ Whether or not tunneling is supported
- ✔ Whether the connection is to clients or other WebLogic Servers

Network channels are created using the Network Access Point section of Administration Console.

WebLogic uses the terms network access point and network channel interchangeably — sometimes even on the same screen, as shown in Figure 4-3. I refer to them as network channels.

Before you can work with a network channel, you must create one. Follow these steps:

1. **Log on to Administration Console.**

2. **On the left side of the Administration Console screen, click the Servers folder, and then click your server.**

   The information on the right side of the screen changes to reflect the configuration area you selected.

3. **Click the Protocols tab and then click the Channels subtab.**

   The screen shown in Figure 4-3 appears.

4. **Click the <u>Configure a new Network Channel</u> link.**

   The screen shown in Figure 4-4 appears.

5. **Configure your network channel.**

   Notice the caution icon. It simply means that if you make a change to the option, you might have to restart the server.

   At a minimum, you should specify a listen port and address. (You may have to scroll the screen to see them.) Listen port is the regular port used when a browser accesses a URL that starts with `http`. SSL listen port is used when a secure page is requested with a URL that starts with `https`.

6. **Click Create.**

   You've created the channel.

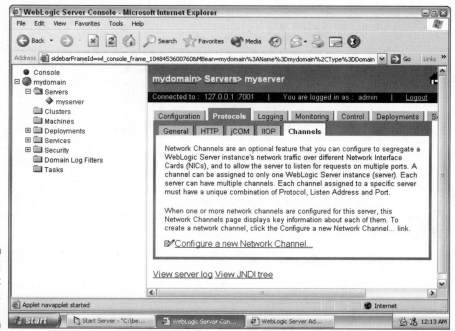

Figure 4-3:
Current
network
channels.

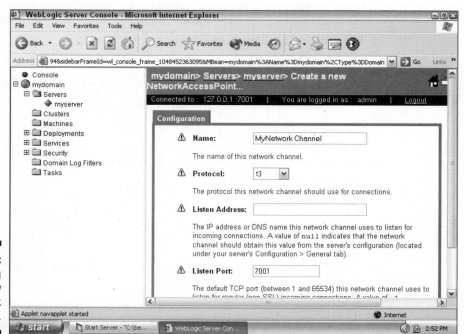

Figure 4-4:
Configuring
a new
network
channel.

Introducing Node Manager

In WebLogic terminology, a *node* is an individual element of a cluster. Earlier in the chapter, I mentioned that clusters are made up of individual WebLogic Servers. Thus, *nodes* and *servers* are essentially synonymous. In addition, because a one-to-one relationship often exists between servers and machines, the term *node* can be used also to refer to an individual machine. A node controlled by Node Manager is called a *managed server*.

You use Node Manager only when you need to manage a large number of nodes. Node Manager can be somewhat tricky to configure because it runs on multiple machines and relies heavily on script files and environmental variables. If you're going to be working with only a single WebLogic Server, you don't need to concern yourself with Node Manager.

Node Manager has the following two main components:

- **Node Manager,** which runs on each managed server
- **Administration Server,** which runs on one computer and coordinates all Node Managers

Under a Node Manager system, you have a network of computers running Node Manager and a single machine running Administration Server. Node Manager is most useful when you're using a cluster (a group of servers that appear as one server). By having more than one server, your system gains greater reliability and performance. Clustering is covered in Chapter 16.

One of the jobs of Administration Server is to restart Node Manager computers when they lock up, so it's a good idea to make sure that Administration Server is running on a computer that's not also running Node Manager. If Administration Server was running on a server that crashed, Administration Server would be down as well. And because Administration Server can't restart itself, it would be unable to restart the server.

In particular, Node Manager allows you to

- Start remote managed servers
- Restart managed servers that have shut down unexpectedly or crashed
- Automatically monitor the health of managed servers and restart the server when appropriate
- Force the shutdown of a managed server that has failed to respond to a shutdown request

In this section, you find out how to set up Node Manager and use it to perform various tasks.

Setting Up Node Manager

To set up Node Manager, you must perform the following tasks:

1. **Set up the Node Manager hosts file.**
2. **Configure SSL for Node Manager.**
3. **Configure a control machine to use Node Manager.**
4. **Configure startup arguments for managed servers.**

You can perform all these tasks from Administration Console. After these pre-requisite tasks have been performed, Node Manager is ready for use and is available from Administration Console. You'll then be able to start and stop managed servers and configure exactly how Node Manager operates.

Setting up the Node Manager hosts file

Node Manager will accept commands only from servers running on trusted hosts. You can identify a trusted host by an IP address, such as 192.168.1.1, or by a domain name, such as www.mycompany.com.

Only machines that have their IP address or domain name in the hosts file will be allowed to connect. By default, the hosts file is named nodemanager. hosts and is installed in the following directory:

```
c:\bea\weblogic81\common\nodemanager\config
```

To specify a different name and location for the trusted hosts file, you simply use a Node Manager command-line argument. For more information, see the upcoming "Configuring startup arguments for managed servers" section.

The nodemanager.hosts file contains one line for each trusted host on which Administration Server runs. The nodemanager.hosts file provided with WebLogic contains the following:

```
localhost
127.0.0.1
```

The hosts file is an ordinary text file that can be edited with any text editor. Using this text editor, you can easily add or remove hosts.

If you want to identify a trusted host by its host name, you must enable reverse DNS lookup. This option is specified when starting Node Manager by including the following command-line option:

```
-Dweblogic.nodemanager.reverseDnsEnabled=true
```

Without the command-line parameter, the default is to disable reverse DNS lookup.

In a typical production environment, Node Manager should not be on the same machine as Administration Server. Make sure that `nodemanager.hosts` contains only those machines that host Administration Server. Also make sure that your Node Manager machine is not accessible to the outside world through your firewall. Otherwise, it could be used by hackers to compromise your system.

Configuring SSL for Node Manager

Communication between Node Manager and Administration Server must be secure. Because of this, the Secure Socket Layer (SSL) protocol is used. This security is bidirectional, in that messages from both Node Manager and Administration Server are encrypted with SSL.

To make use of SSL encryption, you must use a public key infrastructure, which includes a password-protected private key and an identity certificate. Node Manager uses the same certificate format and public key infrastructure that WebLogic Server uses.

Before you can do much with Node Manager, you must obtain a key and certificate files. These are usually obtained from a vendor such as Verisign. Obtaining SSL keys and certificates is covered in Chapter 18.

For testing, WebLogic includes demonstration key and certificate files named `demokey.pem` and `democert.pem`, respectively. They enable you to set up and use SSL communication. After you install WebLogic, these files are available in various folders on your system, as summarized in Table 4-2.

Table 4-2	Directories for SSL Certificates
Directory	*What It Does*
`\samples\server\config\examples`	Contains the keys used for the `examples` domain
`\samples\server\config\petstore`	Contains the keys used for the `pet store` domain
`\common\nodemanager\config`	Contains the keys for use with the installed Node Manager application

(continued)

Table 4-2 *(continued)*

Directory	What It Does
your domain directory	Contains the sample key and certificate files that are copied to your own domains when you create your domains through Configuration Wizard

It's a good idea to use the sample security files when you're testing and developing your system. They enable you to get up and running quickly without purchasing real SSL certificates.

Using these files, I will now show you how to configure SSL for Administration Server. Authority certificates are stored in a special location known as a *keystore*. You must specify the location of the path to the keystore by using the following startup argument:

```
-Dweblogic.security.SSLtrustedCAKeyStore
```

You must make sure that Administration Server's startup script or service command-line specifies this argument. For example, the following startup command specifies the paths to these two files:

```
java -Xms200m -Xmx200m -classpath
%CLASSPATH% -Dweblogic.Name=myadminserver
-Dbea.home=c:\bea -Djava.security.policy=
c:\bea\weblogic81\server\lib\weblogic.policy
-Dweblogic.security.SSL.trustedCAKeyStore=
c:\bea\weblogic81\server\lib\cacerts
weblogic.Server
```

When calling Java from the command line as just shown, you can't use line breaks as part of the command line. In an actual script file, the preceding command would be represented as one long line.

Configuring a control machine to use Node Manager

Some configuration is required before you can use Node Manager. First, you must create a machine definition for each machine that runs a Node Manager process:

1. **Log on to Administration Console.**

2. **On the left side of the Administration Console screen, click the Machines folder.**

   The information on the right side of the screen changes to reflect the configuration area you selected.

3. **On the right side of the screen, click the <u>Configure a new Machine</u> link.**

4. **Make sure that the General tab (of the Configuration tab) is displayed. Then, in the Name box, type a new name for your machine, as shown in Figure 4-5.**

   Your machine name should be unique, and should make it easy for you to associate the computer with that name.

5. **Click the Create button.**

   WebLogic creates your machine definition.

6. **Click the Node Manager tab.**

   The screen shown in Figure 4-6 appears.

7. **Type the listen address and port that Node Manager uses for requests.**

   Usually, you should accept the default values for the IP address and port. If you use a different IP address and port, you must provide this information to each node.

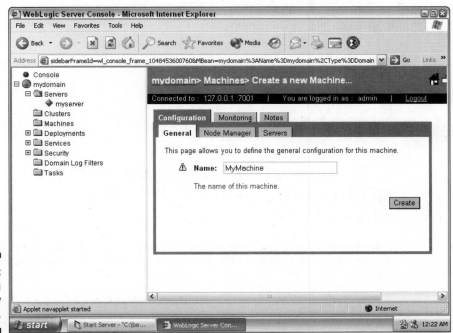

Figure 4-5:
Configuring
a new
machine.

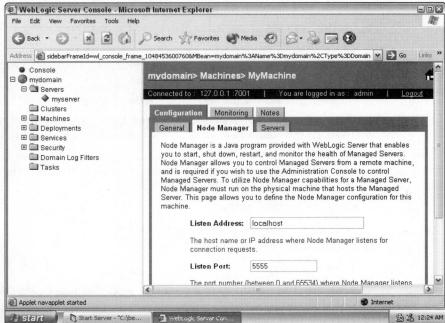

Figure 4-6:
Setting up
an address
and a port.

8. **Click the Apply button to save your changes.**

9. **Click the Servers tab.**

   A screen similar to the one in Figure 4-7 appears.

10. **Specify which of the domain's servers will work with Node Manager.**

    To specify a particular server, click the check box next to that server's name.

11. **Click Apply to apply your changes.**

Configuring startup arguments for managed servers

The Administration Server SSL configuration applies to the domain as a whole. After configuring Administration Server, each Node Manager instance that you run in the domain must specify startup arguments that identify the location of the keystore, password, and certificate files to use for SSL communication.

SSL is configured by providing command-line properties to Node Manager. Table 4-3 lists these command-line properties.

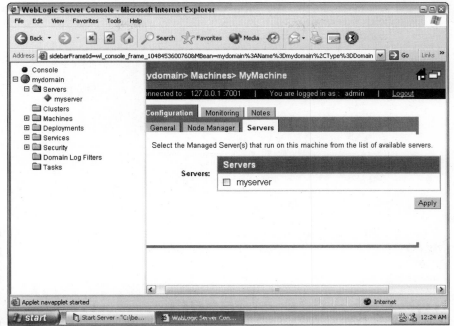

Figure 4-7:
Specifying
servers
for Node
Manager.

Table 4-3	Node Manager SSL Command-Line Properties
Property	**What It Does**
`-Dweblogic.nodemanager.keyFile`	Specifies the path to the key file, which could be encrypted.
`-Dweblogic.nodemanager.keyPassword`	Specifies the password to use if the key file is encrypted.
`-Dweblogic.nodemanager.certificateFile`	Specifies the path to the certificate file.
`-Dweblogic.security.SSL.trustedCAKeyStore`	Specifies the path to the keystore that holds a private key.
`-Dweblogic.nodemanager.sslHostNameVerificationEnabled`	Controls Administration Server host name checks against the nodemanager.hosts file. This should be disabled only when you're using demonstration certificates.

For example, to start Node Manager using the SSL configuration provided with the sample SSL certificate and key, you would use the following lengthy command:

```
java.exe -Xms32m -Xmx200m  -classpath %CLASSPATH%
-Dbea.home=c:\bea
-Dweblogic.nodemanager.keyFile=
c:\bea\user_domains\mydomain\demokey.pem
-Dweblogic.security.SSL.trustedCAKeyStore=
c:\bea\weblogic81\server\lib\cacerts
-Dweblogic.nodemanager.certificateFile=
c:\bea\user_domains\mydomain\democert.pem
-Djava.security.policy=
c:\weblogic81\server\lib\weblogic.policy
-Dweblogic.nodemanager.sslHostNameVerificationEnabled=false
weblogic.nodemanager.NodeManager
```

Although the preceding code looks like more than one line, you must enter it as a single command.

Starting Node Manager

Node Manager is a Java program and can be started by simply using the `java` command. In a production environment, you should automate this process by specifying that Node Manager be started as either a Windows service or a UNIX daemon.

In this section, you find out how to start Node Manager both from start scripts and as a Windows service. For more information about starting programs as UNIX daemons, refer to Chapter 3.

Starting Node Manager using start scripts

WebLogic includes some sample start scripts that you can use to start Node Manager. These start scripts are installed in the following directory:

```
c:\bea\weblogic81\server\bin
```

The name of your start script is as follows.

- `startNodeManager.cmd` for Windows
- `startNodeManager.sh` for UNIX

Both scripts set the required Node Manager environment values and start the Node Manager process.

When the script is executed, the current directory is changed to the following:

```
c:\bea\weblogic81\common\nodemanager
```

This directory will be used as a working directory for storing output and log files. If you want to specify a different working directory, edit the start script with a text editor and set the value of the NODEMGR_HOME variable to the directory that you would like to use.

It's also necessary to edit the sample start script to ensure that Node Manager startup arguments are set to the correct listen address and port number for your Node Manager process.

Starting with a start script is useful in a development environment, where you may need to stop and start Node Manager frequently.

Starting Node Manager as a Windows service

The c:\bea\weblogic81\ server\bin directory also contains scripts to install and uninstall Node Manager as a Windows service. These scripts are named installNodeMgrSvc.cmd and uninstallNodeMgrSvc.cmd. You can invoke either script from the command line.

In a production environment, it's a good idea to run Node Manager as a service. This ensures that no one has to be logged on to the server for Node Manager to be running.

When you run installNodeMgrSvc.cmd, it creates a default Windows service for Node Manager named NodeManager_localhost_5555. You may want to edit installNodeMgrSvc.cmd before running the script to change the service name or to use nondefault environment variables or startup arguments. If you edit installNodeMgrSvc.cmd to change the listen port or host name, make the same change to uninstallNodeMgrSvc.cmd so that it removes the correct service name.

Setting Node Manager environment variables

You can set many of the options of Node Manager by using environmental variables. You are not required to use all the features of Node Manager. By default, Node Manager performs as follows:

✔ The automatic restarting of managed servers is enabled.

✔ The automatic shutdown of managed servers is disabled.

✔ Node Manager monitors the managed servers that it has started.

In this section, you see how to change these settings.

Environmental variables are operating system variables that hold configuration information. Node Manager uses environmental variables to specify configuration settings. These are already set up for you when you run the startup scripts described previously. If you will be modifying the startup scripts, however, you must know the meanings of these environmental variables. A complete list of these variables is given in Table 4-4.

Table 4-4	Node Manager Environmental Variables
Variable	*What It Does*
CLASSPATH	Specifies the location of JAR files.
JAVA_HOME	Specifies the JVM that you will use for Node Manager. This should be set to the directory that Java is installed to.
PATH	The PATH environment variable should include the WebLogic Server bin directory as well as the path to your Java executable. This specifies the path to executables that must run.
WL_HOME	Specifies the directory that WebLogic was installed into (for example, c:\bea\weblogic81)

You can also set several Java properties when starting Node Manager. The following command shows the format for starting Node Manager using properties:

```
java [java_property=value ...] -D[nodemanager_property=value]
-D[server_property=value]
weblogic.nodemanager.NodeManager
```

A nodemanager_property begins with the prefix weblogic.property and directly affects the behavior of the Node Manager process. Table 4-5 summarizes these properties.

If you specify your own options for Java, always specify a minimum heap size of 32MB (-Xms32m) to avoid running out of memory. If you're using the scripts provided with WebLogic, this value is set automatically.

Table 4-5	Node Manager Properties	
Property	*Default*	*What It Does*
weblogic.ListenAddress	localhost	Specifies the address where Node Manager listens for connection requests.
weblogic.ListenPort	5555	Specifies the TCP port number where Node Manager listens for connection requests.
weblogic.nodemanager.certificateFile	./config/democert.pem	Specifies the path to the certificate file used for SSL authentication.
weblogic.nodemanager.javaHome	none	Specifies the Java home directory that Node Manager uses to start Managed Servers.
weblogic.nodemanager.keyFile	./config/demokey.pem	Specifies the path to the private key file to use for SSL communication with Administration Server.
weblogic.nodemanager.keyPassword	password	Specifies the password used to access the encrypted private key in the key file.
weblogic.nodemanager.nativeVersionEnabled	true	For UNIX systems other than Solaris or HP-UX, set this property to false to run Node Manager in non-native mode.
weblogic.nodemanager.reverseDnsEnabled	false	Specifies whether entries in the trusted hosts file can contain DNS names (instead of IP addresses).
weblogic.nodemanager.savedLogsDirectory	./NodeManagerLogs	Specifies the path in which Node Manager stores log files. Node Manager creates a subdirectory in savedLogsDirectory named NodeManagerLogs.

(continued)

Table 4-5 *(continued)*

Property	Default	What It Does
weblogic.nodemanager.sslHostNameVerificationEnabled	false	Specifies whether or not Node Manager performs host name verification.
weblogic.nodemanager.startTemplate	./nodemanager.sh	For UNIX systems, specifies the path of a script file used to start managed servers.
weblogic.nodemanager.trustedHosts	./nodemanager.hosts	Specifies the path to the trusted hosts file that Node Manager uses. See the "Setting up the Node Manager hosts file" section.
weblogic.nodemanager.weblogicHome	n/a	Specifies the root directory of the WebLogic Server installation. This is used as the default value of -Dweblogic.RootDirectory for servers that do not have a configured root directory.

Monitoring the Server

Monitoring is an important part of WebLogic administration. Monitoring allows you to quickly see an overview of how different parts of WebLogic are performing. WebLogic allows you to monitor the following areas:

- CORBA connection pools
- EJB
- HTTP
- JDBC
- JMS
- JNDI
- JTA subsystem

✔ Security

✔ Servers

All monitoring activity takes place through Administration Console. The monitoring functions of Administration Console are not isolated to one specific area. Rather, these functions are placed in the same area as the system that they're monitoring.

In general, to find the monitoring page for a specific service in WebLogic, follow these steps:

1. **Log on to Administration Console.**

2. **In the Services folder (on the left side of the screen), click the folder representing the service you want to monitor.**

   The information at the right side of the console changes to reflect the service you selected.

3. **On the right side of the screen, click the Monitoring tab.**

   The monitoring page shown in Figure 4-8 appears.

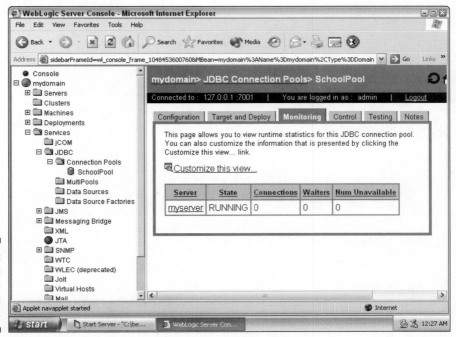

Figure 4-8: Beginning the monitoring process.

The monitoring page shows you how many connections are active, how many threads are waiting on a connection, and how many connections are unavailable. From here, you can monitor your connection.

Part II

Understanding
WebLogic
Components

In this part . . .

WebLogic Server can make use of many different components. In this part, you find out about these components and how they interact. You begin by constructing a web application. This application becomes the foundation upon which you build many of your other components.

Next, you're introduced to EJBs — Enterprise JavaBeans. EJBs allow you to create models that perform specific tasks. You find out about two types of EJBs — stateful and stateless session beans — as well as BMP (bean-managed persistence) and CMP (container-managed persistence) entity beans.

Then you create the one component that ties together all the other components: an enterprise application. The enterprise application can hold a web application and the EJBs used by that web application. In this way, you can package your application as one complete application.

Chapter 5

Creating Web Applications

● ●

In This Chapter

▶ Finding out the differences between web and application servers

▶ Setting up your first web application

▶ Understanding what's in a web application

▶ Using JSP, servlets, and JSTL

● ●

A web server can send a wide range of files to a client, on request. These files are the HTML, JSP, servlet, and other files needed to display your web site. These files, taken collectively, are referred to as a *web application*. Creating a web application is the topic of this chapter.

Server Basics

The difference between a web server and an application server can be confusing. As web and application servers continue to evolve, considerable overlap is created between the roles of these two types of software.

A *web server* is a program that sends web pages to a browser so that they can be displayed to users. For example, when you use your browser to visit a search engine, the browser requests the web page containing the search form. The server provides the form to your browser, which in turn displays the form for you to use. When you fill out the form, your browser sends your information to the web server. In short, the web server's primary job is interacting with the client software, such as your web browser.

Following are examples of programs commonly thought of as web servers:

✔ **Apache:** One of the oldest web servers and the leading one as measured by its installed base. Apache is open source and freely available.

✔ **Microsoft Internet Information Server (IIS):** Microsoft's web server, commonly used to run active server pages (ASP). IIS is the second largest web server, as measured by its installed base.

✔ **Tomcat:** A freely available open-source web server. Tomcat can be used either as a stand-alone server or with another web server that doesn't support JSP on its own.

An *application server* is a program whose primary purpose is to process data entered by the user. The application server does this by managing connections to the database. The user doesn't see the application server directly. The web server accesses the application server, and the user sees only the results of the application server's work through the web server. An application server can't be used alone to create an application, so most application servers, such as WebLogic and WebSphere, include their own web server as well. This allows you to deliver a complete application with both the web and application servers.

The following programs are commonly thought of as application servers, though some are capable of functioning also as web servers:

✔ **WebLogic.** A commercial application and web server developed by BEA Systems.

✔ **WebSphere.** An application and web server developed and marketed by IBM and usually used with IBM's Visual Age products.

✔ **JBoss.** An open-source application server. JBoss does not have the market share of WebLogic or WebSphere, but it's gaining in popularity.

Setting Up a Web Application

WebLogic is a great tool for setting up web applications. And in this section, you discover how to use WebLogic to do just that. The following steps are involved in setting up a web application:

1. **Create your server.** You create a server instance in WebLogic's Administration Console.

2. **Create your web application.** You create the web application in Administration Console. This will be a simple web application that doesn't yet have any content.

3. **Test your web application.** After you create your web application, you start your server and make sure that you set up the basic web application properly.

4. **Program your web application.** Now that your web application is working correctly, you can add some content. Programming your web application is a lengthy process that uses several technologies. This is by far the most time-consuming step. The amount of time that it takes is determined by the complexity of your web application.

5. **Package your web application.** You can optionally decide to package your web application into a WAR file — a single module file that contains nearly all your web application. (Only external resources such as databases are not included.) This can make it very easy to distribute your web application.

6. **Deploy your web application.** After you package your web application, you can deploy it to any number of servers. After your web application is deployed, it's ready to be used.

Creating, testing, packaging, and deploying your web application take little time compared to programming your web application. At the end of the chapter, I present an overview of the technologies available for programming your web application. More detailed information on individual technologies that you can use to build your web application can be found in other chapters.

The three steps of creating, testing, and deploying your server could be considered initial setup tasks. However, you create your server only once, but you test and deploy it repeatedly as you change your web application.

Creating your server

To run a web application, you need a server. One server can host multiple web applications. The easiest way to create a server is to use Domain Configuration Wizard. In Chapter 2, I go into the details of creating a server using Configuration Wizard, so refer to that chapter for more information.

Creating your web application

In this section, I show you how to create a web application. A web application can come in one of two forms. In this section, you create an *exploded web application,* which is made up of actual directories on your server computer. The other form of web application is a *web archive (WAR) file,* which contains the directory structure of an exploded web application.

Usually, you begin with an exploded web application, because it's easier to work with the files in a regular directory structure. Then you package your exploded web application into a WAR file.

Follow these steps to create a web application:

1. **Make sure that WebLogic is *not* running.**

   If you started WebLogic from the Start menu, simply close WebLogic's window. If you started WebLogic as a service, stop the service.

2. **Create your application directory.**

   Choose a name for your web application and create a directory of the same name in your domain's `applications` directory. For example, if you wanted to create an application named `myapp`, you would create a directory named

   ```
   c:\bea\user_projects\mydomain\applications\myapp
   ```

3. **Create an index file named index.html.**

   Create an index file that will be displayed when the user visits your web site. Listing 5-1 shows a sample index file.

4. **Create your `WEB-INF` directory.**

   The `WEB-INF` directory holds configuration files needed by your web application. You should create a `WEB-INF` directory within the directory you created in Step 2. If your web application were named `myapp`, for example, your `WEB-INF` directory would be named

   ```
   c:\bea\user_projects\mydomain\applications\myapp\WEB-INF
   ```

5. **Create a web application descriptor named web.xml and save it in the `WEB-INF` directory.**

   Listing 5-2 shows a sample web.xml file.

Listing 5-1: Sample index.html File

```
<html>
<head>
<title>Welcome</title>
</head>
<body>
<h1>Welcome</h1>
</body>
</html>
```

Listing 5-2: Sample web.xml File

```
<?xml version="1.0" encoding="UTF-8" ?>

  <!DOCTYPE web-app PUBLIC
    "-//Sun Microsystems, Inc.//DTD Web Application 2.3//EN"
    "http://java.sun.com/dtd/web-app_2_3.dtd" >

<web-app>
    <display-name>Example Application</display-name>

</web-app>
```

Now that you've created your web application, you're ready to test it.

Testing your web application

To test your web application, you need to first start your server. You can start a web server in several ways; see Chapter 3 for the details.

If you decided to have your web server start as a Windows service, the server will start automatically when you reboot (and on all subsequent reboots). If you want to start your server as a Windows service without rebooting, open the Windows Control Panel, double-click Administrative Tools, and then double-click the Services icon. Your new server begins with the prefix *beasvc* followed by the domain and server name that you chose in Chapter 2.

If you didn't set up your server as a Windows service, you should start your server using its icon. Choose Start➪BEA WebLogic Platform 8.1➪ User Projects➪(*Your Domain Name*)➪Start Server. (*Your Domain Name*) is the name of the domain that you created in Chapter 2. The screen shown in Figure 5-1 appears.

Now, to verify that your web application is running, open your favorite browser and type the following in the URL box:

```
http://localhost:7001/myapp
```

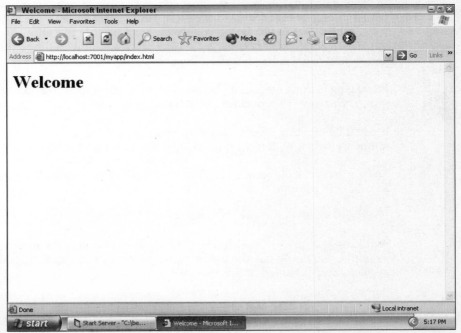

Figure 5-1:
Your
new web
application.

This URL assumes that you used the default port when you created your server. If you used a different number for your port (see Chapter 2), replace 7001 with that number.

Programming your web application

Assuming that you followed the steps outlined earlier in the chapter (and that you named the domain for your server `mydomain`), the root directory for this web application is

```
C:\bea\user_projects\mydomain\applications\myapp
```

You may want to simply use this web application on your single WebLogic Server. However, now is the time that you would normally begin programming your web application. You can use many different technologies to do this. Later in this chapter, I introduce you to some of them. Other chapters are dedicated to showing you how to use WebLogic and J2EE technologies to construct your web application.

Packaging your web application

At this point, you haven't created much of a web application. Other chapters show you how to create more advanced web applications. After you've created a more advanced web application, you'll likely want to package it as a web archive (WAR) file. Doing so means you'll be able to rapidly deploy your application on another server by simply copying the WAR file to the new server and using Administration Console to deploy the file.

Packaging is not a step that you do only once. As your web application grows, you have to repackage it each time you need an up-to-date WAR file.

If you'll be creating an enterprise application, you need to package your web application as a WAR file. Enterprise applications are discussed in Chapter 8.

To create a WAR file from `DefaultWebApp`, issue the following command from a command prompt:

```
jar cvf MyWebApp.war -C web-app-dir *.*
```

replacing `web-app-dir` with the root directory of your web application. For example, you could use the following to create a WAR file for the sample application developed in this chapter:

```
jar cvf MyWebApp.war -C
          C:\bea\user_projects\mydomain\applications\Default
          WebApp *.*
```

If you haven't added the JDK `bin` directory as part of your system path, you must use the full path name of the `jar` command, as shown here:

```
c:\bea\jdk131_03\bin\jar cvf MyWebApp.war -C
          C:\bea\user_projects\mydomain\applications\Default
          WebApp *.*
```

Deploying your web application

Now that you've packaged your web application, you can deploy it to any WebLogic Server that you want. You can also make it part of an enterprise application, as discussed in Chapter 8. WebLogic includes a program called Administration Console that can help you with most of the work necessary to deploy your web application. (For more on Administration Console, see Chapter 4.)

After you create your web application, you may want to change some of its options. Fortunately, these settings are not set in stone. You can change them by configuring your web application. The best way to find out how to configure your server is to just jump right in and do it:

1. **Log on to Administration Console.**

   If you need a refresher on how to do this, refer to Chapter 4. Here, however, you need to use your administrative username and password to actually log on.

2. **In the left pane, click the Deployments folder, and then click the Web Application Modules folder.**

   The right pane looks similar to Figure 5-2.

3. **In the right pane, click the <u>Deploy a new Application</u> link.**

4. **Click the <u>upload your file(s)</u> link.**

   This link is in the right pane, in the "Step 1" section. The screen shown in Figure 5-3 appears.

5. **Locate and open the WAR file that you want to add.**

   Click the Browse button, locate your WAR file, and then click Open.

6. **Upload the WAR file.**

   WebLogic reads the WAR file and displays a directory at the bottom of the right pane, as shown in Figure 5-4.

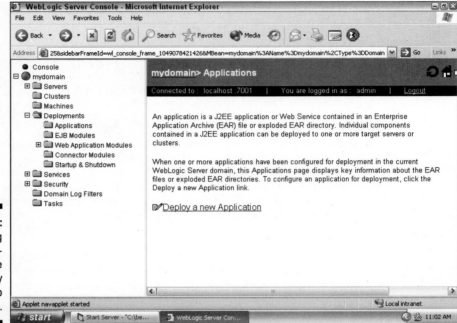

Figure 5-2:
Using
Administra-
tion Console
to modify
your web
applications.

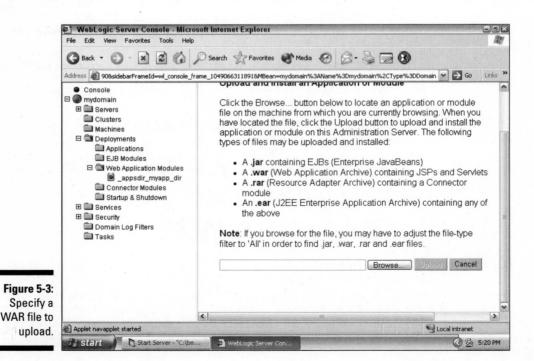

Figure 5-3:
Specify a
WAR file to
upload.

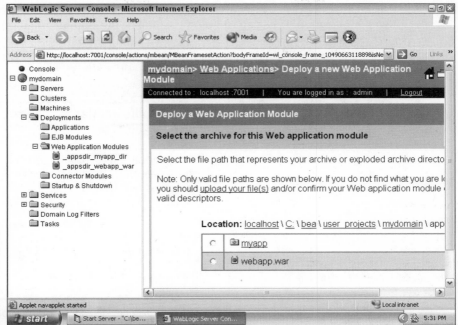

Figure 5-4:
Selecting
your
uploaded
WAR file.

7. **In the directory tree, click the radio button link to the left of the JAR file name.**

   You may have to scroll to see the radio button and WAR file name.

8. **Type a name for your web application.**

   The name can contain letters and numbers.

9. **Click Deploy.**

Now that you've seen how to create and deploy a web application, it's time to look at some of the technologies that you can include in a web application.

Directory Structure for Your Web Application

Earlier in this chapter (in the section "Creating your server"), you created a directory to hold your web application. This is only the root-level directory for your application. You should create other directories — in fact, an entire directory structure — to help organize the information in your application.

As an administrator, you must be aware of the directory structure of your web application. Doing so will help you make your application more efficient and economical on space, as well as more logical for you and others who must work with your application. Table 5-1 shows some of the important directories and files contained in your web application.

Table 5-1	WEB-INF Subdirectories and Files
Directory and File	*What It Is*
WEB-INF/web.xml	The main web application deployment configuration file. This file contains many configuration settings and has a standard format, so it can be used by many different web servers.
WEB-INF/weblogic.xml	This file is similar to web.xml except it contains settings specific to WebLogic.
WEB-INF/classes	Contains server-side class files, such as servlets.
WEB-INF/lib	Contains JAR files used by the web application. JAR files contain Java classes that will be used by your web application.

The WEB-INF directory is a private directory in your domain's root directory. *Private directories* are not accessible to users who browse your web site. All configuration information for your web application is stored in this directory. Later, when you want to deploy your web application, you copy this directory structure or archive it to a web archive (WAR) file.

Now that you have an overview of the technologies that make up a web application, it's time to see how to use some of them.

The Files in a Web Application

Now you have a generic web application that's like any web application created with WebLogic. In this section, you make your web application perform a task by adding different types of custom files to it. Following are some of these custom files:

✔ **JSP (JavaServer Pages).** Similar to HTML files in that they contain HTML formatting information that defines how to display the page. However, JSP can contain embedded Java that further defines the appearance of a page, so JSP is dynamic. For more information about how to program JSP, see *Making Use of JSP* by Madhushree Ganguli (published by Wiley Publishing, Inc.).

✓ **JSTL (JSP Standard Tag Library).** Another way of programming JSP. Instead of using Java commands, however, you use special tags, like HTML. The result is a more consistent JSP file. For more on programming JSTL, see my book on JSTL, *JSP Standard Tag Library Kick Start* (published by Sams).

✓ **Servlet.** A Java program that produces HTML output. Most functions of the servlet have been replaced by JSP and JSTL. For more information about how to program servlets, check out *Java Servlet Programming Bible* by Suresh Rajagopalan (Editor), Ramesh Rajamani, Ramesh Krishnaswamy, and Sridhar Vijendran (published by Wiley Publishing, Inc.).

Using JSP

One common way to create web applications is to use Java Server Pages (JSP). With JSP, you can generate web pages that pull their content from a variety of sources, such as user input or a database. Unlike HTML pages, which remain the same from view to view (they're static), JSPs can change their content (they're dynamic). JSPs usually form the front line of your web application because they're the level that the user directly interacts with.

Finding a home for JSPs

When you create JSP files, you store them in the root directory of your web application, but they're not limited to that location. You can also create subdirectories and place JSP files there as well. You determined the location of your web application's root directory when you created your web application.

You can also create additional directories under the root directory. For example, you might want to create a directory named `images` to hold all graphic files used with your web application.

Creating a JSP file

JSP files are ordinary text files, so you can create a JSP file with any text file editor.

You can create JSP files also with HTML editing tools such as FrontPage or Dreamweaver. Although HTML editors such as these are of little help writing the Java source code part of a JSP, they can help you to create the HTML that provides the look and feel of your JSP.

JSPs are a blend of HTML and Java code. If you know Java, it won't take you long to figure out how to create JSPs. This book doesn't attempt to teach you JSP. To find out more about JSP, refer to *Making Use of JSP* by Madhushree Ganguli (published by Wiley Publishing, Inc.).

Figure 5-5 shows an example of a web page created using JSP. This page displays a form that allows the user to enter an ID and a password. The program then displays that same information. This simple example shows the dynamic nature of JSP, in that the JSP can integrate the data that you enter with the HTML that it displays.

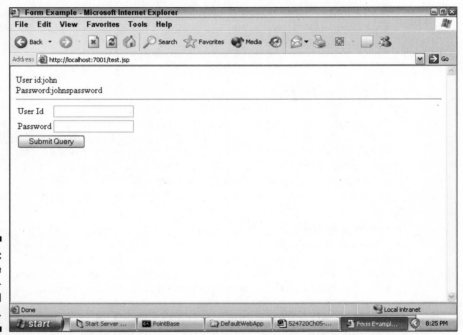

Figure 5-5:
An example
of a JSP-
generated
web page.

The source code for this page is shown in Listing 5-3. The JSP code is not very long, but it runs quite handily on WebLogic.

Listing 5-3:   JSP to Prompt the User for an ID and a Password

```
<html>
  <head>
    <title>Form Example</title>
  </head>
  <body>
<%
```

```
if( request.getMethod().equalsIgnoreCase("post"))
{%>
User id:<%=request.getParameter("uid")%><br/>
Password:<%=request.getParameter("pwd")%><br/>
<hr/>
<%}
%>
    <table border=0>
      <form method="post">
        <tr><td>User Id</td>
        <td><input type="text" name="uid"></td>
        </tr>
        <tr><td>Password</td>
        <td><input type="text" name="pwd"></td>
        </tr>
        <tr><td colspan="2"><input type="submit"/>
        </td></tr>
      </form>
    </table>
  </body>
</html>
```

The JSP is a mix of HTML and Java code. When Java code appears in JSP, the code is enclosed by <% and %>. This is true for both large blocks of code, spanning several lines, or a small block containing a single statement (as in <%=i%>).

The following steps summarize how the JSP in Listing 5-3 executes:

1. The example page is loaded into the browser. No POST is detected, so the form is displayed.

2. The user enters data.

3. The form POSTs the entered data back to itself.

4. The example page begins again. A POST is detected, so the POSTed variables are displayed.

You may be wondering what I mean by POSTing data. HTTP (the underlying protocol of the Web) has three basic types of requests: POST, GET, and HEAD. HEAD simply verifies that a page still exists. Search engines typically use the HEAD request to purge their lists of dead links. The two request types that you need to understand are GET and POST.

The GET request is the most common request type. When a browser requests a web page, it uses a GET request. When you type a URL in a browser or follow a hyperlink, you're performing a GET request. Step 1 of this JSP page checks to see whether a POST request is being performed, by using this line:

```
if( request.getMethod().equalsIgnoreCase("post"))
```

If this is the first request for the page, the request method is a GET request, not a POST request. Thus, the JSP simply displays the form to request user information.

When Step 3 is performed, however, the page is retrieved using a POST request. The POST request is similar to a GET request. In both the POST and GET requests, you request a URL and get a page back. The main difference is that the POST request allows you to supply additional information with the request. In Listing 5-3, the extra information is the data that the user entered. When you reach Step 3, the JSP detects that a POST request is in progress and displays the results of the POST request rather than the form.

Step 4 now begins. The user may enter information and begin the process again.

You can save time by designing a JSP to POST back to itself. Otherwise, you need two JSPs: one to display the form and a second to process the data returned by the form. POSTing to the JSP that created the form saves having to have two JSPs for each form.

JSP pages are converted to Java source files. These source files are then compiled to servlets and presented to the user as the application runs.

A quick look at servlets

A *servlet* is nothing more than a Java class constructed so that it can output to a web server. In the old days (before JSPs), you could create interactive Java web pages only by using servlets.

A JSP file is actually a servlet. The code in a JSP file is first translated to a .java file. This .java file contains a servlet. When you create the servlet yourself, the translation step is eliminated, resulting in faster execution time.

Listing 5-4 shows a simple "Hello World" servlet.

Listing 5-4:   Servlet to Display "Hello World"

```
import javax.servlet.*;
import java.io.*;

public class ExampleServlet extends GenericServlet
{
  public void service(ServletRequest request, ServletResponse
          response)
  {
    response.setContentLength(helloString.length());
    response.setContentType("text/plain");
```

```
    try
    {
      PrintStream rs = new
          PrintStream(response.getOutputStream());
      rs.print("Hello, world\r\n");
    }
    catch (IOException e)
    {
    // handle any errors
    }
  }
}
```

If you're familiar with Java, you might notice in Listing 5-4 that a servlet is simply a regular Java program. The `service` method fulfills the same purpose as `main` in a regular Java program.

The servlet communicates by using the `ServletRequest` parameter that's passed in. To send data back to the web browser, you use the `ServletResponse` object, which is passed to the `service` method. For more information on servlets, you might want to read *Java Servlet Programming* by Jason Hunter and William Crawford (published by O'Reilly & Associates).

Using JSTL

One of the main disadvantages of both JSP and servlets is that they mix regular Java program code and HTML-type tags, which display the page layout. JSP Standard Tag Library (JSTL), however, eliminates this difference by requiring the use of tags, rather than Java code. Because of this, Java programmers find JSTL not as familiar as JSP. In many ways, JSTL is a new web programming language separate from JSP.

Installing JSTL

To use JSTL, you must have a JSP 1.2 (or higher) server installed, such as WebLogic. (Isn't it handy that you just happen to have such a server?) WebLogic doesn't include JSTL support by default; it must be added. You can obtain JSTL from the following URL:

```
http://java.sun.com/products/jsp/jstl/
```

From here, you can download and discover more about JSTL.

To use JSTL, you must unzip the distribution files and install them in the correct locations in WebLogic. Follow these three steps:

1. **Copy the JSTL JAR files to WebLogic's `lib` directory.**

   If you're using Windows, the likely location of your `lib` directory is `\WEB-INF\lib`. A number of JAR files are included with the JSTL release; copy each of these files to the WebLogic `lib` directory.

2. **Copy the JSTL TLD files to WebLogic's `WEB-INF` directory.**

   The `WEB-INF` directory is probably at this location: `\WEB-INF`. If you look at the JSTL distribution files, you should notice eight files with the .tld extension. Copy all eight files to your `WEB-INF` directory.

3. **Modify the web.xml file to include the TLD files.**

   JSTL is made up of eight tag libraries. Add an entry for each library by adding `<taglib>` directives inside the main `<web-app>` directive. The entries you should add are shown in Listing 5-5.

Listing 5-5: web.xml Entries Used for JSTL

```
<taglib>
  <taglib-uri>http://java.sun.com/jstl/fmt</taglib-uri>
  <taglib-location>/WEB-INF/fmt.tld</taglib-location>
</taglib>

<taglib>
  <taglib-uri>http://java.sun.com/jstl/fmt-rt</taglib-uri>
  <taglib-location>/WEB-INF/fmt-rt.tld</taglib-location>
</taglib>

<taglib>
  <taglib-uri>http://java.sun.com/jstl/core</taglib-uri>
  <taglib-location>/WEB-INF/c.tld</taglib-location>
</taglib>

<taglib>
  <taglib-uri>http://java.sun.com/jstl/core-rt</taglib-uri>
  <taglib-location>/WEB-INF/c-rt.tld</taglib-location>
</taglib>

<taglib>
  <taglib-uri>http://java.sun.com/jstl/sql</taglib-uri>
  <taglib-location>/WEB-INF/sql.tld</taglib-location>
</taglib>

<taglib>
  <taglib-uri>http://java.sun.com/jstl/sql-rt</taglib-uri>
  <taglib-location>/WEB-INF/sql-rt.tld</taglib-location>
</taglib>

<taglib>
```

```
    <taglib-uri>http://java.sun.com/jstl/x</taglib-uri>
    <taglib-location>/WEB-INF/x.tld</taglib-location>
</taglib>

<taglib>
    <taglib-uri>http://java.sun.com/jstl/x-rt</taglib-uri>
    <taglib-location>/WEB-INF/x-rt.tld</taglib-location>
</taglib>
```

You're now ready to test your installation of JSTL. To do so, create a JSP file that uses JSTL. I will show you how to do this in the next section.

If JSTL is not installed correctly and you try to view a JSTL page, you probably won't see an error message. If JSTL is not interpreting your tags, they're passed through directly to the web browser. The web browser interprets these tags as unknown HTML tags, which most browsers simply ignore.

A JSTL example

JSTL code is stored in a JSP file. Because of this, you can easily mix JSTL code with both HTML and Java code, as shown in Listing 5-6, a simple JSTL example that counts to ten.

Listing 5-6:   Count to Ten Using JSTL

```
<%@ taglib uri="http://java.sun.com/jstl/core" prefix="c" %>
<html>
  <head>
    <title>If with Body</title>
  </head>

  <body>
    <c:if test="${pageContext.request.method=='POST'}">
      <c:if test="${param.guess=='Java'}">You guessed it!
      <br />

      <br />

      <br />
      </c:if>

      <c:if test="${param.guess!='Java'}">You are wrong
      <br />

      <br />

      <br />
      </c:if>
```

(continued)

Listing 5-6 *(continued)*

```
    </c:if>

    <form method="post">Guess what computer language
                        I am thinking of?
    <input type="text" name="guess" />

    <input type="submit" value="Try!" />

    <br />
    </form>
  </body>
</html>
```

As you can see from Listing 5-6, there's no Java code on the page. Tag programming determines whether you guessed the correct word. A good example of tag programming is the method JSTL uses for an if statement. The body of the if statement is enclosed in <c:if> and </c:if> tags. The expression that the <c:if> tag evaluates is provided by the var attribute.

Complete coverage of JSTL is beyond the scope of this book. For more information on JSTL, you might want to check out a book I wrote called *JSP Standard Tag Library Kick Start* (published by Sams).

Chapter 6

Using EJBs

*E*nterprise JavaBeans, or EJBs, are individual units that you break your web application into and host using WebLogic Server. In this chapter, you create (and install) an EJB. These individual units represent functional areas of your web application, making your web application easy to maintain and increasing the likelihood of reusing the code.

Creating EJBs, however, is only half of the story. Your EJBs must ultimately be used somewhere. In this chapter, you also find out how to use these EJBs in web applications that you've created with WebLogic.

Several types of EJBs are available:

✔ **Stateful session beans.** An EJB that holds information from one invocation to the next. Holding this information requires overhead, so stateful session beans should be used sparingly.

✔ **Stateless session beans.** An EJB that doesn't hold any information from one invocation to the next. This is the most commonly used EJB.

✔ **Entity beans.** A bean that represents some form of persistent data. An entity bean usually corresponds to one record of data.

✔ **Message beans.** An EJB that receives JMS messages.

In this chapter, I focus on session beans, presenting an example of both a stateful and stateless EJB. These are the two most basic types of EJBs supported by WebLogic. Entity beans are described in Chapter 7. Message beans are introduced here and discussed in Chapter 15.

Creating Stateless Session Beans

In the world of Enterprise JavaBeans, a *stateless session bean* simply means that the bean doesn't remember anything from one invocation to the next. This is useful because it takes some overhead to maintain this memory. You should use stateless session beans whenever possible.

To create a stateless session bean, you must include five components:

- **Remote interface.** The client class uses this interface to call your EJB.

- **Home interface.** The client program uses this interface to create instances of the EJB.

- **Bean class.** The bean class holds the functionality of the bean. Most of your code will be placed in this class.

- **Deployment descriptor.** The deployment descriptor is an XML file that contains the names of all the classes that make up your EJB.

- **Client class.** The client class is not part of the EJB. This is a class that calls the EJB.

In this section, you find out what you must do to create each of these components.

Creating the remote interface

The process of creating a bean begins with the creation of a remote interface. Your remote interface must extend (using the Java keyword `extends`) the `javax.ejb.EJBObject` interface and define the methods that you want to make available with your EJB. The client uses the remote interface to access your EJB. The remote interface is only a template to specify how to access the bean class. You will have only method templates — no actual code.

Your remote interface is implemented as a Java interface. A Java interface explains something that can be accomplished but never explains how to accomplish it. An interface does not contain program logic. It contains only method headers that list the methods available to any class that implements the interface. The remote interface for your stateless session bean is shown in Listing 6-1.

Listing 6-1:   Remote Interface for Your Stateless EJB

```
// Sample.java
package com.dummies.ejb;

import javax.ejb.*;
import java.rmi.*;

public interface Sample extends EJBObject
{
  public String sampleMethod(int n)
    throws RemoteException;
}
```

I created a class named `Sample` that contains a single method named `sampleMethod`. Although this EJB has only one method, you can add as many methods as needed to create your EJB.

Creating the home interface

After you create the remote interface, the next step is to create a home interface. The home interface is a Java class that extends the `EJBHome` class. It's called a home interface because it's used by the client to instantiate instances of the EJB.

The home interface defines the creation and removal of session beans. Fortunately, you don't need to write all the methods of the parent `EJBHome` interface. You need to write only a `create` method that returns the type of remote interface.

The home interface is shown in Listing 6-2. For stateless session beans, your home interface will always be this simple.

Listing 6-2:   Home Interface for Your Stateless EJB

```
// SampleHome.java
package com.dummies.ejb;

import javax.ejb.*;
import java.rmi.*;

public interface SampleHome extends EJBHome
{
  public Sample create()
    throws RemoteException,CreateException;

}
```

Creating the bean class

Up to this point in your stateless session bean creation, you've created only two interfaces. In this section, you create the bean class, where all the real work takes place. The bean class is a regular Java class that implements the SessionBean class. Listing 6-3 shows the bean class for your bean.

Listing 6-3:   Class for Your Stateless EJB

```
// SampleBean.java
package com.dummies.ejb;

import javax.ejb.*;
import java.rmi.*;
import javax.swing.*;

public class SampleBean implements SessionBean
{

  private SessionContext stx;

  //Required methods, not used by this type of bean
  public void ejbCreate(){}
  public void ejbRemove(){}
  public void ejbActivate(){}
  public void ejbPassivate(){}

  // setter for the SessionContext
  public void setSessionContext(SessionContext ctx)
  {
    ctx = this.stx;
  }

  // the sample method

  public String sampleMethod(int num)
    throws RemoteException
  {
    switch(num)
    {
      case 1:return "One";
      case 2:return "Two";
      case 3:return "Three";
      case 4:return "Four";
      case 5:return "Five";
      case 6:return "Six";
      case 7:return "Seven";
      case 8:return "Eight";
      case 9:return "Nine";
```

```
      case 10:return "Ten";
      default:return "Some Number";
   }
  }
}
```

The bean class is more complex than the interfaces you created previously in the chapter. The `setSessionContext` method receives `javax.ejb.SessionContext`, which you need for stateful beans.

The `SessionContext` object stores information that you want to hold between calls to your EJB. WebLogic passes `SessionContext` to the `setSessionContext` method. The `SessionContext` object is stored to a `class` property, as we did in `setSessionContext`.

Creating deployment descriptors

Deployment descriptors are the configuration files that allow WebLogic to know about your EJBs. WebLogic uses two EJB-specific deployment descriptors; both are XML files:

- ✓ `ejb-jar.xml`. Required by J2EE, this descriptor remains the same whether you're using WebLogic or another application server. The primary purpose of this file is to map your bean to its class files and to define the type of bean.

- ✓ `weblogic-ejb-jar.xml`. This descriptor includes configuration information required by WebLogic but not by J2EE. This file is specific to WebLogic and would have no meaning to another application server. This file contains information for performance, clustering, and security.

The `ejb-jar.xml` descriptor required for the example stateless bean is shown in Listing 6-4.

Listing 6-4:   J2EE Deployment Descriptor for Your Stateless EJB

```
<!DOCTYPE ejb-jar PUBLIC
'-//Sun Microsystems, Inc.//DTD Enterprise JavaBeans 2.0//EN'
'http://java.sun.com/dtd/ejb-jar_2_0.dtd'>
<ejb-jar>
  <enterprise-beans>
    <session>
      <ejb-name>SampleObject</ejb-name>
        <home>com.dummies.ejb.SampleHome</home>
        <remote>com.dummies.ejb.Sample</remote>
        <ejb-class>com.dummies.ejb.SampleBean</ejb-class>
```

(continued)

Listing 6-4 *(continued)*

```
            <session-type>Stateless</session-type>
            <transaction-type>Container</transaction-type>
        </session>
    </enterprise-beans>
</ejb-jar>
```

The elements you must configure are summarized in Table 6-1. The primary purpose of these elements is to name the home, interface, and bean classes that you created previously.

Table 6-1	Selected EJB Deployment Descriptor Elements
Element	**What It Is**
ejb-name	The name of the EJB.
home	The class that implements the home interface for the bean.
remote	The class that implements the remote interface for the bean.
ejb-class	The class that implements the logic for the bean.
session-type	The type of session that this bean supports. This value is Stateless or Stateful.
transaction-type	This property specifies whether the bean or the container will manage persistence for an entity bean. Should be container or bean. See Chapter 7.

In addition to the standard EJB deployment descriptor, you must create a WebLogic-compatible deployment descriptor. An example of a WebLogic deployment descriptor is shown in Listing 6-5. You must configure a number of elements, primarily enterprise elements. These are covered in Chapter 8.

Listing 6-5: WebLogic Deployment Descriptor for Your Stateless EJB

```
<!DOCTYPE weblogic-ejb-jar PUBLIC
'-//BEA Systems, Inc.//DTD WebLogic 6.0.0 EJB//EN'
'http://www.bea.com/servers/wls600/dtd/weblogic-ejb-jar.dtd'>

<weblogic-ejb-jar>
    <weblogic-enterprise-bean>
        <ejb-name>SampleObject</ejb-name>
        <jndi-name>SampleObject</jndi-name>
    </weblogic-enterprise-bean>
</weblogic-ejb-jar>
```

Creating the client class

Up to this point, you've focused on how to configure the application server. However, the reason you put an EJB on an application server is so a client program can access the functionality in the EJB. In this section, you create a client that can access your EJB. Listing 6-6 shows a simple client that accesses the EJB that you just created.

When I refer to *client* and *server*, you may think that this means two different machines. This is not necessarily the case. The client and server could be the same machine.

Listing 6-6:   Java Program to Access Your Stateless EJB

```
package com.dummies.ejb;

import javax.ejb.*;
import javax.rmi.*;
import java.rmi.*;
import java.util.*;
import javax.swing.*;
import javax.naming.*;

public class SampleClient
{
  public static void main(String[] args)
  {
    try
    {
      Properties h = new Properties();
      h.put(Context.INITIAL_CONTEXT_FACTORY,
        "weblogic.jndi.WLInitialContextFactory");
      h.put(Context.PROVIDER_URL, "t3://localhost:7001" );
      Context initial = new InitialContext( h );
      Object obj = initial.lookup("SampleObject");

      SampleHome samplehome = (SampleHome)
      PortableRemoteObject.narrow(obj , SampleHome.class);
      Sample sample = samplehome.create();
      String str =
        JOptionPane.showInputDialog("Enter your number");
      JOptionPane.showMessageDialog(null,
        sample.sampleMethod(Integer.parseInt(str)) );
    }
    catch(Exception e)
    {
      System.out.println( e );
      JOptionPane.showMessageDialog(null ,
        "Exception:"+e);
    }
  }
}
```

To access the EJB using the client program, you must first create a `Properties` object that will contain information specifying which WebLogic Server you will connect to:

```
Properties h = new Properties();
h.put(Context.INITIAL_CONTEXT_FACTORY,
  "weblogic.jndi.WLInitialContextFactory");
h.put(Context.PROVIDER_URL, "t3://localhost:7001" );
```

The server that you're connecting to is on port 7001 of the localhost server. The localhost address specifies the current computer.

After you've constructed your properties, you must obtain a `Context` object. To obtain a `Context` object, you initialize `IntialContext` with the `Properties` object that you just created (h):

```
Context initial = new InitialContext( h );
```

Now that you have a `Context` object, you can use it to access your EJB:

```
Object obj = initial.lookup("SampleObject");
SampleHome samplehome = (SampleHome)
PortableRemoteObject.narrow(obj , SampleHome.class);
```

Finally, you're ready to create your EJB as an object. To do this, you call the `create` method of the `samplehome` object:

```
Sample sample = samplehome.create();
```

Now that you have the object, you can use it. The user is prompted for a number, which is then passed to the `sample` object:

```
String str =
  JOptionPane.showInputDialog("Enter your number");
JOptionPane.showMessageDialog(null,
  sample.sampleMethod(Integer.parseInt(str)) );
```

The result returned from the EJB is then displayed. As you can see from this example, you call the EJB just like any other Java object. The most complex part of creating EJBs on the client is obtaining the object.

Building the Stateless Session Bean EJB

In the preceding section, you created the files necessary to construct an EJB. In this section, you bring these files together and compile the EJB. The final output from the compilation process is a JAR file. You can then deploy this JAR file to WebLogic Server, a process shown in the next section.

To properly compile the EJB, you must have J2SE and J2EE installed on your computer. You can download them from http://java.sun.com. These are two separate downloads. Make sure that you install J2SE first.

Building an EJB requires several steps. To make this process easier, these steps are often put in a script file, which you can then execute to build the EJB JAR file whenever it's needed. To build the example, you would use a build script similar to the one shown in Listing 6-7. This script first compiles the Java files to class files. The EJB is then built from these class files.

Listing 6-7:   Script to Build Your Stateless EJB

```
@rem buildStatelessEJB.cmd
@echo off

@rem Set this to the location of your JDK installation
set JDK_HOME=C:\j2sdk1.4.1_01

@rem Set this to the location of your J2EE JAR file
set CLASSPATH=C:\j2sdkee1.4\lib\j2ee.jar

@rem Set this to the location for storing the class files
set CLASSES=.\CLASSES

@rem set up the directory structure
rmdir /q /s %CLASSES%
mkdir %CLASSES%
mkdir %CLASSES%\META-INF

@rem compile the classes
"%JDK_HOME%"\bin\javac .\src\com\dummies\ejb\*.java -
           classpath %CLASSPATH% -d %CLASSES%

@rem copy the config files
xcopy /y .\src\META-INF\*.* %CLASSES%\META-INF\

@rem JAR it up
cd %CLASSES%
"%JDK_HOME%"\bin\jar -cvf ..\EJBSample.jar *.*
cd ..
```

You should change the first few lines of the build script to reflect the correct paths on your computer. The first variable, JDK_HOME, contains the directory that JDK was installed into. The second variable, CLASSPATH, contains a list of all external JAR files required to compile this class:

```
set JDK_HOME=C:\j2sdk1.4.1_01
set CLASSPATH=C:\j2sdkee1.4\lib\j2ee.jar
```

The only external JAR file that's referenced is the J2EE JAR file. This file should have been installed automatically when you installed J2EE.

Next, the path that the class files will be compiled to is set. Don't change this directory:

```
@rem Set this to the location for storing the class files
set CLASSES=.\CLASSES
```

The script is now ready to create the directory structure. If a classes directory already exists, it is deleted. Next, you create the classes directory as well as a directory named META-INF inside the classes directory. The META-INF directory is where you will store the ejb-jar.xml and weblogic-ejb-jar.xml files:

```
@rem set up the directory structure
rmdir /q /s %CLASSES%
mkdir %CLASSES%
mkdir %CLASSES%\META-INF
```

Now that you've set the paths and created the directory structure, you can begin to compile the files:

```
@rem compile the classes
"%JDK_HOME%"\bin\javac .\src\com\dummies\ejb\*.java -
classpath %CLASSPATH% -d %CLASSES%
```

Next, you copy the two XML files to the classes directory so that they can be included in the JAR file build:

```
@rem copy the config files
xcopy /y .\src\META-INF\*.* %CLASSES%\META-INF\
```

Finally, after all the code has been compiled, the script creates a JAR file to contain the entire EJB:

```
@rem JAR it up
cd %CLASSES%
"%JDK_HOME%"\bin\jar -cvf ..\EJBSample.jar *.*
cd ..
```

When the process is finished, you're left with a file named EJBSample.jar. This file contains your EJB and will be used when the EJB is deployed. When you execute Listing 6-7, the screen shown in Figure 6-1 appears.

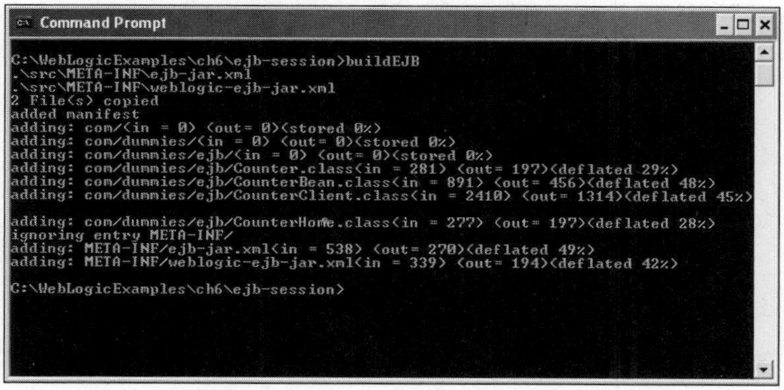

Command Prompt

C:\WebLogicExamples\ch6\ejb-session>buildEJB
.\src\META-INF\ejb-jar.xml
.\src\META-INF\weblogic-ejb-jar.xml
2 File(s) copied
added manifest
adding: com/(in = 0) (out= 0)(stored 0%)
adding: com/dummies/(in = 0) (out= 0)(stored 0%)
adding: com/dummies/ejb/(in = 0) (out= 0)(stored 0%)
adding: com/dummies/ejb/Counter.class(in = 281) (out= 197)(deflated 29%)
adding: com/dummies/ejb/CounterBean.class(in = 891) (out= 456)(deflated 48%)
adding: com/dummies/ejb/CounterClient.class(in = 2410) (out= 1314)(deflated 45%)

adding: com/dummies/ejb/CounterHome.class(in = 277) (out= 197)(deflated 28%)
ignoring entry META-INF/
adding: META-INF/ejb-jar.xml(in = 538) (out= 270)(deflated 49%)
adding: META-INF/weblogic-ejb-jar.xml(in = 339) (out= 194)(deflated 42%)

C:\WebLogicExamples\ch6\ejb-session>

Figure 6-1:
Building
the EJB.

Deploying the Stateless Session EJB

Now that you've created your stateless session EJB, you must deploy it. Then you can use the EJB in client programs. The following steps show you how to deploy the EJB:

1. **Start WebLogic Server.**

   To do so, choose Start⇨All Programs⇨BEA WebLogic Platform 8.1⇨ User Projects⇨*mydomain*. Replace *mydomain* with the name of the domain to which you want to deploy the EJB.

2. **Start WebLogic Server Console.**

   To do so, access the URL `http://localhost:7001/console`.

3. **Type your user name and password.**

4. **On the left, under your domain, click Deployments and then click EJB Modules.**

   The screen shown in Figure 6-2 appears.

5. **Click the <u>Deploy a new EJB Module</u> link.**

6. **In the Step 1 section, choose to upload the EJBSample.jar file by clicking the <u>upload file(s)</u> link.**

   After the upload, your JAR file is visible under Step 2.

7. **In the Step 2 section, select the EJBSample.jar file.**

8. **In the Step 3 section, select your server from the Available Servers list and click the right arrow to move it to the Target Servers list.**

9. **In the Step 4 section, type a name for the application.**

   You can enter any name you like. To follow along with the example, type **EJBSample**.

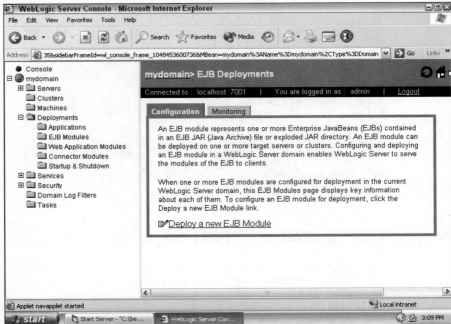

Figure 6-2:
Deploying
the EJB.

10. **Click Configure and Deploy to complete the process.**

Your EJB is now deployed and ready to be accessed. In the next section, you
create a simple class that tests the EJB.

Testing the Stateless Session EJB

Now that you've created your EJB, you need a class that calls it. You created
this class in Listing 6-6. Now you execute the class to see the stateless session EJB in action. Just as you did when building the EJB, you will also create
a script that runs the EJB client. This program is shown in Listing 6-8.

Listing 6-8:   Script to Run Your Stateless EJB Client

```
@rem runEJB.bat
@echo off

@rem Set this to the location of your JDK installation
set JDK_HOME=C:\j2sdk1.4.1_01

@rem Set this to the location of your J2EE JAR file
set CLASSPATH=C:\j2sdkee1.4\lib\j2ee.jar;.\EJBSample.jar;
```

```
  C:\bea\weblogic81\server\lib\weblogic.jar

@rem compile the classes
"%JDK_HOME%"\bin\java com.dummies.ejb.SampleClient -classpath
   %CLASSPATH%
```

The process for running a class that makes use of EJBs is similar to the process you'd use for any other Java class. The only additional step that you must be aware of is making sure that the correct JAR files are in CLASSPATH:

```
set CLASSPATH=C:\j2sdkee1.4\lib\j2ee.jar;.\EJBSample.jar;
   C:\bea\weblogic81\server\lib\weblogic.jar
```

If you issue this command, you'll have all three required JAR files in CLASSPATH. Of course, if you've stored these JAR files elsewhere, you must change the preceding path.

You might need to change this CLASSPATH depending on the path structure of your computer. As you can see, you must include three JAR files:

- ✔ J2EE JAR file (j2ee.jar)
- ✔ WebLogic JAR file (weblogic.jar)
- ✔ EJB JAR file (for example, EJBSample.jar)

For most EJB clients, you will need at least these three files. The name of the EJB JAR file depends on what you called the EJB for your own application.

Adding State

The EJBs that you've seen so far are stateless, which means they remember nothing from one page to the next. After the JSP on which you used the EJB has finished displaying, any data stored in the bean is lost. You can add state by creating a session EJB.

A *session EJB* holds the information stored in the bean until the user's session is terminated. (A user's *session* is a special area of memory created for each user who logs on to the web server.) This session information allows the web server to store basic information about the current user.

Although session EJBs are a convenient way to store information about a user, they should not be overused. Every piece of information that you add to the session bean is additional information that the web server must store for every user who logs on to the system. This can result in a large amount of data if your system has a large number of simultaneous users.

For the example session EJB, you'll create an EJB that implements a simple counter. The class, named `Counter`, contains three methods named `count`, `reset`, and `getCount`. The `count` method is called with an integer as the parameter. This integer is added to `Counter`'s internal counter. To access the value in this counter, you call the `getCount` method. The counter holds its value as the EJB is used. You can use the `reset` method to set this count back to 0.

You can specify an EJB as a session EJB with the J2EE deployment descriptor. Whereas Listing 6-4 is a deployment descriptor for a stateless EJB, Listing 6-9 is a deployment descriptor for a session EJB.

Listing 6-9: J2EE Deployment Descriptor for Your Session EJB

```
<!DOCTYPE ejb-jar PUBLIC
'-//Sun Microsystems, Inc.//DTD Enterprise JavaBeans 2.0//EN'
'http://java.sun.com/dtd/ejb-jar_2_0.dtd'>
<ejb-jar>
  <enterprise-beans>
    <session>
      <ejb-name>CounterObject</ejb-name>
        <home>com.dummies.ejb.CounterHome</home>
        <remote>com.dummies.ejb.Counter</remote>
        <ejb-class>com.dummies.ejb.CounterBean</ejb-class>
        <session-type>Stateful</session-type>
        <transaction-type>Container</transaction-type>
    </session>
  </enterprise-beans>
</ejb-jar>
```

The one line that changes an EJB to a session EJB is the `session-type` tag. Because the tag type is specified as `Stateful`, the EJB becomes a session EJB.

Just as was the case with the stateless EJB, the session EJB must also have a WebLogic deployment descriptor. Listing 6-10 is a WebLogic deployment descriptor that works with the session EJB that you're creating.

Listing 6-10: WebLogic Deployment Descriptor for Your Session EJB

```
<!DOCTYPE weblogic-ejb-jar PUBLIC
'-//BEA Systems, Inc.//DTD WebLogic 6.0.0 EJB//EN'
'http://www.bea.com/servers/wls600/dtd/weblogic-ejb-jar.dtd'>

<weblogic-ejb-jar>
  <weblogic-enterprise-bean>
    <ejb-name>CounterObject</ejb-name>
    <jndi-name>CounterObject</jndi-name>
  </weblogic-enterprise-bean>
</weblogic-ejb-jar>
```

The WebLogic deployment descriptor for a session EJB is the same as the one for a stateless bean. Aside from the difference in the name of the EJB (`SampleObject` **versus** `CounterObject`), Listing 6-10 is the same as Listing 6-5.

Now that the configuration files are out of the way, you can construct the EJB. Stateless and session EJBs have the same three Java files. The three files that implement the `Counter` interface are shown in Listing 6-11.

Listing 6-11:   Remote Interface for Your Session EJB

```
// Counter.java
package com.dummies.ejb;

import javax.ejb.*;
import java.rmi.*;

public interface Counter extends EJBObject
{
  public void reset()
    throws RemoteException;

  public void count(int n)
    throws RemoteException;

  public int getCount()
    throws RemoteException;
}
```

Here the signatures are given for all three methods used by the `Counter` EJB. (The *signature* is the method header that specifies the method parameters, return type, and exceptions thrown.) The interface for a session EJB is no different than that for a stateless EJB.

The next file to be considered is the home class, which is shown in Listing 6-12. Compare this listing with Listing 6-2, and you can see that the home class for a session EJB and a stateless EJB is the same.

Listing 6-12:   Home Interface for Your Session EJB

```
// CounterHome.java
package com.dummies.ejb;

import javax.ejb.*;
import java.rmi.*;

public interface CounterHome extends EJBHome
{
  public Counter create()
    throws RemoteException,CreateException;

}
```

Next is the session bean class, where you place all the work performed by the session bean. This class, which is shown in Listing 6-13, must remember the data stored in the session bean.

Listing 6-13:   Class for Your Session EJB

```
// CounterBean.java
package com.dummies.ejb;

import javax.ejb.*;
import java.rmi.*;
import javax.swing.*;

public class CounterBean implements SessionBean
{

  private SessionContext stx;

  //Required methods, not used by this type of bean
  public void ejbCreate(){}
  public void ejbRemove(){}
  public void ejbActivate(){}
  public void ejbPassivate(){}

  // setter for the SessionContext
  public void setSessionContext(SessionContext ctx)
  {
    ctx = this.stx;
  }

  // the session information
  private int count = 0;

  // the sample method

  public void reset()
    throws RemoteException
  {
    count = 0;
  }

  public void count(int n)
    throws RemoteException
  {
    count+=n;
  }

  public int getCount()
    throws RemoteException
```

```
    {
      return count;
    }

}
```

The session EJB uses properties, also known as class-level variables, to store the data that will be remembered. In the case of the `Counter` EJB, the session information is stored in the `count` variable, as seen here:

```
private int count = 0;
```

Next you see how to call the session bean. The process is similar to calling a stateless EJB. The client program calls the session bean. The client is shown in Listing 6-14.

Listing 6-14:   Client for Your Session EJB

```
// CounterClient.java
package com.dummies.ejb;

import javax.ejb.*;
import javax.rmi.*;
import java.rmi.*;
import java.util.*;
import javax.swing.*;
import javax.naming.*;

public class CounterClient
{
  public static void main(String[] args)
  {
    try
    {
      Properties h = new Properties();
      h.put(Context.INITIAL_CONTEXT_FACTORY,
        "weblogic.jndi.WLInitialContextFactory");
      h.put(Context.PROVIDER_URL, "t3://localhost:7001" );
      Context initial = new InitialContext( h );
      Object obj = initial.lookup("CounterObject");

      CounterHome counterhome = (CounterHome)
      PortableRemoteObject.narrow(obj , CounterHome.class);
      Counter counter = counterhome.create();

      int i = 1;

      while(i!=0)
      {
```

(continued)

Listing 6-14 *(continued)*

```
        String str =
          JOptionPane.showInputDialog("Enter your number");
        if(str==null)
          i=0;
        else
          i = Integer.parseInt(str);
        counter.count(i);
        JOptionPane.showMessageDialog(null,
          "Current count = " + counter.getCount()  );
      }
    System.exit(0);
    }
  catch(Exception e)
  {
    System.out.println( e );
    JOptionPane.showMessageDialog(null ,
      "Exception:"+e);
  }
  }
}
```

Session and stateless EJBs are instantiated in the same way. (*Instantiation* is the process by which the EJB is allocated and assigned to a variable.) All information about the fact that this is a session bean is contained in the EJB itself.

The client program works by displaying a dialog box in which the user types a number. As the user types more and more numbers, they're added to the `counter` bean. This program can be seen in Figure 6-3.

Figure 6-3:
Testing the
stateless
EJB.

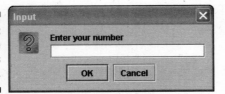

Accessing Data with Entity Beans

One powerful feature of EJBs is their capability to represent data stored in relational databases. This type of bean is called an *entity bean*. The process of storing this data is called *persistence*. Two types of entity beans follow:

✔ **Bean-managed persistence (BMP).** BMP EJBs contain code inside the bean class that allow the beans to be persisted. The beans may be persisted to a relational database or some other source. If the beans are persisted to a relational database, the EJB classes will contain methods used to write the contents of the bean to the database. If a means other than a relational database is used to persist the beans, the appropriate methods must be included.

✔ **Container-managed persistence (CMP).** CMP EJBs don't contain code inside their classes to persist the data stored in them. Rather, CMP EJBs are persisted to a relational database by using the SQL commands embedded in the EJB's configuration files.

Chapter 7 describes how to use both types of beans to interact with your database and shows you how to decide which of the two types you should use in your programs.

Configuring Message-Driven Beans

The EJBs discussed up to this point are all accessed like normal Java objects. You can also configure EJBs to be accessed through messages. Using messages with EJBs requires Java Message Services (JMS). This type of EJB is discussed in Chapter 15.

Chapter 7

Using Entity Beans

*I*n this chapter, you discover how to use J2EE entity beans. Entity beans provide a convenient interface between your program and the database. These beans are used to hold data that must eventually be stored in some permanent form, most commonly a relational database. J2EE has two types of entity beans: bean-managed persistence (BMP) beans and container-managed persistence (CMP) beans. BMP entity beans open connections directly to the database, whereas CMP entity beans rely on the server (container) for interacting with the database. I discuss both types of beans in this chapter.

Understanding WebLogic Database Access

The purpose of an entity bean is to allow Java data to move between memory and permanent storage, such as a database. The entity bean examples in this chapter write their data to a database, so you need to understand the basics of connecting a database to WebLogic. A basic familiarity with SQL and relational databases is assumed. A book such as Allen G. Taylor's *SQL For Dummies* (published by Wiley Publishing, Inc.) would be helpful for understanding the finer points of SQL.

You can use nearly any sort of database with WebLogic. For the examples in this book, I use the ODBC-JDBC bridge driver. Open Database Connectivity (ODBC) is a common standard on the Microsoft platform. Java Database Connectivity (JDBC) is the Java database standard. Using the ODBC-JDBC bridge allows you to use ODBC drivers from Java. Everything that you need to use the ODBC-JDBC bridge is already built into Java.

If you're using a database such as Oracle, DB2, MySQL, or SQL Server, you should use the appropriate driver. This will give better performance than the ODBC-JDBC bridge. For specific instructions on how to use a particular database with JDBC, refer to that database's documentation. Database access is covered in Chapter 12. More information about MySQL can be found at http://www.mysql.org.

Regardless of which database you use, you must set up the appropriate tables. In SQL, a *table* is a database construct that holds individual rows. For example, if you were keeping an address book, the address book is the table with individual names stored in rows. Listing 7-1 shows the SQL code necessary to create the tables used in this chapter. For more information about SQL, see Chapter 12.

Listing 7-1:   Script to Create the Example Database

```
CREATE TABLE T_STUDENT (
   F_ID INTEGER NOT NULL PRIMARY KEY,
   F_FIRST VARCHAR(40),
   F_LAST VARCHAR(40))

CREATE TABLE T_DEPARTMENT (
   F_ID INTEGER NOT NULL PRIMARY KEY,
   F_NAME VARCHAR(40))

CREATE TABLE T_COURSE (
   F_ID INTEGER NOT NULL PRIMARY KEY,
   F_NAME VARCHAR(40),
   F_CREDIT INTEGER,
   F_DEPARTMENT_ID INTEGER NOT NULL)
```

The SQL in Listing 7-1 should be generic enough to work with most databases. Note that each table name is prefixed with T_ and each field name is prefixed with F_. This notation ensures that a table or field name does not accidentally use a reserved word. This is important when designing for multiple databases, in which the collection of reserved words is different from database to database.

As you can see from Listing 7-1, each table is made up of several fields. For example, T_DEPARTMENT holds F_ID and F_NAME as fields. Every row in the T_DEPARTMENT table will hold these two values.

Creating the connection pool

WebLogic communicates with the database through a connection pool. The connection pool enables WebLogic to use a fixed number of connections to databases rather than incur the overhead of constantly creating and disposing of connections. Because of this, you must establish a data connection pool that accesses your database. To do so, follow these steps:

1. **Start Administrative Console.**

   For more information on this step, see Chapter 4.

2. **On the left side of the screen, click the Services folder, and then click the JDBC folder.**

   On this page, you can choose connection pools and choose to create a connection pool.

3. **Type a name for the connection pool.**

   To follow along with the example, type **SchoolPool** for the connection pool name. This name needs to be given to the data source you create in the next section.

4. **Choose your database type.**

   Your database type should match the database you're using. To follow along with the example, choose Other.

5. **Set the driver class name and URL to whatever is appropriate for your database.**

   The driver class name and URL in Figure 7-1 are for an ODBC DSN named school.

6. **Add this pool to your server.**

   To do so, click the Targets tab. Select your server, and then click the right arrow button to assign it.

Creating the data source

After you create a connection pool, you must attach it to a data source. It is through this data source that WebLogic can access your database. To create a data source, follow these steps:

1. **In Administrative Console, click the Services folder and then click the data source you want to use.**

   If you choose the JDBC data source, the screen shown in Figure 7-2 appears.

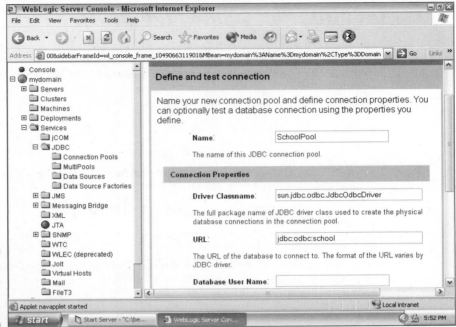

Figure 7-1:
Create a
connection
pool.

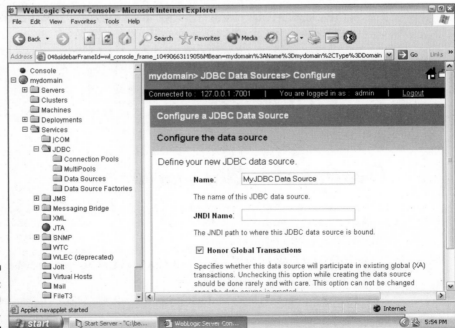

Figure 7-2:
Create a
data source.

2. **Type a name for your data source.**

   You can choose any name you want; the name is for your reference only.

3. **Type a JNDI name.**

   To follow along with the example, type **jdbc/SchoolDataSource** for the JNDI name.

4. **Type a pool name.**

   This is the name you typed in Step 3 in the preceding section. To follow along with the example, type **SchoolPool** for the pool name.

5. **Add this data source to your server.**

   To do so, click the Targets tab. Select your server, and then click the right arrow button to assign it.

The life cycle of a bean

Two types of beans are available for your use: bean-managed persistence (BMP) and container-managed persistence (CMP). With BMP beans, the bean handles the process of saving data. With CMP beans, the container, in this case WebLogic, handles the saving of bean data. In addition, CMP beans, unlike BMP beans, allow relationships between beans.

Regardless of which type of bean you use, it's helpful to understand the EJB life cycle, which represents the stages that an entity bean goes through as it's used.

The first step in an entity bean's life is its creation by WebLogic. When the bean is created, the `newInstance` method is called. This call is followed by a call to `setEntityContext`, which gives the entity bean access to WebLogic. At this point, the bean doesn't contain data. It has just been created and is said to be in a *pooled* state.

To create a new instance of the entity bean, you call a `create` method in the bean's home interface. Before the bean can be useful, it must load its data from the database or become a new object. To load an existing bean, you make a call to a `findBy` method in the bean's home interface. (Both methods are discussed in this chapter.)

Now that the bean has been created or loaded, it's ready for use. At this point, the programmer can read data from the bean or change the field values held inside the bean.

The bean can revert from a ready state to a pooled state in three ways:

✓ You can call the `ejbPassive` method, which disassociates the bean from the persistent data. The bean is now free to be used for another purpose.

✓ You can call the `remove` method, which removes the bean from permanent storage.

✓ You can roll back the transaction. A *rollback* allows all the steps to either fail or succeed as a whole.

As you create BMP and CMP beans, you'll see that the entity bean classes are similar. This can make creating EJBs by hand tedious. To alleviate this, use a development tool, such as Borland JBuilder or WebLogic EJBGen, to automatically generate your entity bean classes.

Now that you've set up the database connection, you're ready to use beans that interact with that database.

Constructing a BMP Bean

The first entity bean you'll create is a BMP bean that represents a student. You can use the student BMP bean to store and retrieve information about students at a school. With a BMP bean, the bean class performs all the SQL needed to read the object from and write the object to the database. Several source files are needed to create a BMP bean. In this section, you find out how to create each of them, starting with the bean interface.

Constructing the bean interface

The *bean interface* is what a programmer who is using your bean has access to. Listing 7-2 shows the student bean interface. The bean interface contains mainly getters and setters for the student data: `getId`, `getFirst`, `getLast`, `setFirst`, and `setLast`. ID doesn't have a `set` method because it's the *primary key* in the database — the value that uniquely identifies the student — and can't be changed.

Listing 7-2:   Student Bean Interface

```
package com.dummies.ejb;

import javax.ejb.EJBObject;
import java.rmi.RemoteException;

public interface Student extends EJBObject {
   public int getId() throws RemoteException;
   public String getFirst() throws RemoteException;
   public void setFirst(String first) throws RemoteException;
   public String getLast() throws RemoteException;
   public void setLast(String last) throws RemoteException;
}
```

Constructing the home interface

The *home interface* is used to gain access to student entity beans. The main task of the student home interface, which is shown in Listing 7-3, is to create and access objects. Creating objects is accomplished by calling one of the `create` methods. You should provide one `create` method for each of the methods in which you would like to create an entity bean. By *methods,* I mean the data that you would like to provide to create your bean. You may create a method that accepts all the necessary information, and a second method that accepts no information and creates a blank bean.

Listing 7-3:   Student Home Interface

```
package com.dummies.ejb;

import javax.ejb.*;
import java.rmi.RemoteException;
import java.util.Enumeration;

public interface StudentHome extends EJBHome {
   public Student create(Integer key)
   throws CreateException, RemoteException;
   public Student create(Integer key, String first, String
            last)
   throws CreateException, RemoteException;
   public Student findByPrimaryKey(Integer key)
   throws FinderException, RemoteException;
   public Enumeration findAll()
   throws FinderException, RemoteException;
}
```

In addition to the `create` method, there are two `find` methods. The `findByPrimaryKey` method locates students based on their primary key, which is their student number. The `findAll` method returns all student records in the system.

Constructing the bean implementation

Perhaps the most important file to a BMP bean is the bean implementation file. When the bean is used by a client program, this file performs the main functions of the bean, namely storing and loading data. Listing 7-4 shows the student bean implementation.

Listing 7-4:   Student Bean Implementation

```
package com.dummies.ejb;

import javax.ejb.*;
import javax.naming.*;
import javax.sql.*;
import java.sql.*;
import java.rmi.RemoteException;
import java.util.Vector;
```

(continued)

Listing 7-4 *(continued)*

```java
import java.util.Enumeration;

public class StudentBean implements EntityBean {

  private EntityContext context;

  // student attributes
  private int id;
  private String first;
  private String last;

  public int getId() { return id;}
  public String getFirst() { return first;}
  public void setFirst(String first) { this.first = first;}
  public String getLast() { return last;}
  public void setLast(String last) { this.last = last;}

  public void setEntityContext(EntityContext context) {
          this.context = context;}
  public void unsetEntityContext() { this.context = null;}

  public void ejbActivate() {}
  public void ejbPassivate() {}
  public void ejbPostCreate(Integer id) {}
  public void ejbPostCreate(Integer id, String first,String
          last) {}

  public Integer ejbCreate(Integer key) throws
          CreateException {
    return ejbCreate(key, "","");
  }

  public Integer ejbCreate(Integer key, String first, String
          last) throws CreateException {
    // set the beans fields
    this.id = key.intValue();
    this.first = first;
    this.last = last;
    Connection conn = null;
    PreparedStatement ps = null;

    try {
      conn = getConnection();
      String sql = "INSERT INTO t_student(f_id, f_first,
          f_last) VALUES(?,?,?)";
      ps = conn.prepareStatement(sql);
      ps.setInt(1,id);
      ps.setString(2,first);
      ps.setString(3,last);
      ps.executeUpdate();
```

```java
    } catch ( Exception e ) {
      System.out.println("Error:" + e );
      e.printStackTrace();
      throw new CreateException(e.getMessage());
    } finally {
      handleCleanup(conn,ps,null);
    }
    return key;
}

public void ejbLoad() {
  Connection conn = null;
  PreparedStatement ps = null;
  ResultSet rs = null;

  try {
    Integer key = (Integer)context.getPrimaryKey();
    conn = getConnection();
    String sql = "SELECT f_id, f_first,f_last FROM
        t_student WHERE f_id=?";
    ps = conn.prepareStatement(sql);
    ps.setInt(1,key.intValue());
    rs = ps.executeQuery();

    if ( !rs.next() ) {
      // not found in database
      throw new NoSuchEntityException();
    }
    // set the beans fields with the data from the DB row
    this.id = rs.getInt(1);
    this.first = rs.getString(2);
    this.last = rs.getString(3);
  } catch ( Exception e ) {
    System.out.println("Error:" + e );
    e.printStackTrace();
    throw new EJBException(e.getMessage());
  } finally {
    handleCleanup(conn,ps,rs);
  }
}

public void ejbStore() {
  Connection conn = null;
  PreparedStatement ps = null;
  try {
    conn = getConnection();
    String sql = "UPDATE t_student SET f_first=?,f_last=?
        WHERE f_id=?";
    ps = conn.prepareStatement(sql);
    ps.setString(1,first);
```

(continued)

Listing 7-4 *(continued)*

```
      ps.setString(2,last);
      ps.setInt(3,id);
      ps.executeUpdate();
    } catch ( Exception e ) {
      System.out.println("Error:" + e );
      e.printStackTrace();
      throw new EJBException(e.getMessage());
    } finally {
      handleCleanup(conn,ps,null);
    }
  }

  public void ejbRemove() throws RemoveException {
    Connection conn = null;
    PreparedStatement ps = null;
    try {
      conn = getConnection();
      String sql = "DELETE FROM t_student WHERE f_id=?";
      ps = conn.prepareStatement(sql);
      ps.setInt(1,id);
      ps.executeUpdate();
    } catch ( Exception e ) {
      System.out.println("Error:" + e );
      e.printStackTrace();
      throw new RemoveException(e.getMessage());
    } finally {
      handleCleanup(conn,ps,null);
    }
  }

  public Integer ejbFindByPrimaryKey(Integer key) throws
          FinderException {
    Connection conn = null;
    PreparedStatement ps = null;
    ResultSet rs = null;
    try {
      conn = getConnection();
      String sql = "SELECT f_id FROM t_student WHERE f_id=?";
      ps = conn.prepareStatement(sql);
      ps.setInt(1,key.intValue());
      rs = ps.executeQuery();
      if ( !rs.next() ) {
        throw new ObjectNotFoundException();
      }
    } catch ( Exception e ) {
      System.out.println("Error:" + e );
      e.printStackTrace();
      throw new FinderException(e.getMessage());
    } finally {
      handleCleanup(conn,ps,rs);
```

```
    }
    return key;
  }

  public Enumeration ejbFindAll() throws FinderException {
    Connection conn = null;
    PreparedStatement ps = null;
    ResultSet rs = null;
    Vector keys = null;
    try {
      conn = getConnection();
      String sql = "SELECT f_id FROM t_student ORDER BY
          f_id";
      ps = conn.prepareStatement(sql);
      rs = ps.executeQuery();
      keys = new Vector();
      while ( rs.next() ) {
        keys.add(new Integer(rs.getInt(1)));
      }
    } catch ( Exception e ) {
      System.out.println("Error:" + e );
      e.printStackTrace();
      throw new FinderException(e.getMessage());
    } finally {
      handleCleanup(conn,ps,rs);
    }
    return keys.elements();
  }

// internal utility methods

  private Connection getConnection() throws NamingException,
          SQLException {
    InitialContext ic = new InitialContext();
    DataSource ds =
          (DataSource)ic.lookup("java:comp/env/jdbc/SchoolDa
          taSource");
    return ds.getConnection();
  }

  private void handleCleanup(Connection
          conn,PreparedStatement ps,ResultSet rs)
  {
    // make sure the connection is returned to the connection
          pool
    try {
      if ( rs!=null )
        rs.close();
      if ( ps!=null )
        ps.close();
```

(continued)

Listing 7-4 *(continued)*

```
        if ( conn!=null )
          conn.close();
      } catch ( SQLException e ) {
      }
   }
}
```

Two methods deal directly with the data source: getConnection and handleCleanup. The getConnection method opens a connection to the data source that you created earlier in this chapter. This connection is returned to the method that called getConnection. All methods in the bean implementation class call getConnection to gain access to the database. The handleCleanup method closes the database objects created by these methods.

Also implemented in this file are various find methods as well as methods that handle the creation, deletion, modification, and retrieval of the student records. Most of these methods do no more than use JDBC and SQL to access the correct data. Chapter 12 covers JDBC in greater detail.

Constructing the bean configuration files

Finally, the BMP bean requires two configuration files. The first file, ejb-jar.xml, is a J2EE standard file. It's shown in Listing 7-5.

Listing 7-5:   Student J2EE Configuration File

```xml
<?xml version="1.0"?>
<!DOCTYPE ejb-jar PUBLIC '-//Sun Microsystems, Inc.//DTD
            Enterprise JavaBeans 1.1//EN'
            'http://java.sun.com/j2ee/dtds/ejb-jar_1_1.dtd'>
<ejb-jar>
  <enterprise-beans>
    <entity>
      <ejb-name>StudentObject</ejb-name>
      <home>com.dummies.ejb.StudentHome</home>
      <remote>com.dummies.ejb.Student</remote>
      <ejb-class>com.dummies.ejb.StudentBean</ejb-class>
      <persistence-type>Bean</persistence-type>
      <prim-key-class>java.lang.Integer</prim-key-class>
      <reentrant>False</reentrant>
      <resource-ref>
        <description>The reference to the
          DataSource.</description>
        <res-ref-name>jdbc/SchoolDataSource</res-ref-name>
        <res-type>javax.sql.DataSource</res-type>
```

```
          <res-auth>Container</res-auth>
        </resource-ref>
      </entity>
    </enterprise-beans>
    <assembly-descriptor>
      <container-transaction>
        <method>
          <ejb-name>StudentObject</ejb-name>
          <method-name>*</method-name>
        </method>
        <trans-attribute>Required</trans-attribute>
      </container-transaction>
    </assembly-descriptor>
</ejb-jar>
```

This XML file has many settings, all of which are summarized in Table 7-1.

Table 7-1	J2EE Settings for BMP Beans
Entry	*What It Is*
ejb-class	The name of the bean implementation class. This should be a full package name such as com.mycompany.MyImplementationClass.
ejb-name	The name of this bean. This can be any name, but it should not be duplicated elsewhere in your program.
home	The name of the home class. This should be a full package name such as com.mycompany.MyHomeClass.
persistence-type	The type of persistence supported. This will be bean for BMP and container for CMP.
prim-key-class	The type used by the primary key. This will usually be one of the wrapper classes, such as java.lang.Integer or java.lang.String.
reentrant	Whether the class thread is safe. As long as you don't call classes that are not thread safe or use static variables, your code should be thread safe.
remote	The name of the bean interface. This is the class that implements the bean.
res-ref-name	The data source to use. You set up this data source in Administration Console.
res-type	The object type of this data source. This is almost always javax.sql.DataSource.

In addition to the J2EE standard configuration file, WebLogic adds some configuration information that you must also provide. You store this information in the weblogic-ejb-jar.xml file, which is shown in Listing 7-6. Only a few additional configuration items are stored in this file. The most important additional piece of information for a BMP bean is the JNDI name, which your client programs use to access the bean.

Listing 7-6:   Student WebLogic Configuration File

```
<?xml version="1.0"?>
<!DOCTYPE weblogic-ejb-jar PUBLIC '-//BEA Systems, Inc.//DTD
          WebLogic 5.1.0 EJB//EN'
             'http://www.bea.com/servers/wls510/dtd/weblogic-
             ejb-jar.dtd'>

<weblogic-ejb-jar>
  <weblogic-enterprise-bean>
    <ejb-name>StudentObject</ejb-name>
    <reference-descriptor>
      <resource-description>
        <res-ref-name>jdbc/StudentDataSource</res-ref-name>
        <jndi-name>StudentDataSource</jndi-name>
      </resource-description>
    </reference-descriptor>
    <jndi-name>StudentObject</jndi-name>
  </weblogic-enterprise-bean>
</weblogic-ejb-jar>
```

Compiling a BMP Bean

You've seen how to construct the BMP bean, so now you're ready to compile and test it. To do this, you need to construct a client program. This client program will create an instance of the bean and cause it to load its data from the database. Listing 7-7 is a short client program that uses the BMP bean.

Listing 7-7:   Client Program

```
package com.dummies.ejb;

import javax.ejb.*;
import javax.rmi.*;
import java.rmi.*;
import java.util.*;
import javax.swing.*;
import javax.naming.*;

public class StudentClient {
  public static void main(String[] args)
```

```
    {
      try {
        Properties h = new Properties();
        h.put(Context.INITIAL_CONTEXT_FACTORY,
            "weblogic.jndi.WLInitialContextFactory");
        h.put(Context.PROVIDER_URL, "t3://localhost:7001" );
        Context initial = new InitialContext( h );
        Object obj = initial.lookup("StudentObject");

        StudentHome studentHome = (StudentHome)

            PortableRemoteObject.narrow(obj ,
            StudentHome.class);

// First attempt to locate student number 1
        Student student = null;

        try {
          student = studentHome.findByPrimaryKey(new
              Integer("1"));
        } catch ( FinderException e ) {
          System.out.println( "Does not yet exist" );
        }

        if ( student!=null ) {
          System.out.println("User already existed, delete
              him!");
          student.remove();
        }

        student = studentHome.create(new
            Integer("1"),"John","Smith");
        System.out.println("Created user");
        student.setLast("Jones");
        System.out.println("Change user's last name to Jones");

        System.out.println("Now find user by primary key");

        try {
          student = studentHome.findByPrimaryKey(new
              Integer("1"));
        } catch ( FinderException e ) {
          System.out.println( "Something is not working, we did
              not find him!" );
        }

        System.out.println("Found:" + student.getLast() + "," +
            student.getFirst() );

      } catch ( Exception e ) {
        System.out.println( e );
```

(continued)

Listing 7-7 *(continued)*

```
        JOptionPane.showMessageDialog(null ,
                                    "Exception:"+e);
    }
  }
}
```

The client program first gains access to the home interface for the bean. (Home interfaces are discussed in Chapter 6.) After the home interface is accessed, you can create and load beans. The program begins by trying to load a student record with the ID number of 1. If the load is successful, the student record is deleted. Next, a new student record with an ID of 1 is created. This student's last name is then modified and resaved. The last name is modified as an example of how to process a change such as a correction.

Listing 7-8 shows a script that compiles the CMP bean into a JAR file. For more information on this process, see Chapter 6.

Listing 7-8:   Script to Compile the Student EJB

```
@echo off

@rem Set this to the location of your JDK installation
set JDK_HOME=C:\j2sdk1.4.1_01

@rem Set this to the location of your J2EE JAR file
set CLASSPATH=C:\j2sdkee1.4\lib\j2ee.jar

@rem Set this to the location where the class files will be
            stored
set CLASSES=.\CLASSES

@rem set up the directory structure
rmdir /q /s %CLASSES%
mkdir %CLASSES%
mkdir %CLASSES%\META-INF

@rem compile the classes
"%JDK_HOME%"\bin\javac .\src\com\dummies\ejb\*.java -
            classpath %CLASSPATH% -d %CLASSES%

@rem copy the config files
xcopy /y .\src\META-INF\*.* %CLASSES%\META-INF\

@rem JAR it up
cd %CLASSES%
"%JDK_HOME%"\bin\jar -cvf ..\BMPBean.jar *.*
cd ..
```

After you've built the JAR file, you must deploy it. For more information on this task, see Chapter 6. After the bean has been deployed, you can test it.

Listing 7-9 shows how to properly set up `classpath` so that the client program can run.

Listing 7-9:   Script to Test the Student EJB

```
@echo off

@rem Set this to the location of your JDK installation
set JDK_HOME=C:\j2sdk1.4.1_01

@rem Set this to the location of your J2EE JAR file
set CLASSPATH=C:\j2sdkee1.4\lib\j2ee.jar;
.\BMPBean.jar;C:\bea\weblogic81\server\lib\weblogic.jar

@rem run the test client
"%JDK_HOME%"\bin\java com.dummies.ejb.CMPClient -classpath
          %CLASSPATH%
```

Constructing a CMP Bean

As you saw in the preceding section, BMP beans must be saved and loaded by the bean itself. In this section, you find out about CMP beans as well as the capability of establishing relationships between CMP beans. The main difference between a CMP bean and a BMP bean is that a BMP bean stores its own data, but a CMP bean uses WebLogic to store its data. As a result, the CMP bean has less code than the BMP bean.

You'll create two CMP beans called `Department` and `Course` and give the `Department` class a one-to-many relationship with the `Course` class.

Constructing the value objects

As was the case with a BMP bean, several classes make up a CMP bean. However, a CMP bean has a few additional class types. One of these is the value object. Value objects in a CMP bean have only one job: storing all data contained by the bean. The value object beans for both `Course` and `Department` are shown in Listings 7-10 and 7-11.

Listing 7-10:   Value Object for `Course`

```
package com.dummies.ejb;

public class CourseVO implements java.io.Serializable {
  private Integer id;
  private String name;
```

(continued)

Listing 7-10 *(continued)*

```
  private int credit;

  public CourseVO() {
  }

  public CourseVO(Integer id) {
    this.id = id;
  }

  public Integer getId() {
    return id;
  }

  public void setName(String name) {
    this.name = name;
  }

  public String getName() {
    return name;
  }

  public void setCredit(int credit)    {
    this.credit = credit;
  }

  public int getCredit() {
    return credit;
  }
}
```

Listing 7-11:   Value Object for Department

```
package com.dummies.ejb;

public class DepartmentVO implements java.io.Serializable {
  private Integer id;
  private String name;

  public DepartmentVO()
  {
  }

  public DepartmentVO(Integer id)
  {
    this.id = id;
  }

  public Integer getId()

  {
    return id;
```

```
    }

    public void setName(String newName)
    {
        name = newName;
    }
    public String getName()
    {
        return name;
    }
}
```

Constructing the local bean interfaces

EJB 2.0 introduced the concept of local and remote interfaces. The main purpose of these interfaces is to alleviate some of the overhead in having to call every bean as though it were on a remote computer. Both the `Course` and `Department` beans use local bean interfaces.

For the local interface to work, the bean must be called from the same Java Virtual Machine (JVM) as the client program. This eliminates all overhead in calling from one JVM to another. The `Department` and `Course` examples use the local interface to enable fast access between the `Department` and `Course` classes. The local interface for the `Course` and `Department` classes are shown in Listings 7-12 and 7-13, respectively.

Listing 7-12:   Local Bean Interface for `Course`

```
package com.dummies.ejb;

import javax.ejb.*;

public interface CourseLocal extends EJBLocalObject {
    public CourseVO getCourseData();
    public void setCourseData(CourseVO course);

    public void setDepartment(DepartmentLocal dept);
    public DepartmentLocal getDepartment();
}
```

Listing 7-13:   Local Bean Interface for `Department`

```
package com.dummies.ejb;

import javax.ejb.*;

public interface DepartmentLocal extends EJBLocalObject {

}
```

The `Course` local bean contains methods required for `Department` to add courses to itself. No local methods are made public in `Department` because it is the top-level object and is not added to anything.

Constructing the remote bean interface

Because none of the methods were exposed for the `Department` bean interface, they must be exposed in the remote interface for the `Department` bean, which is shown in Listing 7-14. Most of these methods have already been discussed. A new one, the `addCourse` method, is used to add courses to the department. To remove courses from the department, you simply call the `remove` method for those particular courses.

Listing 7-14:   Remote Bean Interface for `Department`

```
package com.dummies.ejb;

import java.rmi.*;
import java.util.*;
import javax.ejb.*;
import javax.naming.*;

public interface DepartmentRemote extends EJBObject {
   public DepartmentVO getDepartmentData()
   throws RemoteException;
   public void setDepartmentData(DepartmentVO dept)
   throws RemoteException;

   public void addCourse(CourseVO courseData)
   throws NamingException, CreateException, RemoteException;

   public CourseVO[] getAllCourses() throws RemoteException;
}
```

Constructing the local home interfaces

The local interface for the `Course` bean contains `create` and `findBy` methods. These methods enable the `Department` bean to both create and locate `Course` beans. The source code for the `Course` bean is shown in Listing 7-15.

Listing 7-15:   Local Home Interface for `Course`

```
package com.dummies.ejb;

import javax.ejb.*;
```

```
import java.util.*;

public interface CourseLocalHome extends EJBLocalHome {

   public CourseLocal create(CourseVO course)
   throws CreateException;

   public CourseLocal findByPrimaryKey(Integer primaryKey)
   throws FinderException;
}
```

The Department local bean needs to expose only the findByPrimaryKey method, because Course never creates Department. The source code for the Department bean's local home interface is shown in Listing 7-16.

Listing 7-16: **Local Home Interface for** Department

```
package com.dummies.ejb;

import javax.ejb.*;
import java.util.*;

public interface DepartmentLocalHome extends EJBLocalHome {
   public DepartmentLocal findByPrimaryKey(Integer primaryKey)
   throws FinderException;
}
```

Constructing the remote home interface

The only bean that requires a remote home interface is the Department bean. This is because the client program directly accesses the Department beans, not the Course beans. The Course beans are owned by the Department beans, and all access to the Course beans are through the Department beans. The source code for the remote home interface is shown in Listing 7-17.

Listing 7-17: **Remote Home Interface for** Department

```
package com.dummies.ejb;

import java.util.*;
import java.rmi.*;
import javax.ejb.*;

public interface DepartmentRemoteHome extends EJBHome {

   public DepartmentRemote create(DepartmentVO Department)
```

(continued)

Listing 7-17 *(continued)*

```
  throws CreateException, RemoteException;

  public DepartmentRemote findByPrimaryKey(Integer
        primaryKey)
  throws FinderException, RemoteException;

  public Collection findAll()
  throws FinderException, RemoteException;

  public DepartmentRemote findByName(java.lang.String name)
  throws FinderException, RemoteException;
}
```

Constructing the abstract bean implementation

Finally, you come to the abstract bean implementation. It's abstract because you haven't defined all the required methods of its parent class, which is `javax.ejb.EntityBean`. WebLogic uses the abstract class internally and makes it complete by adding the required methods. This is all accomplished behind the scenes, so you don't need to be concerned with it. The bean classes are simply shortened versions of the bean classes used for the BMP beans. Listings 7-18 and 7-19 show the abstract bean classes for the `Course` bean.

Listing 7-18:   Abstract Bean Class for the `Course` **Bean**

```
package com.dummies.ejb;

import java.io.Serializable;
import java.util.*;

import javax.ejb.*;
import javax.naming.*;
import javax.sql.*;

abstract public class CourseEJB implements EntityBean {
  private EntityContext ctx;

  public void setEntityContext(EntityContext ctx) {
    this.ctx = ctx;
  }

  public void unsetEntityContext() {
    this.ctx = null;
  }

  public void ejbActivate() {}
```

```
public void ejbPassivate() {}
public void ejbLoad() {}
public void ejbStore() {}

public void ejbRemove()
throws RemoveException
{}

abstract public Integer getId();
abstract public void setId(Integer id);

abstract public String getName();
abstract public void setName(String name);

abstract public int getCredit();
abstract public void setCredit(int credit);

abstract public void setDepartment(DepartmentLocal dept);
abstract public DepartmentLocal getDepartment();


public Integer ejbCreate(CourseVO course)
throws CreateException
{
  setCourseData(course);
  return null;
}

public void ejbPostCreate(CourseVO course){}
public CourseVO getCourseData()
{
  CourseVO course = new CourseVO(this.getId());
  course.setName(this.getName());
  course.setCredit(this.getCredit());
  return course;
}

public void setCourseData(CourseVO course)
{
  setName(course.getName());
  setCredit(course.getCredit());
}
}
```

Listing 7-19: Abstract Bean Class for the Department **Bean**

```
package com.dummies.ejb;

import java.util.*;
import javax.ejb.*;
```

(continued)

Listing 7-19 *(continued)*

```java
import javax.naming.*;

abstract public class DepartmentEJB implements EntityBean {
  private EntityContext ctx;

  public void setEntityContext(EntityContext ctx) {
    this.ctx = ctx;
  }
  public void unsetEntityContext() {
    this.ctx = null;
  }
  public void ejbActivate() {}
  public void ejbPassivate() {}
  public void ejbLoad() {}
  public void ejbStore() {}
  public void ejbRemove() throws RemoveException
  {
  }

  abstract public Integer getId();
  abstract public void setId(Integer id);

  abstract public String getName();
  abstract public void setName(String val);

  abstract public Collection getCourses();
  abstract public void setCourses(Collection courses);

  public DepartmentVO getDepartmentData()
  {
    DepartmentVO dept = new DepartmentVO(this.getId());
    dept.setName(this.getName());
    return dept;
  }

  public void setDepartmentData(DepartmentVO dept)
  {
    setName(dept.getName());
  }

  public Integer ejbCreate(DepartmentVO dept)
  throws CreateException
  {
    setDepartmentData(dept);
    return null;
  }

  public void ejbPostCreate(DepartmentVO dept)
  throws CreateException
```

```
    {
    }

  public CourseVO[] getAllCourses()
  {
    Collection courses = getCourses();
    CourseVO[] courseArray = new CourseVO[courses.size()];
    Iterator courseIterator = courses.iterator();
    for ( int i=0; courseIterator.hasNext(); i++ ) {
      CourseLocal course = (CourseLocal)
            courseIterator.next();
      courseArray[i] = course.getCourseData();
    }

    return courseArray;
  }

  public void addCourse(CourseVO courseData) throws
          NamingException, CreateException
  {
    Context ctx = new InitialContext();
    CourseLocalHome courseHome = (CourseLocalHome)
          ctx.lookup("cmp.Course");
    CourseLocal course = courseHome.create(courseData);
    getCourses().add(course);
  }
}
```

As you can see in Listings 7-18 and 7-19, the abstract bean classes are implemented as abstract Java classes. WebLogic extends these classes and adds the appropriate methods to access the objects. These methods perform the same functions as the BMP bean.

Constructing the bean configuration files

CMP beans use a total of three configuration files: the `ejb-jar.xml` and `weblogic-ejb-jar.xml` files as were used by BMP beans and a database mapping file called `weblogic-rdbms-jar.xml`. I start with the `ejb-jar.xml` file, which is shown in Listing 7-20.

Listing 7-20:   J2EE Standard Bean Configuration File

```
<?xml version="1.0"?>
<!DOCTYPE ejb-jar PUBLIC
'-//Sun Microsystems, Inc.//DTD Enterprise JavaBeans 2.0//EN'
'http://java.sun.com/j2ee/dtd/ejb-jar_2_0.dtd'>
<ejb-jar>
  <enterprise-beans>
```

(continued)

Listing 7-20 *(continued)*

```
<entity>
  <ejb-name>DepartmentEJB</ejb-name>
  <home>com.dummies.ejb.DepartmentRemoteHome</home>
  <remote>com.dummies.ejb.DepartmentRemote</remote>
  <local-home>com.dummies.ejb.DepartmentLocalHome</local-
        home>
  <local>com.dummies.ejb.DepartmentLocal</local>
  <ejb-class>com.dummies.ejb.DepartmentEJB</ejb-class>
  <persistence-type>Container</persistence-type>
  <prim-key-class>java.lang.Integer</prim-key-class>
  <reentrant>False</reentrant>
  <cmp-version>2.x</cmp-version>
  <abstract-schema-name>DepartmentSchema</abstract-
        schema-name>
  <cmp-field>
    <field-name>id</field-name>
  </cmp-field>
  <cmp-field>
    <field-name>name</field-name>
  </cmp-field>
  <primkey-field>id</primkey-field>
  <query>
    <query-method>
      <method-name>findByName</method-name>
      <method-params>
        <method-param>java.lang.String</method-param>
      </method-params>
    </query-method>
    <ejb-ql><![CDATA[SELECT OBJECT(d) FROM
        DepartmentSchema AS d WHERE d.name = ?1]]></ejb-
        ql>
  </query>
  <query>
    <query-method>
      <method-name>findAll</method-name>
      <method-params/>
    </query-method>
    <ejb-ql><![CDATA[SELECT OBJECT(d) FROM
        DepartmentSchema AS d]]></ejb-ql>
  </query>
</entity>
<entity>
  <ejb-name>CourseEJB</ejb-name>
  <local-home>com.dummies.ejb.CourseLocalHome</local-
        home>
  <local>com.dummies.ejb.CourseLocal</local>
  <ejb-class>com.dummies.ejb.CourseEJB</ejb-class>
  <persistence-type>Container</persistence-type>
  <prim-key-class>java.lang.Integer</prim-key-class>
  <reentrant>False</reentrant>
```

```xml
        <cmp-version>2.x</cmp-version>
        <abstract-schema-name>CourseSchema</abstract-schema-
            name>
        <cmp-field>
          <field-name>id</field-name>
        </cmp-field>
        <cmp-field>
          <field-name>name</field-name>
        </cmp-field>
        <cmp-field>
          <field-name>credit</field-name>
        </cmp-field>
        <primkey-field>id</primkey-field>
     </entity>
  </enterprise-beans>
  <relationships>
    <ejb-relation>
      <ejb-relation-name>Department-Course</ejb-relation-
          name>
      <ejb-relationship-role>
        <ejb-relationship-role-name>
          Department-Has-Courses
        </ejb-relationship-role-name>
        <multiplicity>one</multiplicity>
        <relationship-role-source>
          <ejb-name>DepartmentEJB</ejb-name>
        </relationship-role-source>
        <cmr-field>
          <cmr-field-name>courses</cmr-field-name>
          <cmr-field-type>java.util.Collection</cmr-field-
              type>
        </cmr-field>
      </ejb-relationship-role>
      <ejb-relationship-role>
        <ejb-relationship-role-name>
          Course-Has-Department
        </ejb-relationship-role-name>
        <multiplicity>many</multiplicity>
        <cascade-delete/>
        <relationship-role-source>
          <ejb-name>CourseEJB</ejb-name>
        </relationship-role-source>
        <cmr-field>
          <cmr-field-name>department</cmr-field-name>
        </cmr-field>
      </ejb-relationship-role>
    </ejb-relation>
  </relationships>
  <assembly-descriptor>
    <container-transaction>
```

(continued)

Listing 7-20 *(continued)*

```
      <method>
        <ejb-name>DepartmentEJB</ejb-name>
        <method-name>*</method-name>
      </method>
      <trans-attribute>Required</trans-attribute>
    </container-transaction>
    <container-transaction>
      <method>
        <ejb-name>CourseEJB</ejb-name>
        <method-name>*</method-name>
      </method>
      <trans-attribute>Required</trans-attribute>
    </container-transaction>
  </assembly-descriptor>
</ejb-jar>
```

Many of these entries are the same as those in the BMP version of the file. The first difference to note is the cmp-field tags, which specify the property names for each bean. These fields are not database fields, but rather fields mapped to the database. The cmp-field tags contain only the field names:

```
<cmp-field>
  <field-name>...field name...</field-name>
</cmp-field>
```

Queries are also included that show WebLogic how to provide information to the findBy methods in the home classes. This allows the findBy methods to construct SQL queries to find the appropriate record. The following query shows how you can implement findByName for the Department bean:

```
<query>
  <query-method>
    <method-name>findByName</method-name>
    <method-params>
      <method-param>java.lang.String</method-param>
    </method-params>
  </query-method>
  <ejb-ql><![CDATA[SELECT OBJECT(d) FROM DepartmentSchema AS
          d WHERE d.name = ?1]]></ejb-ql>
</query>
```

You can specify multiple parameters in the ejb-ql tag. These will be filled in with the value that you're searching on. For example, the preceding code is filling in the ?1 parameter to specify a name that's being searched for. The ejb-relationship-role tag specifies how the tables relate to each other. The multiplicity tag specifies whether the relationship is to one object or multiple objects. If the cascade-delete tag is specified, child objects are deleted when the parent object is deleted.

The WebLogic-specific configuration file, which is shown in Listing 7-21, contains additional information for CMP beans.

Listing 7-21:   WebLogic Bean Configuration File

```xml
<?xml version="1.0"?>
<!DOCTYPE weblogic-ejb-jar PUBLIC '-//BEA Systems, Inc.//DTD
          WebLogic 6.0.0 EJB//EN'
          'http://www.bea.com/servers/wls600/dtd/weblogic-
          ejb-jar.dtd'>

<weblogic-ejb-jar>

  <weblogic-enterprise-bean>
    <ejb-name>DepartmentEJB</ejb-name>
    <entity-descriptor>
       <persistence>
<persistence-type>
   <type-identifier>WebLogic_CMP_RDBMS</type-identifier>
   <type-version>6.0</type-version>
   <type-storage>META-INF/weblogic-cmp-rdbms-jar.xml</type-
          storage>
       </persistence-type>
<persistence-use>
   <type-identifier>WebLogic_CMP_RDBMS</type-identifier>
   <type-version>6.0</type-version>
</persistence-use>
       </persistence>
    </entity-descriptor>
    <jndi-name>cmp.Department</jndi-name>
    <local-jndi-name>cmp.Department-Local</local-jndi-name>
  </weblogic-enterprise-bean>

  <weblogic-enterprise-bean>
    <ejb-name>CourseEJB</ejb-name>
    <entity-descriptor>
       <persistence>
<persistence-type>
   <type-identifier>WebLogic_CMP_RDBMS</type-identifier>
   <type-version>6.0</type-version>
   <type-storage>META-INF/weblogic-cmp-rdbms-jar.xml</type-
          storage>
</persistence-type>
<persistence-use>
   <type-identifier>WebLogic_CMP_RDBMS</type-identifier>
   <type-version>6.0</type-version>
</persistence-use>
       </persistence>
    </entity-descriptor>
    <local-jndi-name>cmp.Course</local-jndi-name>
  </weblogic-enterprise-bean>

</weblogic-ejb-jar>
```

You need to configure the `persistence-type` tags. Inside these tags, leave the `type-identifier` and `type-version` tags as they are. You need to set the `type-storage` tag to the path of your mapping file. Mapping files are discussed next.

The last configuration file is the database mapping file, which is shown in Listing 7-22. This file specifies the table names and maps the bean properties to the correct fields.

Listing 7-22:   Database Mapping for WebLogic

```
<!DOCTYPE weblogic-rdbms-jar PUBLIC
'-//BEA Systems, Inc.//DTD WebLogic 6.0.0 EJB RDBMS
         Persistence//EN'
'http://www.bea.com/servers/wls600/dtd/weblogic-rdbms20-
         persistence-600.dtd'>
<weblogic-rdbms-jar>
  <weblogic-rdbms-bean>
    <ejb-name>DepartmentEJB</ejb-name>
    <data-source-name>jdbc/SchoolDataSourceTX</data-source-
         name>
    <table-name>t_department</table-name>
    <field-map>
       <cmp-field>id</cmp-field>
       <dbms-column>f_id</dbms-column>
    </field-map>
    <field-map>
       <cmp-field>name</cmp-field>
       <dbms-column>f_name</dbms-column>
    </field-map>

  </weblogic-rdbms-bean>

  <weblogic-rdbms-bean>
    <ejb-name>CourseEJB</ejb-name>
    <data-source-name>jdbc/SchoolDataSourceTX</data-source-
         name>
    <table-name>t_course</table-name>
    <field-map>
       <cmp-field>id</cmp-field>
       <dbms-column>f_id</dbms-column>
    </field-map>
    <field-map>
       <cmp-field>name</cmp-field>
       <dbms-column>f_name</dbms-column>
    </field-map>
    <field-map>
       <cmp-field>credit</cmp-field>
       <dbms-column>f_credit</dbms-column>
```

```
      </field-map>

   </weblogic-rdbms-bean>

   <weblogic-rdbms-relation>
      <relation-name>Department-Course</relation-name>
      <weblogic-relationship-role>
         <relationship-role-name>Course-Has-
             Department</relationship-role-name>
         <column-map>
            <foreign-key-column>f_department_id</foreign-key-
            column>
            <key-column>f_id</key-column>
         </column-map>
      </weblogic-relationship-role>
   </weblogic-rdbms-relation>
</weblogic-rdbms-jar>
```

Tables are defined inside `weblogic-rdms-bean` tags. The tag contains the
following information:

```
<table-name>...the name of the table...</table-name>
<field-map>
   <cmp-field>...property name of first field...</cmp-field>
   <dbms-column>...database field name...</dbms-column>
</field-map>
<field-map>
   ...the second field...
</field-map>
```

By creating one `field-map` tag for each field in your table, you can map the
entire table. For every foreign key, you must also create a `weblogic-rdbms-
relation` tag. This specifies the foreign key relationship. As you can see,
`weblogic-rdbms-relation` specifies the foreign key using the `foreign-
key-column` tag and maps it to the primary key of that table.

Compiling a CMP Bean

You compile a CMP bean in the same way you compile a BMP bean. Listing 7-23
is a script that uses the correct names for the CMP bean you just created.

Listing 7-23: Script to Compile the CMP Bean

```
@echo off

@rem Set this to the location of your JDK installation
```

(continued)

Listing 7-23 *(continued)*

```
set JDK_HOME=C:\j2sdk1.4.1_01

@rem Set this to the location of your J2EE JAR file
set CLASSPATH=C:\j2sdkee1.4\lib\j2ee.jar

@rem Set this to the location that the class files will be
            stored
set CLASSES=.\CLASSES

@rem setup the directory structure
rmdir /q /s %CLASSES%
mkdir %CLASSES%
mkdir %CLASSES%\META-INF

@rem compile the classes
"%JDK_HOME%"\bin\javac .\src\com\dummies\ejb\*.java -
            classpath %CLASSPATH% -d %CLASSES%

@rem copy the config files
xcopy /y .\src\META-INF\*.* %CLASSES%\META-INF\

@rem JAR it up
cd %CLASSES%
"%JDK_HOME%"\bin\jar -cvf ..\CMPBean.jar *.*
cd ..
```

CMP and BMP beans enable you to make data persistent, so you can isolate your database code to the beans and keep it away from other beans dedicated to business processing logic. This isolation means that you have fewer places to change if you alter the structure of your database.

Chapter 8

Stepping Up to Enterprise Applications

In This Chapter

▶ Getting your directories in order

▶ Creating deployment descriptors with tools or by hand

▶ Packaging an enterprise application

▶ Deploying an enterprise application

The term *enterprise application* is used by a variety of products. For WebLogic and J2EE, an enterprise application is comprised of one or more of the following technologies:

✓ Web application

✓ Enterprise JavaBeans

✓ Client application

If you're already creating applications that use these components, you may be wondering why you'd need an enterprise application. Well, enterprise applications provide a way to package all these components in a single archive. The main advantage is that you would then have one file to manage and deploy. If you're still working on your application, however, you'll find it easier to work with the expanded version of your application, not one packaged into a single enterprise application file.

Because it's easier to develop an application using individual files and directories, compress your application into an enterprise archive file only after you complete the development stage.

In this chapter, you discover how to create an enterprise application. Rather than showing you how to create the components that make up an enterprise application, however, I show you how to connect these pieces in an enterprise application. To create the components of an enterprise application, refer to Chapter 5 for details on web applications and Chapters 6 and 7 for information on EJBs and client applications.

Creating an enterprise application consists of four major steps:

1. **Arrange the components that make up the enterprise application into the proper directory structure.**

2. **Create your deployment descriptors.**

3. **Compress the entire structure into a JAR file.**

4. **Deploy your enterprise application.**

You go through each of these steps in this chapter.

Organizing Your Directories

The first step in creating an enterprise application is to organize your directories. You must move the files that make up your EJBs into a single directory structure. If you've been developing your application's individual components, you're probably close to finishing this step.

The structure of the WebLogic directory

Understanding the WebLogic directory structure is important when creating an enterprise application because it helps you know where to place specific file types. When you first create your WebLogic domain, as discussed in Chapter 4, you specify a root directory for it. This directory is usually a subdirectory of `c:\bea\user_projects\`.

The web applications directory (described in detail in Chapter 5) is stored in a subdirectory named `applications`, which is in your domain directory. WebLogic provides you with at least one web application, which is named `DefaultWebApp`.

In this chapter, I assume that you're using a web application named `MyWebApp`. If you're using the default web application, the instructions remain the same except you use `DefaultWebApp` as the name of your web application.

The root directory of your web application forms the base from which you package your enterprise application. For example, if you created a domain named `mydomain` and are using the default web application, this root is

```
C:\bea\user_projects\mydomain\applications\DefaultWebApp
```

If your web application is named `MyWebApp`, the root is

```
C:\bea\user_projects\mydomain\applications\MyWebApp
```

These are Windows paths. UNIX users have a /user_projects subdirectory to the directory that holds WebLogic.

The root directory

Everything that you store in the root directory of your WebLogic server can be accessed by the user. Consider the example of WebLogic Server installed in the following directory:

```
C:\bea\user_projects\mydomain\applications\MyWebApp
```

Your root directory is MyWebApp. Every file that you place in this directory is exposed to the Internet. For example, if you stored the myfile.asp file in MyWebApp, you could see this file by accessing the following page:

```
http://localhost:7001/myfile.asp
```

The same is true of directories that you place in the DefaultWebApp directory. For example, if you create a directory named images and place into it a file named photo.jpg, you could see this file by accessing the following URL:

```
http://localhost:7001/images/photo.jpg
```

However, one directory is not exposed to the Internet: WEB-INF, which is in your root directory. This directory holds configuration information and other important subdirectories used by WebLogic.

Because every other directory in the root directory is exposed to the Internet, be careful about what you place there. Configuration and other sensitive information should be kept in the WEB-INF directory so that the information can't be downloaded by a malicious user.

Now that you've seen the purpose of the root and WEB-INF directories, you can take a look at the directories inside the WEB-INF directory.

The WEB-INF/classes directory

This is the directory where you place the .class files, which are used to implement servlets. Any .class file in this directory is automatically available to WebLogic.

When creating an enterprise application, make sure that your individual .class files and servlets are in the WEB-INF/classes directory. This ensures that they're packaged to the correct location and that WebLogic can find them when you deploy your enterprise web application.

You can't just place the .class files in this directory. Like any Java .class file, they must be placed in a subdirectory that corresponds to their package. For example, if your .class file is in the com.dummies.ejb package, you have to create the com/dummies/ejb directory structure under your classes directory. You then place your .class file in the ejb subdirectory.

The WEB-INF/lib directory

Your web application may use a variety of JAR files to perform its operations. JAR files contain class libraries that give your program additional functionality. These JAR files may have been created by you or by a third party. Regardless of their source, JAR files must be placed in the WEB-INF/lib directory if WebLogic is to make use of them.

One common use for the WEB-INF/lib directory is to store the JAR files associated with tag libraries. A *tag library* is a class library contained in a JAR file. Including the tag library in your application gives you access to additional tags that you can use in your JSP pages.

The WEB-INF/tlds directory

Tag libraries require additional setup beyond just placing their JAR files into the lib directory. Tag libraries also require tag library descriptor (TLD) files. These TLD files are placed in the WEB-INF/tlds directory.

Examining the directory structure

Now that you've seen the directories that make up an enterprise application, it's time to see how the files in those directories are laid out. Table 8-1 shows some of the files in a typical enterprise application. This application has two primary areas: the main area of the application, which stores its JSP files in the root, and an administration area. The administration area would likely be secured with a password by using logic contained in the JSP pages. This application also makes use of one servlet and a tag library.

Table 8-1	File Structure of a Typical Web Application
File or Directory	*What It Is*
MyWebApp/	The root directory of your web application
MyWebApp/index.jsp	The index for your web application
MyWebApp/main.jsp	A JSP page that's part of your web application
MyWebApp/admin	A programmer-defined directory containing the JSP pages needed for the administration section of your web application

File or Directory	What It Is
`MyWebApp/admin/index.jsp`	The index page displayed for the administration section
`DefaultWebApp/admin/info.html`	An HTML file that's part of your web application
`MyWebApp/images`	A programmer-defined directory that contains the image files for your web application
`MyWebApp/images/logo.gif`	A graphics file used by your web application
`MyWebApp/WEB-INF`	A directory that is not visible to the Internet and that holds configuration files and other system directories
`MyWebApp/WEB-INF/web.xml`	J2EE standard configuration information for your web application
`MyWebApp/WEB-INF/weblogic.xml`	WebLogic-specific configuration information for your web application
`MyWebApp/lib`	A directory that contains the JAR files for your application
`MyWebApp/lib/mytag lib.jar`	A JAR file needed by your web application
`MyWebApp/classes`	A directory that contains the .class files for your application
`MyWebApp/classes/com/dummies/servlet/myservlet.class`	A class file needed by your web application
`MyWebApp/tlds`	A directory that contains the tag library descriptors for your web application
`MyWebApp/tlds/my tags.tld`	A tag library definition file for your web application

Note that throughout the folders used by this web application are numerous configuration files, which are called *descriptors*. In the next section, you find out the part that descriptors play in an enterprise application.

Creating Deployment Descriptors

The second step in creating an enterprise application is perhaps your biggest task: creating your deployment descriptors. *Deployment descriptors* are XML files that contain configuration information about your enterprise application and its components. This section begins with an introduction to the individual deployment descriptors that WebLogic uses.

Understanding deployment descriptors

Deployment descriptors are not unique to WebLogic; they're a J2EE concept. However, WebLogic contains features that extend the capabilities of J2EE. You can't put non-compliant J2EE information in a J2EE deployment descriptor, so WebLogic introduced a special XML file that contains WebLogic-specific information. Because of this, all deployment descriptor files come in pairs: the J2EE deployment descriptors and the WebLogic deployment descriptors. Table 8-2 summarizes these deployment descriptors.

Table 8-2	J2EE and WebLogic Deployment Descriptors	
Purpose	*J2EE Descriptor*	*WebLogic Descriptor*
Client applications	application-client.xml	client-application.runtime.xml
Enterprise applications	../META-INF/application.xml	META-INF/application.xml
Enterprise JavaBeans	../META-INF/ejb-jar.xml	../META-INF/weblogic-ejb-jar.xml, ../META-INF/weblogic-cmp-rdbns.xml
Resource adaptors	../META-INF/ra.xml	META-INF/weblogic-ra.xml
Web applications	../WEB-INF/web.xml	WEB-INF/weblogic.xml

When creating descriptors, you have two choices: You can use utilities provided with WebLogic to create your descriptors automatically or you can create the descriptors by hand.

Even if you choose to create descriptors automatically, you still have to do some configuration. When you use a tool to generate your descriptors, that tool examines your files and directory structure and makes its best guess as to how the deployment descriptor should be constructed. You can't entirely escape the process of creating descriptor files because the tool may not always properly determine every unique aspect of your application. It would be impossible for BEA to create a tool that can handle every conceivable way that an enterprise application could be set up.

Although automatic generators often do not create perfect deployment descriptors, they do generate descriptors that are a closer match to your ideal descriptors than any sort of template descriptor. Because of this, you should use the descriptor generators to generate the first version of your deployment descriptors.

Creating descriptors using tools

WebLogic includes several tools that you can use to automatically generate descriptors for your enterprise application. These tools are implemented as command-line Java utilities. Before you can use these utilities, however, you must make sure that CLASSPATH is set correctly.

Setting CLASSPATH

The utility classes are located in the weblogic.jar file, and you must make this file part of CLASSPATH. You can do this by issuing the following command to your command prompt:

```
set CLASSPATH=
%CLASSPATH%;C:\bea\weblogic81\server\lib\weblogic.jar
```

This adds the weblogic.jar file to CLASSPATH for the current command prompt. If you close the command-prompt window, you must reissue the preceding command to use the utility classes again.

If you find that you're using the descriptor generation utilities frequently, you may want to permanently add weblogic.jar to your system CLASSPATH. To do so, modify the CLASSPATH environmental variable on your system. The instructions for doing this vary depending on your operating system, so refer to your operating system instructions for more information.

Invoking the descriptor generation utilities

WebLogic has four descriptor generation utilities, as shown in Table 8-3. Which utility you should use depends on the type of descriptor that you want to generate.

You invoke these utilities just as you would any other Java utility: by specifying the main class. For example, to generate the web.xml and weblog.xml descriptors for the web application stored at the following location:

Table 8-3	Deployment Descriptor Utilities
Application	*Main Class*
Enterprise application	weblogic.ant.taskdefs.ear.DDInit
Enterprise JavaBeans (EJB) 1.0	weblogic.ant.taskdefs.ejb.DDInit
Enterprise JavaBeans (EJB) 2.0	weblogic.ant.taskdefs.ejb20.DDInit
Web application	weblogic.ant.taskdefs.war.DDInit

```
C:\bea\user_projects\mydomain\applications\MyWebApp
```

you would issue the following command:

```
java weblogic.ant.taskdefs.war.DDInit c:\bea\user_projects
\mydomain\applications\MyWebApp
```

Although this command spans more than one line, it must be entered as one command. This command generates the web.xml and weblogic.xml files for MyWebApp and places them in the WEB-INF directory.

Creating descriptors manually

In this section, you create by hand the application.xml file, the J2EE enterprise descriptor for an enterprise application. You may include the weblogic.xml descriptor as well. Both files are covered in this section.

The J2EE enterprise descriptor

The J2EE enterprise descriptor is named application.xml. An example application.xml file is shown in Listing 8-1.

Listing 8-1:   J2EE Enterprise Descriptor

```
<?xml version="1.0" encoding="UTF-8"?>

<!DOCTYPE application PUBLIC
'-//Sun Microsystems, Inc.//DTD J2EE Application 1.3//EN'
'http://java.sun.com/dtd/application_1_3.dtd'>

<application>
  <display-name>HomeMethods ejb20</display-name>
```

```
<description>HomeMethods ejb20</description>

<module>
  <ejb>ejb20_homemethods.jar</ejb>
</module>

</application>
```

The main purposes of the application.xml file are to identify the EJBs used with your web application and to tie together all the components that make up the application. Table 8-4 lists the components in application.xml.

Table 8-4	XML Elements for application.xml
Element	*What It Does*
application	Contains the other elements described in this table. This is the root element of the application deployment descriptor.
icon	Specifies the locations of small and large images that represent the application in a GUI tool. Currently, WebLogic Server doesn't use this element, so its inclusion is optional.
small-icon	Specifies the location for a small (16x16 pixel) .gif or .jpg image that represents the application in a GUI tool. Currently, WebLogic Server doesn't use this element, so its inclusion is optional.
large-icon	Specifies the location for a large (32x32 pixel) .gif or .jpg image that represents the application in a GUI tool. Currently, WebLogic Server doesn't use this element, so its inclusion is optional.
display-name	Describes the name of the application displayed by GUI tools.
description	Describes the application displayed by GUI tools.
module	This element specifies EJBs, servlets, and other components. One module element exists for every module in WebLogic.
alt-dd	Specifies an optional URI to the post-assembly version of the deployment descriptor file for a particular J2EE module. The URI must specify the full path name of the deployment descriptor file relative to the application's root directory. If you do not specify alt-dd, the deployer must read the deployment descriptor from the default location and file name required by the respective component specification.

(continued)

Table 8-4 *(continued)*

Element	What It Does
connector	Specifies the URI of a resource adapter (connector) archive file, relative to the top level of the application package.
ejb	Defines an EJB module in the application file. Contains the path to an EJB JAR file in the application.
web-uri	Defines the location of a web module in the application.xml file. This is the name of the WAR file.
context-root	Specifies the context root for the web application.
description	Describes the security role.
role-name	Defines the name of a security role or principal used for authorization in the application.

As you can see from Table 8-4, you can specify security information as well as information about the components of the enterprise application. Security is discussed in Chapter 18.

The WebLogic-specific descriptor

The WebLogic-specific enterprise descriptor is named weblogic.xml. This descriptor allows you to specify security settings that are not part of the J2EE descriptor. You can use this descriptor to create security roles that govern the abilities of users. An example weblogic.xml file is shown in Listing 8-2.

Listing 8-2:   WebLogic Enterprise Descriptor

```
<?xml version="1.0" encoding="UTF-8"?>
<!DOCTYPE weblogic-web-app PUBLIC
"-//BEA Systems, Inc.//DTD Web Application 7.0//EN"
"http://www.bea.com/servers/wls700/dtd/weblogic700-web-
          jar.dtd" >
<weblogic-web-app>

    <security-role-assignment>
        <role-name>GoodRole</role-name>
        <principal-name>larry</principal-name>
        <principal-name>moe</principal-name>
    </security-role-assignment>

</weblogic-web-app>
```

Many of these elements are related to security, a topic discussed in Chapter 18. Table 8-5 offers a brief description of the WebLogic elements.

Table 8-5	XML Elements for weblogic.xml
Element	*What It Does*
`weblogic-web-app`	Contains the other elements described in this table. This is the root element of the WebLogic deployment descriptor.
`description`	Describes this enterprise application.
`weblogic-version`	Specifies the version of WebLogic for which this file was designed.
`security-role-assignment`	Specifies a security role assignment that can be used in the J2EE enterprise application descriptor.
`reference-descriptor`	Matches `resource-ref` elements in the web.xml descriptor to JNDI names.
`session-descriptor`	Determines how WebLogic configures each session.
`jsp-descriptor`	Determines how WebLogic handles JSP files.
`auth-filter`	Specifies the full class name of a servlet that handles authentication.
`charset-params`	Determines `charset` mappings for GETs and POSTs.

Packaging Your Enterprise Application

The third step in creating an enterprise application is to package, or archive, your enterprise application. The enterprise application is stored in a JAR file, which is a special archive file used by Java. The file format of a JAR file is the same as the format for a ZIP archive. JAR files usually end with the .jar extension, but the extension can be changed to anything you want.

Although enterprise applications are stored as JAR files, they use the .ear extension, not the .jar extension. In this section, you find out how to convert your enterprise application's directory structure to an EAR file.

Follow these steps to package your enterprise application:

1. **Create a temporary directory anywhere on your hard drive.**

   You'll use this directory to stage the directories and files in your enterprise application.

2. **Copy all web archives (WAR files) and EJB archives (JAR files) to the staging directory.**

3. **Create a** META-INF **subdirectory in the staging directory.**

4. **Set up your shell environment.**

   If you're using Windows, execute the setenv.cmd command, which is in the "WebLogic Home"\bin\setenv.cmd directory. If you're using UNIX, execute the setenv.sh command, which is in the "WebLogic Home"/bin/setenv.sh directory. For Windows or UNIX, replace "WebLogic Home" with the directory that you installed WebLogic to.

5. **Create the application.xml deployment descriptor file and place it in the** META-INF **directory.**

   For more information on this step, see the preceding section.

6. **Optionally create the weblogic.xml file and place it in the** META-INF **directory.**

   For more information on this step, see the preceding section.

7. **Create the Enterprise archive (EAR file) for the application, using the following** jar **command:**

   ```
   jar cvf application.ear -C staging-dir
   ```

   where *application* is the name of your application and *staging* is your staging directory.

Now that you've created an EAR file, it's time to deploy it.

JAR, WAR, and EAR files have the same format as a ZIP file. Therefore, you can simply copy each to a new file — renaming it as .zip — and then use WinZip to view the contents of the file. This is a fast way to look inside the archive.

Deploying Your Enterprise Application

The fourth step in creating an enterprise application is to deploy it to WebLogic Server.

After you've packaged your web application to an EAR file, you deploy it as many times as needed. This provides a convenient way to distribute your enterprise application to any number of servers.

Follow these steps to deploy an enterprise application:

1. **Ensure that WebLogic Server is running.**

2. **Log on to Administration Console at** http://localhost:7001/console.

3. **In the left pane, click the Deployments folder, and then click the Applications folder.**

   The screen shown in Figure 8-1 appears.

4. **Click the Deploy a new Application link.**

   The screen shown in Figure 8-2 appears.

5. **Click the upload your file(s) link, type the name of the EAR file that you'll be uploading to the server, and then click the Upload button.**

6. **Click the radio button that appears next to your newly uploaded EAR file, and then click Continue.**

7. **Type a name for your application.**

8. **Click the Deploy button.**

   The screen shown in Figure 8-3 appears. After a few moments, the deployed status will go to the value of `completed`.

Your enterprise application is now deployed and ready for use. Now that you've created an enterprise application, you're ready to find out about some of the services that WebLogic provides. That's the topic of the next part of the book.

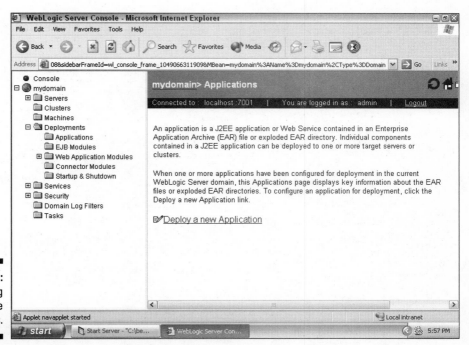

Figure 8-1: Viewing enterprise applications.

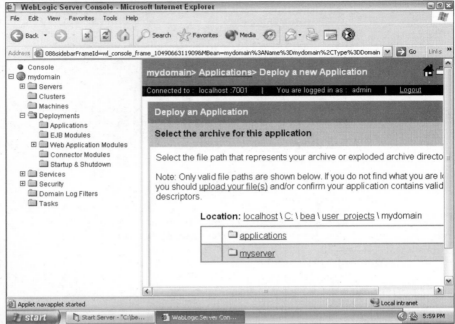

Figure 8-2:
Deploying
a new
application.

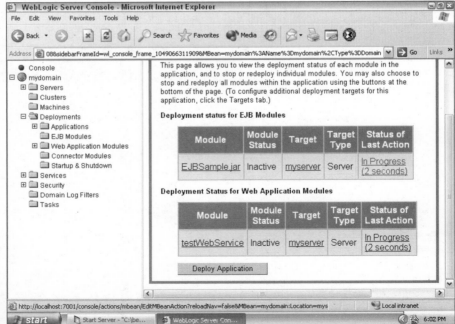

Figure 8-3:
Your
deployed
application.

Part III
Employing Web Services

The 5th Wave   By Rich Tennant

Meditations, Inc.
BOOKS • SEMINARS • TAPES

"Sales on the Web site are down. I figure the server's chi is blocked, so we're fudgin' around the feng shui in the computer room, and if that doesn't work, Ronnie's got a chant that should do it."

In this part . . .

Web applications are programs that run on a web server and are usually accessed by humans. A web service is similar to a web application in that it can run from a web server. However, web services are usually accessed by computer programs, not humans. Additionally, a web service can run over e-mail as well as the web. In this part, you create a simple web service in WebLogic.

After you create a web service, you'll want to access it, so your next task is constructing a client program to do just that.

Finally, you use Resource Workshop to create a web service. Resource Workshop uses a GUI similar to Visual Basic, so you can design your web service graphically.

Chapter 9

Building and Deploying Web Services

*W*eb services have received a lot of media attention lately. But what exactly is a web service? A *web service* is a remote procedure available to clients through TCP/IP, typically using HTTP or SMTP as the transport and XML for encoding. The web service is described using standard XML notation called a *service description*. A web service fulfills a single task or a set of tasks.

All details of the web service are hidden from the user, and the service is both hardware and software independent. This encourages software developers to build applications consisting of small, individual services, which can then be used alone or in groups to perform even more complex tasks.

You can create a web service in two ways: manually, through the creation of Java source and configuration files, or using a GUI system called WebLogic Workshop. In this chapter, you create a web service manually. For more on WebLogic Workshop, see Chapter 11.

WebLogic services are built on the Simple Object Access Protocol (SOAP), a standard protocol upon which XML messages are exchanged between web services and their clients. Generally, WebLogic deals with the details of the SOAP protocol, freeing you to focus on building your web service. However, if you're interested in knowing more about SOAP, go to the site of the World Wide Web consortium, the group that maintains the SOAP standard, at http://www.w3.org/TR/SOAP/.

Understanding SOAP

SOAP is an XML-based, lightweight protocol that's used for information exchange. This protocol works in both decentralized and distributed environments. SOAP is decentralized in that the provider of a SOAP service and the consumer program can be run on two different computers. SOAP is distributed in that many different computers can provide the same SOAP service, which allows these computers to balance the load of requests to achieve maximum performance.

SOAP consists of three main parts:

- **SOAP envelope.** The SOAP envelope portion of the message describes what's in a message and how to process it. It contains a target address specifying the server that the SOAP message is targeted to and a return address specifying where the server should send its response. The encoding rules are specified by the XML attribute `SOAP-ENV:Envelope`.

- **Encoding rules.** For expressing the application's data types. Every SOAP message contains the rules used to encode it. These rules specify what version of SOAP was used and how different components of the SOAP message are represented. The encoding rules are specified by the XML attribute `SOAP-ENV:encodingStyle`.

- **Method call.** When a SOAP message is sent, part of the message specifies the methods that the server should execute. The method being invoked is specified inside the `SOAP-ENV:Body` XML tag.

Although SOAP can be used with a variety of protocols, it's almost always used only with HTTP.

You may be wondering exactly what a SOAP request looks like. The following is a simple SOAP request to get the weather conditions for a specific station. In the following example, I request the weather for KSTL, or St. Louis, Missouri:

```
<SOAP-ENV:Envelope
  xmlns:SOAP-ENV="http://
  schemas.xmlsoap.org/soap/
  envelope/"
  SOAP-ENV:encodingStyle=
  "http://schemas.xmlsoap.org/
  soap/encoding/">
  <SOAP-ENV:Body>
    <m:GetCurrentTemperature
  xmlns:m="Some-URI">

    <symbol>KSTL</symbol>
    </m:
  GetCurrentTemperature >
    </SOAP-ENV:Body>
</SOAP-ENV:Envelope>
```

I called the `GetCurrentTemperature` method, passing it one parameter, which is called `symbol`. This is the weather station I am querying.

Defining a Web Service

Before you create your web service, you should define what it will do. This allows you to properly construct the interface that other applications must adhere to if they want to communicate with your web service.

The most basic design decision is which of the two general types of web services you will create:

> ✔ Synchronous service
> ✔ Asynchronous service

A *synchronous web service,* which is the default, begins when the web service receives a message. This web service responds immediately.

Synchronous web services are most useful when the client program requires the data returned from the request immediately. An example of this type of data is the current stock quote for a particular company.

An *asynchronous* web service is asynchronous, so messages can be exchanged freely between the client and web service. A message from one side does not oblige the other to send a corresponding message. When a client sends a message to an asynchronous web service, the client doesn't wait for a message back from the web service. The web service may send a message back to the client at a later time, but nothing inherently ties this message to the original message that the client sent.

Asynchronous web services are a good choice when you're sending information that doesn't require a response. For example, you may want to a send a message to several of your servers, giving them a new greeting message to display to users.

Choosing and Building a Backend Component

The purpose of your web service is to allow remote clients to access services that you provide. These services, called the *backend component,* take the form of Java code. You can build your backend component as one of the following:

> ✔ A method of a stateless session EJB
> ✔ A method of a Java class
> ✔ A JMS method consumer

WebLogic can make any of these items available as a web service. This makes it convenient to package existing Java code as a web service. If you've already created stateless session EJBs, you can package them as a web service. Or if your code exists in regular Java classes, you can provide access to your class as a web service. You can also use JMS messaging as a backend service for your web service. JMS is covered in Chapter 15.

Building a Synchronous Web Service

In this section, you build a synchronous web service. I cover using and a regular Java class and then using a stateless session EJB. Later, you find out what changes are necessary to make this web service an asynchronous service.

First you must write the backend component. This will be either a Java class, a stateless EJB, or a JMS method consumer.

Working with a Java class backend component

You must follow a few rules when implementing a web service operation using a Java class:

- Do not start any threads. This rule applies to all Java code that runs on WebLogic Server.
- Define a default no-argument constructor.
- Define as public the methods of the Java class that will be exposed as web service operations.

You must write thread-safe Java code because WebLogic Server maintains only a single instance of a Java class that implements a web service operation, and each invocation of the web service uses this same instance.

For an example of implementing a WebLogic web service operation with a Java class, go to the following directory:

```
WL_HOME\samples\server\src\examples\webservices\basic\javacla
       ss
```

where WL_HOME refers to the main directory of your WebLogic Server installation. On a Windows system, this directory is usually C:\bea\weblogic81.

Listing 9-1 shows a Java class that you could use as a backend component. This Java class contains a single method, named sampleMethod, that accepts an int and returns a String.

Listing 9-1: Java Class Backend Component

```
package com.dummies.ejb;

public class SampleBackendComponent
{
```

```
public String sampleMethod(int num)
  {
  switch(num)
  {
    case 1:return "One";
    case 2:return "Two";
    case 3:return "Three";
    case 4:return "Four";
    case 5:return "Five";
    case 6:return "Six";
    case 7:return "Seven";
    case 8:return "Eight";
    case 9:return "Nine";
    case 10:return "Ten";
    default:return "Some Number";
  }
 }
}
```

Working with a stateless session EJB backend component

You may also choose to build your backend component as a stateless session EJB. Writing Java code for a stateless session EJB for a web service is no different than writing a stand-alone EJB.

In the web-services.xml deployment descriptor, you can specify that a web service operation is one way, which means that the client application that invokes the web service doesn't wait for a response. When you write the Java code for the EJB method that implements this type of operation, you must specify that it returns `void`.

When choosing between using an EJB or a Java class backend component, consider the other ways in which your backend component will be used. If your backend component will be commonly accessed as an EJB, build it as an EJB. This allows you to use the same code for both your EJB and web service.

Considerably more resources are required to call a web service than to call an EJB. Because of this, it's common to create all your backend components as EJBs and then allow external applications to access your backend components as web services. Your own local applications, which are running on the same network as your WebLogic server, can use the faster EJB calling method.

For the EJB in this section, you use the stateless EJB developed in Chapter 6. You'll see the highlights of that EJB and how they relate to the web service. For complete information on creating an EJB, refer to Chapter 6.

Listing 9-2 shows the bean file that implements the EJB backend component. The EJB backend component is nearly the same as the Java class backend component. The main difference is the additional code used to support the EJB.

Listing 9-2:   EJB Backend Component

```
package com.dummies.ejb;

import javax.ejb.*;
import java.rmi.*;
import javax.swing.*;

public class SampleBean implements SessionBean
{

  private SessionContext stx;

  //Required methods, not used by this type of bean
  public void ejbCreate(){}
  public void ejbRemove(){}
  public void ejbActivate(){}
  public void ejbPassivate(){}

  // setter for the SessionContext
  public void setSessionContext(SessionContext ctx)
  {
    ctx = this.stx;
  }

  // the sample method
  public String sampleMethod(int num)
    throws RemoteException
  {
    switch(num)
    {
      case 1:return "One";
      case 2:return "Two";
      case 3:return "Three";
      case 4:return "Four";
      case 5:return "Five";
      case 6:return "Six";
      case 7:return "Seven";
      case 8:return "Eight";
      case 9:return "Nine";
      case 10:return "Ten";
      default:return "Some Number";
    }
  }
}
```

You must specify that the bean is a stateless EJB in the ejb-jar.xml file, which is shown in Listing 9-3. You can use many nodes and attributes. For more information on the structure of an ejb-jar.xml file, refer to Chapter 6.

Listing 9-3:   ejb-jar.xml File for a Backend Component

```
<!DOCTYPE ejb-jar PUBLIC '-//Sun Microsystems, Inc.//DTD
           Enterprise JavaBeans 2.0//EN'
'http://java.sun.com/dtd/ejb-jar_2_0.dtd'>
<ejb-jar>
  <enterprise-beans>
    <session>
      <ejb-name>SampleObject</ejb-name>
        <home>com.dummies.ejb.SampleHome</home>
        <remote>com.dummies.ejb.Sample</remote>
        <ejb-class>com.dummies.ejb.SampleBean</ejb-class>
        <session-type>Stateless</session-type>
        <transaction-type>Container</transaction-type>
    </session>
  </enterprise-beans>
</ejb-jar>
```

Building an Asynchronous Web Service

In general, you build the backend component for an asynchronous service just as you would a synchronous service. When creating a backend component for an asynchronous service, keep the following in mind:

- ✔ The backend component that implements the operation must explicitly return void.
- ✔ You can't specify out or in-out parameters to the operation; you can specify only in parameters.

Asynchronous web services do not return a result when sent a request. Your client will not even know whether the web service received the request.

Nearly all web services are synchronous style rather than asynchronous style. Before you choose to create an asynchronous service, make sure that it will truly fit your needs. Pure broadcast communication, in which you expect no result and don't care whether your message was received, is the only appropriate time to choose an asynchronous service.

Packaging Your Web Service

In this section, you find out how to package your web service. *Packaging* is the process that connects your backend component with WebLogic in such a way that WebLogic makes the backend component available as a web service.

The packaging process that WebLogic uses for web services relies heavily on Ant (developed by the Apache Software Foundation). Ant is a tool that executes scripts designed to carry out tasks for Java programs. The most common use for Ant is to create build scripts for Java programs.

The following steps assume that Ant is part of your system path. WebLogic uses a customized version of Ant, and you must use their version.

Packaging a synchronous service

You must create a custom build.xml file to show Ant how to build your web service. Such a build.xml file is shown in Listing 9-4.

Listing 9-4: build.xml File for a Synchronous Web Service

```
<project name="buildWebservice" default="ear">
  <target name="ear">
    <servicegen
      destEar="TestWebService.ear"
      contextURI="testWebService" >
    <service
      ejbJar="EJBSample.jar"
      targetNamespace=
        "http://localhost/webservices/TestWebService"
      serviceName="TestWebService"
      serviceURI="/TestWebService"
      generateTypes="True"
      expandMethods="True"
      style="rpc" >
    <client
      packageName=
        "com.dummies.webservices.TestWebService"
    />
    </service>
    </servicegen>
  </target>
</project>
```

A number of attributes are shown in the build.xml file. Attributes for the `servicegen` node are listed in Table 9-1. Attributes for the `service` node are listed in Table 9-2.

Table 9-1		`servicegen` **Node Attributes**	
Attribute	*Required?*	*Default*	*What It Is*
contextURI	No	value of `warName`	Defines the URI used to access the web service.
destEar	Yes	—	Contains the name of the EAR file that will contain the final web service. This file is deployed to WebLogic when you deploy your web service.
overwrite	No	true	Specifies whether you want to overwrite any previous versions of your web service.
warName	No	web-services. war	Specifies the name of the web application. You should generally stick with the default value for this attribute.

Table 9-2		`service` **Node Attributes**	
Attribute	*Required?*	*Default*	*What It Is*
ejbJar	No	—	Specifies the name of the JAR file that contains the EJB — if the backend component for this web service is an EJB. If you don't specify this attribute, you must include the `javaClass-Components` attribute.
excludeEJBs	No	—	Contains a comma-separated list of EJB names for which non-built-in data type components should not be generated.

(continued)

Table 9-2 *(continued)*

Attribute	Required?	Default	What It Is
expandMethods	No	false	Specifies whether a separate `<operation>` element for each method of the EJB or Java class is used, or whether the task should implicitly refer to all methods. This attribute should be `true` or `false`.
generateTypes	No	true	Specifies whether the serialization class and Java representations for non-built-in data types should be generated. This attribute should be `true` or `false`.
includeEJBs	No	—	Contains a list of the EJB names that use non-built-in data types.
javaClass-Components	No	—	Contains a comma-separated list of classes — if the backend component is one or more Java classes. These classes must be compiled and be part of `CLASSPATH`. If you don't specify this attribute, you must include the `ejbJar` attribute.
JMSAction	Yes, if using JMS	—	Specifies whether the client application that invokes this JMS-implemented web service sends messages to or receives messages from the JMS destination. This attribute should contain the value `Send` or `Receive`.
JMSConnection-Factory	Yes, if using JMS	—	Specifies the JNDI name of `ConnectionFactory` used to create a connection to the JMS destination.

Attribute	Required?	Default	What It Is
JMSDestination	Yes, if using JMS		Specifies the JNDI. This attribute should contain the name of a JMS topic or queue.
JMSDestination-Type	Yes, if using JMS		Specifies the type of JMS destination. This attribute should contain the value Queue or Topic.
JMSMessageType	No	java. lang. String	Specifies the data type of the single parameter to the send or receive operation.
JMSOperation-Name	No	send or receive, depending on the value of the JMSAction attribute	Specifies the name of the operation in the generated Web Service Definition Language (WSDL) file, which is the file that defines the methods of your web service.
protocol	No	http	Contains the protocol over which this web service is deployed. This attribute should be http or https.
serviceName	Yes	—	Contains the name of the web service that will be published in the WSDL file.
serviceURI	Yes	—	Contains the web service URI portion of the URL used by client applications to access your web service. Always include the leading slash (/), for example /TestWebService.
style	No	rpc	Specifies whether RPC- or documents-oriented operations are used. This attribute should be rpc or document.
targetNamespace	Yes	—	Contains the namespace URI of the web service.

(continued)

Table 9-2 *(continued)*

Attribute	Required?	Default	What It Is
typeMappingFile	No	—	Specifies a file that contains additional XML data-type mapping information. This data is added to web-services.xml.

You can also define several attributes for the client node, as shown in Table 9-3. The client node allows you to automatically generate a stub that a client would use to access the web service. A *stub* is a small class used to interface to the web service. The client communicates with the stub, which in turn communicates with the web service. This process is discussed in greater detail in Chapter 10. If you don't want to create an interface for the client to use when accessing your web server, you're not required to include this client node. If you don't create such an interface, you need to use the clientgen utility later when you want to access this web service from a client. Using web service clients is covered in Chapter 10.

Table 9-3 client **Node Attributes**

Attribute	Required?	Default	What It Is
clientJarName	No	serviceName_client.jar	Contains the name of the generated client JAR file.
packageName	Yes	—	Contains the package name into which the generated client interfaces and stub files are packaged.
saveWSDL	No	true	Generates WSDL and stores it in the JAR file. This prevents clients from having to generate WSDL each time.
useServerTypes	No	false	Specifies whether the client should use the definition for any non–built-in types from the EAR file.

To package your web service, follow these steps:

1. **Set your environment.**

   - If you're using Windows, execute the `setEnv.cmd` command, located in `C:\bea\weblogic81\server\bin`.

   - If you're using UNIX, execute the `setEnv.sh` command, located in `C:\bea\weblogic81/server/bin`.

2. **Create a staging directory.**

   You need to create a temporary staging directory to hold the components that will make up your web service. For this example, I assume you're using `c:\staging` as your staging directory.

3. **Package the backend component.**

   - If the backend component is implemented using an EJB, make sure that your EJB is packaged as an EJB JAR file. This is covered in Chapter 6. Place the EJB JAR file in the staging directory.

   - If the backend component is implemented using a Java class, compile it to a Java `.class` file and place the `.class` file in the staging directory.

4. **Create an Ant build file and place it in the staging directory.**

   Create a custom build.xml file, as shown in Listing 9-1.

5. **Execute the Ant build file by typing** ant **from the staging directory.**

   Ant builds your web service as an EAR file, as shown in Figure 9-1. You're now ready to deploy your web service.

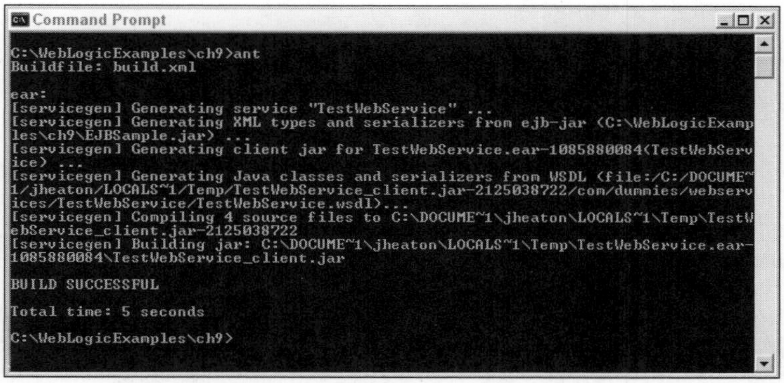

Figure 9-1: Running Ant to generate the web service.

After completing these steps, you have an EAR file that contains your web application. You're now ready to deploy this EAR file to your WebLogic Server.

Packaging an asynchronous service

Packaging an asynchronous web service is nearly the same as building a synchronous web service. The main difference is that the `style` attribute in the build.xml file specifies `message` rather than `rpc`. This designates the web service as an asynchronous web service.

Listing 9-5:   build.xml File for an Asynchronous Service

```
<project name="buildWebservice" default="ear">
  <target name="ear">
    <servicegen
      destEar="TestWebService.ear"
      contextURI="testWebService" >
    <service
      ejbJar="EJBSample.jar"
      targetNamespace=
        "http://localhost/webservices/TestWebService"
      serviceName="TestWebService"
      serviceURI="/TestWebService"
      generateTypes="True"
      expandMethods="True"
      style="rpc" >
    <client
      packageName=
        "com.dummies.webservices.TestWebService"
    />
    </service>
    </servicegen>
  </target>
</project>
```

Deploying Your Web Service

A web service is packaged to an enterprise archive (EAR) file. Because of this, the steps to deploy a web service are nearly the same as deploying an enterprise application, as described in Chapter 8. In this section, I cover the process from a web service point of view.

After you've packaged your web service to an EAR file, you can repeat the deployment step as many times as needed. This provides a convenient way to distribute your web service to any number of servers.

Follow these steps to deploy your web service:

1. **Ensure that WebLogic Server is running, and log on to Administration Console at** `http://localhost:7001/console`.

2. **In the left pane, click the Deployments folder, and then click the Applications folder.**

   The screen shown in Figure 9-2 appears.

3. **Click the <u>Deploy a new Application</u> link.**

   The screen shown in Figure 9-3 appears.

4. **Upload your file.**

   Click the <u>upload your file(s)</u> link, type the name of the EAR file that you'll be uploading to the server, and then click Upload.

5. **Click the radio button that appears next to your newly uploaded EAR file, and then click Continue, as seen in Figure 9-4.**

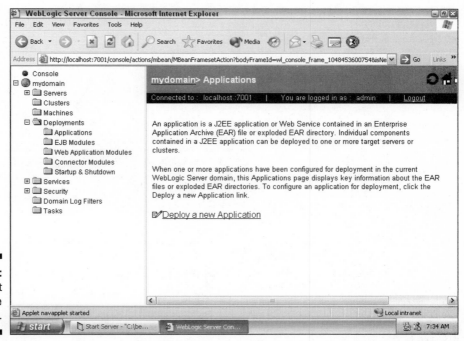

Figure 9-2:
Current
enterprise
applications.

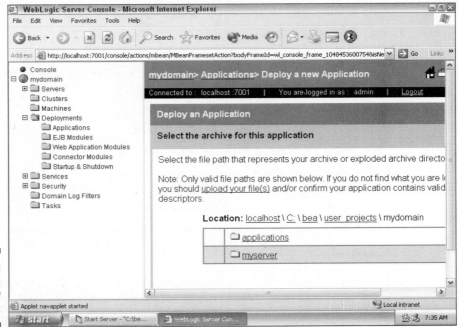

Figure 9-3:
Configuring
a new
application.

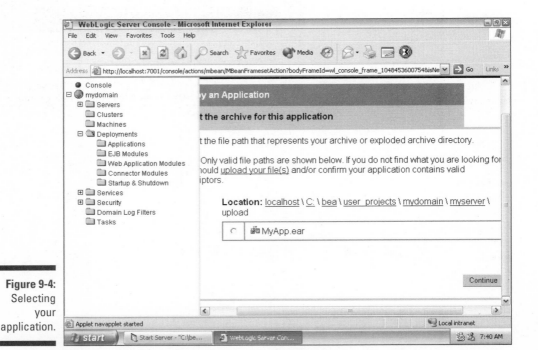

Figure 9-4:
Selecting
your
application.

6. Type a name for your application, and then click Deploy.

After a few moments, the deployed status changes to Success, as shown in Figure 9-5.

Your web service is deployed and ready for use. Chapter 10 describes how to use your newly deployed web service.

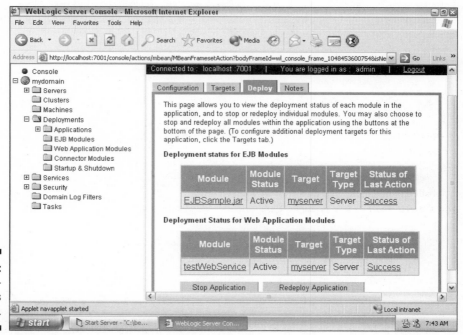

Figure 9-5:
Your application is deployed.

Chapter 10

Accessing Web Services

· ·

· ·

*W*eb services are an increasingly popular way to access remote applications. Web services exchange information with their clients using XML constructed according to the SOAP protocol. (For more on the SOAP protocol, see Chapter 10.) In this chapter, you find out how to access a web service using WebLogic. If you're interested in creating web services, refer to Chapter 9.

You can create two types of web service clients with WebLogic: a static client that uses stub client interfaces created by WebLogic and a dynamic client that learns about the web service as it runs. Static clients are easy to program and use. Dynamic clients require more source code but add flexibility. These are shortcuts that WebLogic provides to make it easier for WebLogic developers to work with web services.

 When accessing a WebLogic web service, always use a static client. Use a dynamic client when you're accessing a non-WebLogic web service or a web service whose interface you may want to change as the program runs. In rare situations, your program may not know the structure of the web service beforehand. A dynamic client can adapt to many types of web services.

Using a Static Client

In this section, you find out how to create a static web service client. A *static client* uses the web service EAR file to generate a client stub that you can use to call the web service, just as if it were a local class. The main difference between a static client and a dynamic client has to do with how you call the web service. In a static client, you call a web service just like any other Java method. In the dynamic client, you must call methods to specify the method name, parameters, and return type. This allows these values to be different each time the client runs.

Understanding WSDL

Web Service Definition Language (WSDL) provides instructions for accessing a web service. You use the WSDL of your target web service to create a client stub. After you generate this client stub, you can access the web service as though it were a regular Java class.

WSDL is an XML-formatted description of a web service. This code contains all the necessary information to access a web service. You can find out more at http://www.w3.org/TR/wsdl.

To access the WSDL file contained in a web service, you first must make sure that you have a web service deployed on WebLogic. For this example, I assume that you're using the TestWebService web service from Chapter 9. You can access this web service with the following URL:

```
http://localhost:7001/testWebService/TestWebService
```

You can see the WSDL file for your web service by accessing the following URL:

```
http://localhost:7001/testWebService/TestWebService?WSDL
```

If your web service has been properly configured, the screen displays something similar to Figure 10-1. (If you don't see your WSDL file, your web service is not up and running. Review Chapter 9 for information on creating and deploying your web service.)

The WSDL file in Figure 10-1 is complex, but you don't need to be able to read the file to access a web service. Reading this file is the job of the WebLogic clientgen application. You find out how to use clientgen in the next section.

Following are the steps you need to take to create a static web service client:

1. **Generate a client stub.**

2. **Create a client program that will use the client stub.**

3. **Start WebLogic Server.**

4. **Run the web service client application.**

In the following sections, I expand upon these steps.

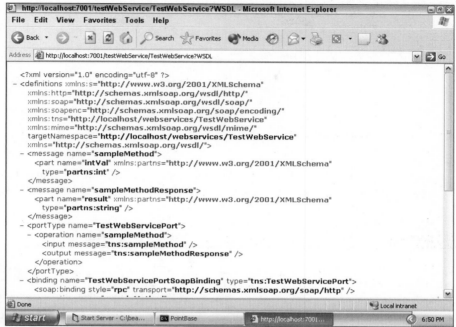

Figure 10-1:
Looking at a
WSDL file.

Generating the client stub

To use the web service created in Chapter 9, you must create a client stub for
that application. This stub allows you to access the web service as though it
were a regular application. The client stub generation process that WebLogic
uses for web services relies heavily on Jakarta Ant. Ant is a tool that executes
scripts that carry out tasks for Java programs. The most common use for Ant
is to create build scripts for Java programs.

WebLogic uses a customized version of Ant, so you must use the version of
Ant provided by WebLogic. Ant is stored in the WebLogic bin directory. The
following steps assume that Ant is part of your system path.

You must create a custom build.xml file to show Ant the URL for which you
want to build a web service. Such a build.xml file is shown in Listing 10-1.

Listing 10-1:   build.xml File for Client Stub Generation

```
<project
  name="buildWebservice"
  default="generate-client">
```

(continued)

Listing 10-1   *(continued)*

```
<target name="generate-client">
  <clientgen
    ear="TestWebService.ear"
    serviceName="TestWebService"
    packageName="com.dummies.webservices.TestWebService"
    useServerTypes="False"
    clientJar="TestWebServiceClient.jar" />
</target>
</project>
```

clientgen automates the creation of the client stub. To use clientgen, you must create an Ant script. You can define quite a few attributes to control the operation of clientgen. These attributes are summarized in Table 10-1.

Table 10-1	clientgen **Attributes**
Attribute	**What It Is**
ear	The enterprise application that contains the web service. For more information on how to generate this file, see Chapter 9.
serviceName	The name of your web service.
packageName	The package name that you want to place your client stub into.
useServerTypes	Determines whether custom data types should be used. This attribute should contain true if you're using the data types of the server or false for customized data types.
clientJar	The name of the JAR file that you want the client stub generated to.

After you create the build.xml file, you can execute it by typing the Ant command from the same directory as the build.xml file. When you do so, the screen shown in Figure 10-2 appears.

Building the client application

Now that you've created the client stub file, you must create an application that makes use of the web service. Listing 10-2 shows such an application.

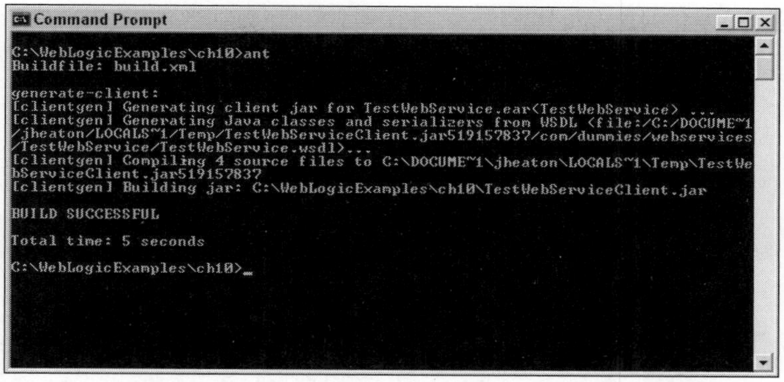

Figure 10-2:
Building the
client file.

Listing 10-2:   Web Service Client

```
import com.dummies.webservices.TestWebService.*;

public class StaticClient {
  public static void main(String[] args) throws Exception {
    // Set up the global JAXM message factory
    System.setProperty("javax.xml.soap.MessageFactory",

        "weblogic.webservice.core.soap.MessageFactoryImpl"
        );
    // Set up the global JAX-RPC service factory
    System.setProperty( "javax.xml.rpc.ServiceFactory",

        "weblogic.webservice.core.rpc.ServiceFactoryImpl")
        ;
    // Parse the argument list
    StaticClient client = new StaticClient();
    String wsdl = (args.length > 0? args[0] : null);
    client.example(wsdl);
  }

  public void example(String wsdlURI) throws Exception {
    TestWebServicePort client = null;
    if ( wsdlURI == null ) {
      client = new
          TestWebService_Impl().getTestWebServicePort();
    } else {
      client = new
          TestWebService_Impl(wsdlURI).getTestWebServicePort
          ();
    }
    // call the method
    System.out.println( trader.sampleMethod(3) );
  }

}
```

The program works as follows. First, you set up the JAXM factory and the RPC factory. A *factory* is a class designed to create other objects. For example, JAXM uses the `javax.xml.soap.MessageFactory` class as a factory to produce messages. You should not change anything in these lines, and they must be included with a client application:

```
// Set up the global JAXM message factory
System.setProperty("javax.xml.soap.MessageFactory",

        "weblogic.webservice.core.soap.MessageFactoryImpl"
        );
// Set up the global JAX-RPC service factory
System.setProperty( "javax.xml.rpc.ServiceFactory",

        "weblogic.webservice.core.rpc.ServiceFactoryImpl")
        ;
```

Next, you create an instance of the `port` class. This object is used to connect to the web service, as seen here:

```
TestWebServicePort client = null;
if ( wsdlURI == null ) {
   client = new TestWebService_Impl().getTestWebServicePort();
} else {
   client = new
        TestWebService_Impl(wsdlURI).getTestWebServicePort
        ();
}
```

In the preceding code, you check to see whether the user has passed in an alternate URL to use with the service. If no alternate URL was passed in, you use the URL built into the web service WSDL:

```
// call the method
System.out.println( trader.sampleMethod(3) );
```

When you compile the program, make sure that both the J2EE and client stub JAR files are in `classpath`. To do so, compile Listing 10-2 with the following command:

```
javac -classpath TestWebServiceClient.jar;
C:\bea\weblogic81\server\lib\webserviceclient.jar
        StaticClient.java
```

I included the webserviceclient.jar file in the command. You may need to include a different version of this JAR file; refer to Table 10-2.

Table 10-2	Web Service Client JAR Files
JAR File	*When to Use It*
webserviceclient.jar	When you don't need SSL to access your web service
webserviceclient+ssl.jar	When you need SSL to access your web service
webserviceclient+ssl_pj.jar	With the CDC profile of J2ME

Running the client application

To run your client application, you must execute it with the WebLogic web services client and the client stub JAR files present. To do so, use the following command:

```
java -classpath TestWebServiceClient.jar;
C:\bea\weblogic81\server\lib\webserviceclient.jar;.
        StaticClient
```

After you execute your application, you'll see the result of calling the web service. Figure 10-3 shows the client program being executed.

Figure 10-3:
Running
the client
application.

You probably noticed a delay of a few seconds before the output was displayed. This is a result of the overhead that the web service incurs as the JVM starts up and data is posted between the web server and web client. The overhead for a web service is considerably more than that for an EJB. As a result, you should use EJBs for your program's internal use. Use web services to allow external applications to access your EJBs through the Internet.

In this section, you found out how to call a client using a static connection to the web service. You can also choose to call your web service dynamically, a topic described in the next section.

Using a Dynamic Client

A *dynamic client* can change virtually anything about the way in which the web service is accessed at run time. All information about which web service to access is given dynamically to Java. I will begin by showing you how to construct the dynamic client.

Constructing the dynamic client

Producing a dynamic client involves fewer steps than producing a static client because a dynamic client doesn't require a client stub file. However, calling methods through the dynamic interface is not as natural for a Java programmer.

In addition, method names and parameters are specified as strings, so you won't catch errors when compiling. If you specify the wrong method name for the dynamic client, you won't know until your program runs. Specifying an invalid method name with a static client would cause a compile error. The complete dynamic client source code is shown in Listing 10-3.

Listing 10-3: Dynamic Client

```
import java.util.Properties;
import java.net.URL;
import javax.naming.Context;
import javax.naming.InitialContext;

import weblogic.soap.WebServiceProxy;
import weblogic.soap.SoapMethod;
import weblogic.soap.SoapType;
import weblogic.soap.codec.CodecFactory;
import weblogic.soap.codec.SoapEncodingCodec;
import weblogic.soap.codec.LiteralCodec;

public class DynamicClient{

  public static void main( String[] arg ) throws Exception{

    CodecFactory factory = CodecFactory.newInstance();
```

```
        factory.register( new SoapEncodingCodec() );
        factory.register( new LiteralCodec() );

        WebServiceProxy proxy = WebServiceProxy.createService(
            new URL(
                "http://localhost:7001/testWebService/TestWebServi
                ce" ) );
        proxy.setCodecFactory( factory );
        proxy.setVerbose( true );

        SoapType param = new SoapType( "intVal", Integer.class );
        proxy.addMethod( "sampleMethod", null, new SoapType[]{
            param } );
        SoapMethod method = proxy.getMethod( "sampleMethod" );

        Object result = method.invoke( new Object[]{ new
            Integer(3)} );
    }
}
```

First, you must register the correct codecs. A WebLogic *codec,* which stands for code/decode, translates Java objects to and from SOAP XML. (When the term *codec* is used with multimedia files such as MPEG and Quicktime, it means compressor/decompressor.) If you're missing a codec, you get an error when you transmit your request:

```
CodecFactory factory = CodecFactory.newInstance();
factory.register( new SoapEncodingCodec() );
factory.register( new LiteralCodec() );
```

A proxy must be set up that will get your method context. The proxy is used as an intermediary to connect to the web service and ultimately to allow you to communicate with the web service. You use the method context to send your method call:

```
WebServiceProxy proxy = WebServiceProxy.createService(
    new URL(
            "http://localhost:7001/testWebService/TestWebServi
            ce" ) );
proxy.setCodecFactory( factory );
```

The method context is very important. The method context is the object that you use to invoke methods on the web service. If any errors are reported, they should be reported *verbosely,* which means with as much detail as possible. The following command sees to this:

```
proxy.setVerbose( true );
```

Next, parameters must be constructed. `sampleMethod` takes one parameter, an `int`, and returns a string:

```
SoapType param = new SoapType( "intVal", Integer.class );
```

Next, `sampleMethod` is obtained using the method name and parameter array:

```
proxy.addMethod( "sampleMethod", null, new SoapType[]{ param
        } );
SoapMethod method = proxy.getMethod( "sampleMethod" );
```

Finally the method is invoked, passing 3 as the parameter. The result is then displayed:

```
Object result = method.invoke( new Object[]{ new Integer(3)}
        );
System.out.println( result );
```

To compile this application, you must make sure that the WebLogic JAR file is in `classpath`. The following command compiles the client:

```
javac -classpath
        TestWebServiceClient.jar;C:\bea\weblogic81\server\
        lib\weblogic.jar DynamicClient.java
```

Now that you've compiled the client, you're ready to run it.

Running the dynamic client

To run the client application, the WebLogic JAR file must be in `classpath`. The following command runs the client application:

```
java -classpath
        TestWebServiceClient.jar;C:\bea\weblogic81\server\
        lib\weblogic.jar;.DynamicClient
```

This program, like the static client example, outputs the word *three* to the console.

In this chapter and in Chapter 9, you create and use web services. In Chapter 11, you use WebLogic Workshop, which is a GUI tool provided by WebLogic to assist in the creation of web services.

Chapter 11

Using WebLogic Workshop

In This Chapter

▶ Creating a web service with Workshop

▶ Debugging your web service

▶ Packaging and deploying your web service

Creating a web service can be difficult, especially for those unfamiliar with J2EE. That's why BEA introduced WebLogic Workshop, a full-featured IDE for creating and debugging web services. WebLogic Workshop was designed to help several groups of people:

✔ Non-J2EE programmers who want to create web services

✔ Non-technical designers who want to create web services

✔ Advanced J2EE developers who want to become more productive by allowing debugging

Many non-Java languages that use web services include similar IDEs. Resource Workshop simplifies Java web service programming. Regardless of which group you're in, read on to find out how to create your own web service using WebLogic Workshop.

Creating a Web Service

The web service you create will be similar to the one in Chapter 9. But in Chapter 9, you create the web service manually. In this chapter, you use Workshop to perform many of the mundane tasks of setting up the web service and the configuration files.

The following general steps are required when creating a web service:

1. **Create a Workshop application.**

2. **Create your web service.**

3. **Add methods to your web service.**

4. **Test your web service.**

Creating a Workshop application and a web service

The first step in creating a web service with Workshop is to create an application file. This file will hold not only web services, but also EJB and database connections.

It's not necessary to have WebLogic Server running to start WebLogic Workshop. Instead, you can start WebLogic Server from WebLogic Workshop.

To create an application file and a web service, follow these steps:

1. **Start BEA WebLogic Workshop.**

   Choose Start⇨BEA WebLogic Platform 8.1⇨WebLogic Workshop. The screen shown in Figure 11-1 appears.

Figure 11-1: The opening screen of BEA WebLogic Workshop.

2. **Create an application by choosing File⇨New⇨Application.**

3. **Type a name for your application, and then click Create.**

   To follow along with the example, type **WorkshopWebService** for the name, as shown in Figure 11-2.

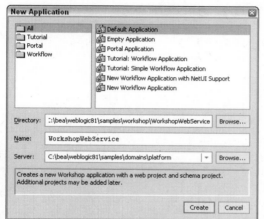

New Application

```
☐ All                    ☐ Default Application
☐ Tutorial               ☐ Empty Application
☐ Portal                 ☐ Portal Application
☐ Workflow               ☐ Tutorial: Workflow Application
                         ☐ Tutorial: Simple Workflow Application
                         ☐ New Workflow Application with NetUI Support
                         ☐ New Workflow Application
```

Directory: `:\bea\weblogic81\samples\workshop\WorkshopWebService` Browse...

Name: `WorkshopWebService`

Server: `C:\bea\weblogic81\samples\domains\platform` ▾ Browse...

Creates a new Workshop application with a web project and schema project. Additional projects may be added later.

Create   Cancel

Figure 11-2: Creating an application.

4. **Right-click WorkshopWebService (from the tree at the left under the Application tab) and choose New⇨Web Service.**

   The Create New File dialog box appears.

5. **Type a name for the web service.**

   To follow along with the example, type **MyService**, as shown in Figure 11-3.

6. **Click OK.**

   The screen shown in Figure 11-4 appears. Your web service is set up.

At this point, you've created your application (WorkshopWebService) and web service (MyService). In the next section, you add some methods.

Adding methods to your web service

For the web service to be of any use, you must add methods to it. Inside the methods, you can place Java code that carries out the tasks needed by your web service. The methods are called by the client programs that access your web service. (For more information on web service clients, see Chapter 10.)

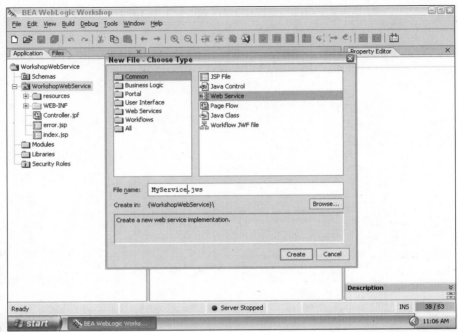

Figure 11-3:
Creating
a web
service.

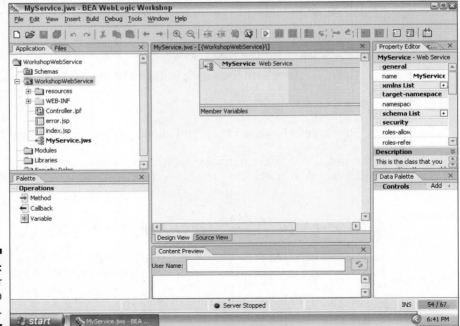

Figure 11-4:
Your
new web
service.

To add a method to the web service, follow these steps:

1. **Add the method.**

   On the Design View tab in the center of the screen (see Figure 11-4), click Add Operation and choose Add Method. A method name appears inside the web service.

2. **Type a new name for your method.**

   To follow along with the example, type **myMethod**. The screen shown in Figure 11-5 appears. Now that you've created your method, you need to give it some parameters and define its body.

3. **Open the code editor.**

   Click the method name to display the code editor.

4. **Program the method.**

   Move the cursor into the body of your method and specify a return type of String and a single integer parameter, as shown in Figure 11-6. All operations performed by the web service are specified using Java code.

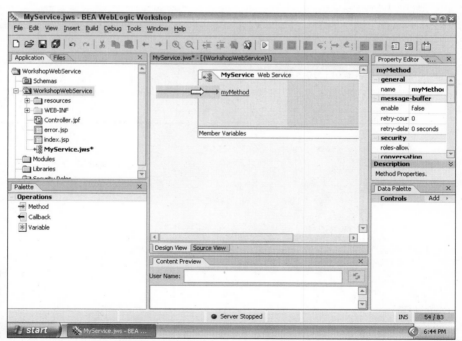

Figure 11-5:
Creating the method.

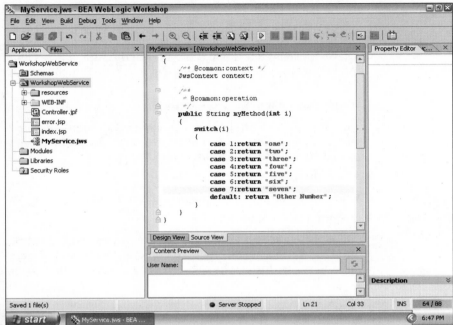

Figure 11-6:
Modifying
the method.

Your method should match Listing 11-1.

Listing 11-1: **The** myMethod **Method**

```
{
    /** @common:context */
    JwsContext context;

    /**
     * @common:operation
     */
    public String myMethod(int i)
    {
        switch(i)
        {
            case 1:return "one";
            case 2:return "two";
            case 3:return "three";
            case 4:return "four";
            case 5:return "five";
            case 6:return "six";
            case 7:return "seven";
            default:return "Other Number";
        }
    }
}
```

Now that you've created a method, you're ready to test your web service by accessing it using a browser.

Testing your web service

To test your web service, you must first start the web server. Simply choose Tools⇨Start WebLogic Server. The server starts and you remain in Workshop, as shown in Figure 11-7.

You could test the web service by using a client program, such as the one in Chapter 10, but a faster way is to use a browser.

The browser interface can be used for any WebLogic web service, not just web services created with Workshop.

When you create a web service, it's often for the benefit of some external entity, such as a client or a vendor. Because of this, you will rarely develop the client applications of a web server. However, you still need a client to test your application.

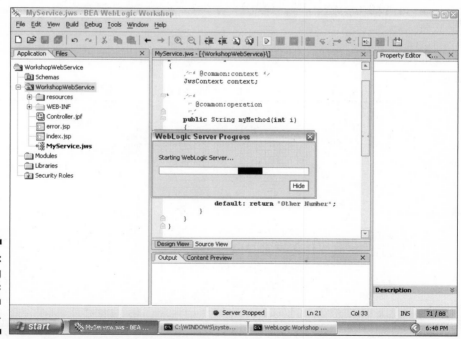

Figure 11-7:
Running
WebLogic
from
Workshop.

If you access the URL of the web service from a browser, you enter a web application that WebLogic provides for testing your web service. Using this approach, you can quickly test your web application without the need to create a client program.

By default, Workshop uses a web server running on the current machine, using port 7001. If you already have WebLogic Server running on that machine and port, Workshop fails to start the server.

Follow these steps to access your web service using its URL and a browser:

1. **Make sure that your web service is running.**

   On the Workshop toolbar, click the light blue arrowhead, which is labeled in Figure 11-8. Workshop automatically opens a browser window to your web service, as shown in Figure 11-9.

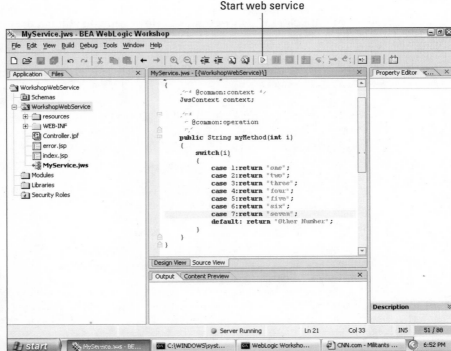

Figure 11-8:
Starting
your web
service.

Figure 11-9:
Accessing
your web
service.

2. **Type the parameters for your web service.**

   Click the Test Form tab. If you're using the example web service developed so far in this chapter, type **1**.

3. **Call your method and observe the results.**

   Click the button that has the same name as your method (myMethod). The results page is shown in Figure 11-10.

4. **End the service.**

   To do so, click the red x icon on the toolbar, which is labeled in Figure 11-11.

These steps show you how to test the output that a web service returns for the specified input. Although this can be a great aid in debugging, you often need more information to debug a program. In the next section, you find out how to use the WebLogic debugger.

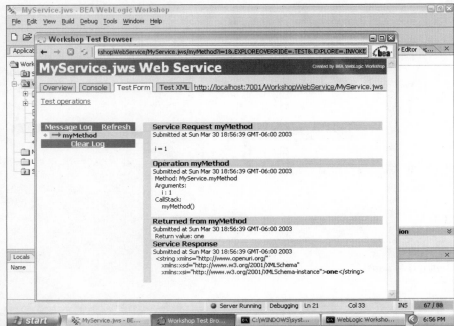

Figure 11-10:
Viewing
the results.

Stop web service

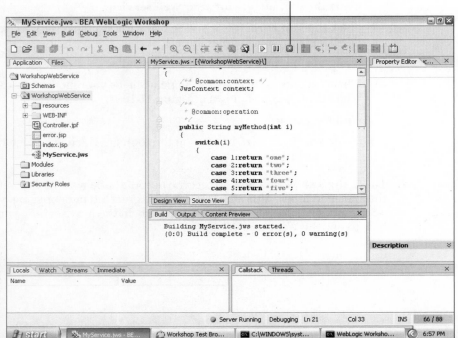

Figure 11-11:
Stopping
your web
service.

Debugging Web Services

Workshop includes features that allow you to perform any of the following debugging tasks:

✔ Set breakpoints to pause the web service on particular lines of code

✔ Inspect the values of variables used by your web service

✔ Evaluate exceptions thrown as your web service runs

In this section, you go through a typical debugging session. During this session, you set a breakpoint in your web service. A *breakpoint* is placed on a single line of code to pause program execution when the breakpoint line is reached during execution. When the program is paused, you will be able to inspect the values of variables and ultimately continue or end execution of the web service.

1. **Start your web service.**

   Click the Start web service icon, which is labeled in Figure 11-8.

2. **Set a breakpoint.**

   Right-click to the left of the `switch` statement and choose Toggle Breakpoint. The screen shown in Figure 11-12 appears.

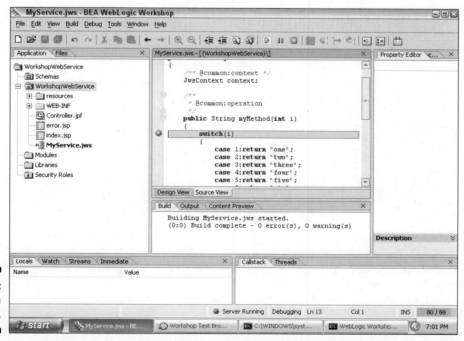

Figure 11-12: Setting a breakpoint.

3. **Use a web browser to execute your web service.**

   For more information, see the "Testing your web service" section. When the web service reaches the breakpoint, the screen shown in Figure 11-13 appears.

4. **Check the values of your variables after the breakpoint.**

5. **To continue execution, click the green arrow. To stop execution, click the red dot.**

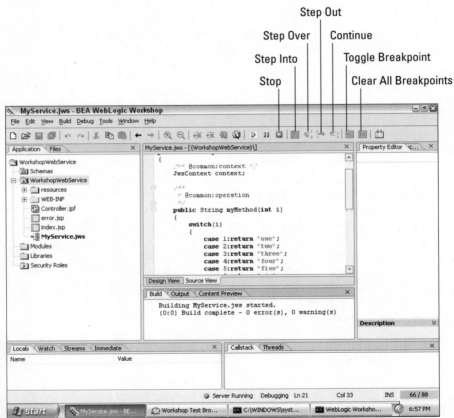

Figure 11-13: The breakpoint is reached.

After you encounter a breakpoint, a number of actions are available by clicking tools on the toolbar:

✓ **Stop.** Stops debugging the web service. After you click Stop, you must restart the web service to continue debugging.

✔ **Step Into.** If you're positioned on a method call, clicking Step Into causes the debugger to enter the method rather than pass over it.

✔ **Step Over.** If you're positioned on a method call, clicking Step Over causes the debugger to skip this method.

✔ **Step Out.** If you're positioned inside a method call, clicking Step Out causes you to leave that method.

✔ **Continue.** Allows the web service to run freely after being stopped. The program continues until it reaches the next breakpoint.

Now that you've used Workshop to create, test, and debug your web service, it's time to see how to package and deploy it.

Packaging and Deploying Web Services

In the previous sections, you found out how to create and make use of web services using only Workshop. Sometimes, however, you'll want to package your files for use elsewhere. For example, you might want to

✔ Archive your newly created web service

✔ Copy your web service to a different development server

✔ Copy your web service to a production server

In this section, you find out how to package and deploy your web service. You begin by examining the directory structure Workshop creates when you create a web service.

Directory locations

When you create a web service using Workshop, it creates a web application to contain your web service. This web application is stored in the `samples` directory of WebLogic. For example, if you created the WorkshopWebService example in this chapter, this web service is stored in the following location:

```
C:\bea\weblogic81\samples\workshop\WorkshopWebService
```

If you examine this directory, you'll see the same folder structure as was used for a web application, as discussed in Chapter 5. The complete directory tree used by a web service is shown in Figure 11-14.

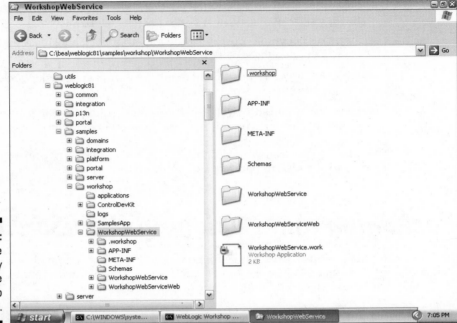

Figure 11-14:
The
directory
structure
of a web
service.

Workshop stores your files in a subdirectory of the `samples` directory. This might be confusing, in that you may assume that the `samples` directory contains only WebLogic examples.

Packaging a web service

In this section, you package a web service created with Workshop. The final product will be an EAR file. This EAR file contains the enterprise application that contains the web service.

To create the EAR file, you use `JwsCompile`. This program, which is invoked from a command prompt, has eighteen command-line options but you need to concern yourself with only a few of them.

If you want to see what command-line options are available for `JwsCompile`, issue the following command:

```
jwscompile -help
```

JwsCompile is in the bin directory of WebLogic Server. This directory must be in your path if you want to execute JwsCompile from the command line.

The following command line compiles the sample web service created in this chapter:

```
JwsCompile -p C:\bea\weblogic81\samples\workshop\
        WebLogicWebService -a -ear
        C:\WebLogicWebService.ear
```

The three options in this command follow:

- ✔ The -p option specifies the directory that contains the application source. WebLogic Workshop placed the example application in the following directory:

  ```
  C:\bea\weblogic81\samples\workshop\WebLogicWebService
  ```

- ✔ The -a option specifies that all the files that make up the application should be compiled by JwsCompile.

- ✔ The -ear option instructs JwsCompile to create an EAR file as its output and tells JwsCompile where to place that file. In this instance, the file is called WebLogicWebService.ear, and it's placed in the root directory of the C: drive. This file contains your web service, packaged and ready to deploy.

Packaging for a different host

When you execute JwsCompile, an EAR file is produced that will work for a server running on a particular host name and port. The host name used is whatever machine JwsCompile runs on. The default port is 7001, which is standard for WebLogic Server. If you want your EAR to run on a different machine, you must place the named weblogic-jws-config.xml configuration file in the application's WEB-INF directory.

In a multi-web service application, you might have more than one weblogic-jws-config.xml file. You can easily allow more than one web service by specifying appropriate parameters on the command line when running JwsCompile. By doing this, you can specify an alternate name for the weblogic-jws-config.xml file.

Listing 11-2 shows sample a weblogic-jws-config.xml file for deploying the WorkshopWebService web service to a machine named MyServer.

Listing 11-2:   Sample weblogic-jws-config.xml File

```
<config>

<protocol>http</protocol>
<hostname>MyServer</hostname>
<http-port>7001</http-port>
<https-port>7002</https-port>

<jws>

   <class-name>WorkshopWebService</class-name>
   <protocol>http</protocol>

</jws>

</config>
```

Table 11-1 describes the purpose of each of the tags in Listing 11-2.

Table 11-1	weblogic-jws-config.xml Attributes
Tag	*What It Is*
protocol	The protocol to use with this web service. This tag usually contains the string http.
hostname	The host name for the computer.
http-port	The port used with the HTTP protocol.
https-port	The port used with the HTTPS protocol.
class-name	The name of the web service.
protocol	The default protocol.

Now that you've seen how to package your web service, it's time to find out how to deploy it.

Deploying web services

Deploying a web service is the same process as deploying an enterprise application. The web service is contained in an EAR file. When the EAR file is deployed, it implements the web service.

The steps to deploy a web service follow:

1. **Make sure that WebLogic Server is running, and log on to Administration Console at** `http://localhost:7001/console`.

2. **Click the Deployments folder and then the Application folder.**

3. **Click the <u>Configure a new Application</u> link.**

4. **Type the name of the EAR file that you'll be uploading to the server.**

5. **Upload your file, and then click the [select] link that appears next to your newly uploaded file.**

6. **Target one or more servers by selecting the server on the left and clicking the arrow to move it to the list on the right. Type a name for your application. Then click Configure and Deploy.**

   After a few moments, the deployed status goes to the value of `true`. Your application is now deployed.

For more information on how to deploy web services, refer to Chapter 8.

Part IV
The Forgotten Services

The 5th Wave   By Rich Tennant

"A centralized security management system sounds fine, but then what would we do with the dogs?"

In this part . . .

Many message services are available with WebLogic. In this part you find out how to use four of them: JMS, JBDC, JTA, and JNDI.

JMS (Java Message Service) allows client programs to send and receive messages. Messages can be sent from one program to one or more programs. JDBC (Java Database Connectivity) allows Java programs to access database services. You set up JDBC for use with WebLogic and use connection pools to more efficiently handle database access.

JTA (Java Transactions) allows database requests to be grouped into transactions, which will succeed or fail as a whole. This allows you to prevent partial transactions from occurring due to an error. JNDI (Java Naming and Directory Interface) allows Java programs to locate named resources on a network. WebLogic uses JNDI to access EJBs, connection pools, and other services.

Chapter 12

Accessing Data with JDBC

● ●

In This Chapter

▶ Configuring a connection pool for your database

▶ Creating a data source for your connection pool

▶ Using your data source and connection pool

▶ Monitoring your connection pool

● ●

Databases are a crucial component of nearly any successful web site or business application. In a distributed application server such as WebLogic, managing the connection between many concurrently executing instances of an EJB and the database can be difficult. WebLogic acts as an intermediary, allowing your EJBs to make the most efficient use of connections to the database.

To use a database from an EJB, you have two options. You can use JDBC to directly connect to the database (also known as bean-managed persistence, or BMP), just like you would in any other Java program, or you can use WebLogic's built-in connection pools to manage your database connections (also known as container-managed persistence, or CMP). Regardless of the strategy you choose, using WebLogic connection pools can enhance the performance of your application considerably. In this chapter, you find out about both approaches.

Creating a Connection Pool

To use a database in Java, you must first open a connection to that database. A database connection is a resource in Java that adds processing overhead, so you want to minimize the number of open connections to the database. You might think that it would be best to open a database connection, perform the operation, and then immediately close the connection. But this approach introduces the overhead of opening and closing database connections. The overhead of opening a connection can be ten to a hundred times as expensive as the requested data transfer. The answer to the problem of opening and closing connections is to use a connection pool.

A *connection pool* is a group of database connections that remains open to the database. When your program needs to access the database, it requests a connection from the connection pool. The program is then given a connection to use for its database operations. To your program, the connection seems like a regular database connection. However, you don't close the database connection when you're finished using it. Instead, you release the database connection back to the connection pool, so it can be used later.

The connection pool prevents Java from having to deal with the overhead of opening and closing connections. Further, the system is kept from creating too many connections and degrading performance. The task of obtaining a proper performance balance with the maximum allowable number of open connections is left to the system administrator, not the web application logic.

To create a connection pool, follow these steps:

1. **Log on to Administration Console as follows:**

    a. **Make sure that WebLogic Server is running.**

    b. **Start your favorite web browser.**

    c. **In the browser, type the URL of your server's Administration Console, at** `http://localhost:7001/console`.

    d. **Type your username and password, and then click Sign In.**

    For more information on using Administration Console, see Chapter 4.

2. **On the left side of the screen, click the Services folder, then click the JDBC folder, and then click the Connection Pools folder.**

    A screen similar to the one in Figure 12-1 appears. If you previously configured any connection pools, they are listed instead, but you can still create another connection pool.

3. **Click the <u>Configure a new JDBC Connection Pool</u> link.**

    The screen shown in Figure 12-2 appears.

4. **Enter the required information for your data source.**

    The two most important pieces of information are the driver class name and the URL. Any database that you use with Java should provide these two values in the documentation. The values entered in Figure 12-2 are for the ODBC bridge driver, which enables you to access any ODBC-compatible driver for which you have a DSN. In a production environment, you'd probably use Oracle, DB2, MySQL, or some other database.

    If you enter invalid data while setting up your connection pool, you won't receive an immediate error. Instead, an exception is thrown when you try to use the connection pool.

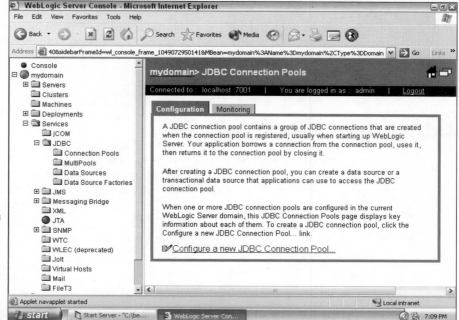

Figure 12-1:
Getting
ready to
create a
connection
pool.

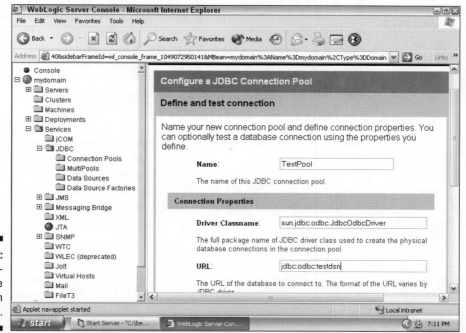

Figure 12-2:
Config-
uring the
connection
pool.

5. Click Create.

You might need to click the scroll bar to see the Create button. Little will change in the window. You'll know that you've successfully created the connection pool by the fact that you can no longer change the name of the data source.

Defining a Data Source

After you have a connection pool, you must attach it to a data source. It's through this data source that WebLogic accesses your database. By having the EJBs connect to data sources directly, you can quickly map data sources to other connection pools. This can be useful if you need to temporarily connect your application to a different database.

To create a data source, follow these steps:

1. Log on to Administration Console.

For details, see Step 1 in the preceding section.

2. On the left side of the screen, click the Services, JDBC, and then Data Sources folders.

A screen similar to the one in Figure 12-3 appears. If you previously created any data sources, they're listed instead, but you can still create another data source.

3. Click the <u>Configure a new JDBC Data Source</u> link.

The screen shown in Figure 12-4 appears.

4. Enter the required information for your data source.

The two most important pieces of information are the data source name and the JNDI name. Administration Console uses the data source name to refer to your data source. Java programs and EJBs use the JNDI name to access your data source. Additionally, you must specify the name of the pool that this data source will reference, which is the pool that you created in the preceding section.

If you enter invalid data while setting up your data source, you won't receive an immediate error. When you try to use your data source, however, an exception will be thrown.

5. Click Create.

After you create your data source, little will change in the window. You will know that the procedure worked by the fact that you can no longer change the name of the data source.

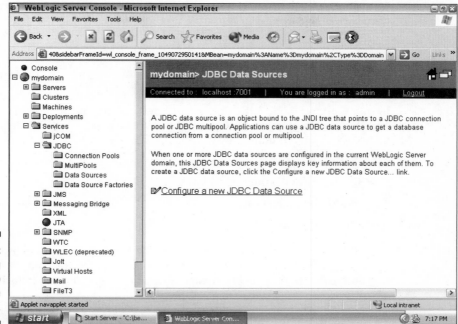

Figure 12-3:
Getting
ready to
create the
data source.

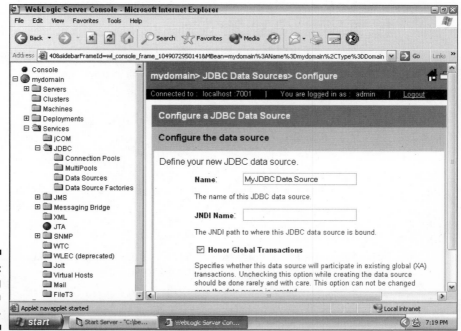

Figure 12-4:
Configuring
the data
source.

Now you're ready to see whether your EJBs can access your newly created data source and connection pool. This topic is covered in the next section.

Using JDBC with EJBs

In this section, you use the data source and connection pool that you just created. You implement a simple EJB that makes use of JDBC. I show you some of the most common ways that JDBC is used, providing examples of the following:

- Executing SQL statements
- Working with a result set
- Using prepared statements

For this example, you need to create an EJB. I show you all the files necessary to create this EJB, but I don't go into the specific steps for compiling, deploying, and executing this bean. For more information about those tasks, see Chapter 6.

To properly compile this bean, you need a J2EE bean descriptor. Listing 12-1 is the J2EE descriptor for the JDBC example.

Listing 12-1:   J2EE EJB Descriptor

```
<!DOCTYPE ejb-jar PUBLIC
'-//Sun Microsystems, Inc.//DTD Enterprise JavaBeans 2.0//EN'
'http://java.sun.com/dtd/ejb-jar_2_0.dtd'>
<ejb-jar>
  <enterprise-beans>
    <session>
      <ejb-name>JDBCSampleObject</ejb-name>
        <home>com.dummies.ejb.JDBCSampleHome</home>
        <remote>com.dummies.ejb.JDBCSample</remote>
        <ejb-class>com.dummies.ejb.JDBCSampleBean</ejb-class>
        <session-type>Stateless</session-type>
        <transaction-type>Container</transaction-type>
    </session>
  </enterprise-beans>
</ejb-jar>
```

To compile the bean, you also need the WebLogic-specific bean descriptor. Listing 12-2 is the WebLogic descriptor for the JDBC example.

Listing 12-2:   WebLogic EJB Descriptor

```
<!DOCTYPE weblogic-ejb-jar PUBLIC
'-//BEA Systems, Inc.//DTD WebLogic 6.0.0 EJB//EN'
'http://www.bea.com/servers/wls600/dtd/weblogic-ejb-jar.dtd'>

<weblogic-ejb-jar>
  <weblogic-enterprise-bean>
    <ejb-name>JDBCSampleObject</ejb-name>
    <jndi-name>JDBCSampleObject</jndi-name>
  </weblogic-enterprise-bean>
</weblogic-ejb-jar>
```

Listing 12-3 is the home class that's compatible with the JDBC example.

Listing 12-3:   JDBC Sample Home Class

```
package com.dummies.ejb;

import javax.ejb.*;
import java.rmi.*;

public interface JDBCSampleHome extends EJBHome
{
  public JDBCSample create()
    throws RemoteException,CreateException;
}
```

Listing 12-4 is the bean interface that's compatible with the JDBC example.

Listing 12-4:   JDBC Example Bean Interface

```
package com.dummies.ejb;

import javax.ejb.*;
import java.rmi.*;
import java.util.*;

public interface JDBCSample extends EJBObject
{
  public void execute()
    throws RemoteException;

  public void prepared()
    throws RemoteException;

  public Collection query()
    throws RemoteException;
}
```

Finally, Listing 12-5 is the complete bean implementation class.

Listing 12-5:   JDBC Example Implementation

```
package com.dummies.ejb;

import javax.ejb.*;
import javax.naming.*;
import javax.sql.*;
import java.sql.*;
import java.rmi.RemoteException;
import java.util.Vector;
import java.util.Enumeration;
import java.util.*;


public class JDBCSampleBean implements SessionBean
{

  private SessionContext stx;

  //Required methods, not used by this type of bean
  public void ejbCreate(){}
  public void ejbRemove(){}
  public void ejbActivate(){}
  public void ejbPassivate(){}

  // setter for the SessionContext
  public void setSessionContext(SessionContext ctx)
  {
    ctx = this.stx;
  }


  public void execute()
    throws RemoteException
  {
    Connection conn = null;
    Statement statement = null;

    try {
      conn = getConnection();
      String sql = "INSERT INTO t_student(f_id, f_first,
          f_last) VALUES(1,'John','Smith')";
      statement = conn.createStatement();
      statement.executeUpdate(sql);
    } catch ( Exception e ) {
      System.out.println(e);
    } finally {
      handleCleanup(conn,null,null,statement);
    }
```

```
  }

public void prepared()
  throws RemoteException
{
  Connection conn = null;
  PreparedStatement ps = null;

  try {
    conn = getConnection();
    String sql = "INSERT INTO t_student(f_id, f_first,
        f_last) VALUES(?,?,?)";
    ps = conn.prepareStatement(sql);
    ps.setInt(1,1);
    ps.setString(2,"John");
    ps.setString(3,"Smith");
    ps.executeUpdate();
  } catch ( Exception e ) {
    System.out.println("Error:" + e );
  } finally {
    handleCleanup(conn,ps,null,null);
  }

}

public Collection query()
  throws RemoteException
{
  Connection conn = null;
  PreparedStatement ps = null;
  ResultSet rs = null;
  Collection result = new ArrayList();

  try {
    conn = getConnection();
    String sql = "SELECT f_id, f_first,f_last FROM
        t_student";
    ps = conn.prepareStatement(sql);
    rs = ps.executeQuery();

    while( rs.next() ) {
      result.add(rs.getString(3));

    }
  } catch ( Exception e ) {
    System.out.println( e );
  } finally {
    handleCleanup(conn,ps,rs,null);
  }
```

(continued)

Listing 12-5 *(continued)*

```
    return result;

}


private Connection getConnection() throws NamingException,
        SQLException {
    InitialContext ic = new InitialContext();
    DataSource ds =
            (DataSource)ic.lookup("java:comp/env/jdbc/SchoolDa
            taSource");
    return ds.getConnection();
}

private void handleCleanup(Connection
        conn,PreparedStatement ps,ResultSet rs,Statement
        statement)
{
    // make sure the connection is returned to the connection
        pool
    try {
      if ( rs!=null )
        rs.close();
      if(statement!=null)
        statement.close();
      if ( ps!=null )
        ps.close();
      if ( conn!=null )
        conn.close();
    } catch ( SQLException e ) {
    }
  }
}
```

Next, I will explain how this example was constructed, beginning with how you obtain a connection from a data source. If you're familiar with JDBC, you'll find that nothing is changed when you use JDBC from a WebLogic data source and connection pool, except the method by which you obtain the connection.

Obtaining the connection

To perform any database operation, you must first obtain a database connection. This is a common process, so it will be placed in a method. This way, you won't have to duplicate the code everywhere that you need a connection. This method will be named `getConnection`, as follows:

```
private Connection getConnection() throws NamingException,
          SQLException {
  InitialContext ic = new InitialContext();
  DataSource ds =
          (DataSource)ic.lookup("java:comp/env/jdbc/TestData
          Source");
  return ds.getConnection();
}
```

The process for obtaining a connection using a WebLogic data source is easy. JDBC data sources are obtained through JNDI, a service that allows string-based names to be associated with services. First, an initial context is obtained; this gives you access to JNDI. Then the data source name is looked up using the `java:comp/env/jdbc/TestData` identifier. Although the data source has this lengthy name, you specify only the `TestData` name when setting up the data source. The `comp/env/jdbc` portion is added automatically. The `java:` portion specifies the protocol; you should always use `java:`. For more information about JNDI, refer to Chapter 13.

Closing the data source

When you're finished with a data source, you should release your data source back to the pool. The following method handles this task:

```
private void handleCleanup(Connection conn,PreparedStatement
          ps,ResultSet rs,Statement statement)
{
  // make sure the connection is returned to the connection
          pool
  try {
    if ( rs!=null )
      rs.close();
    if(statement!=null)
      statement.close();
    if ( ps!=null )
      ps.close();
    if ( conn!=null )
      conn.close();
  } catch ( SQLException e ) {
  }
}
```

`Connection`, `PreparedStatement`, `ResultSet`, and `Statement` are passed in. If any of these values is not null, the `close` method is called on each one. `SQLException` errors are caught but ignored because you're closing the data source.

Executing an SQL statement

In the preceding example, you executed a SELECT statement that returns data. The INSERT, DELETE, and UPDATE SQL statements do not return data. These SQL statements are commands to alter the database, not requests for data. When you execute an INSERT, DELETE, or UPDATE command, you should execute the executeUpdate method, which doesn't expect data to be returned. The following code shows this:

```
public void execute()
   throws RemoteException
{
   Connection conn = null;
   Statement statement = null;

   try {
     conn = getConnection();
     String sql = "INSERT INTO t_student(f_id, f_first,
             f_last) VALUES(1,'John','Smith')";
     statement = conn.createStatement();
     statement.executeUpdate(sql);
   } catch ( Exception e ) {
     System.out.println(e);
   } finally {
     handleCleanup(conn,null,null,statement);
   }
}
```

You begin by getting the connection. Next, the SQL statement is assigned to the sql String. A statement is created and the SQL is passed to the executeUpdate method.

Note that John and Smith are inserted directly into the SQL. Because these values will change, depending on what name you use, you should make them parameters. This will allow you to use the same SQL no matter what name you're inserting. This technique is shown in the next section.

Using prepared statements

A *prepared statement* allows you to insert parameters into an SQL statement. The following method uses a prepared statement named ps:

```
public void prepared()
   throws RemoteException
{
   Connection conn = null;
```

```
    PreparedStatement ps = null;

    try {
      conn = getConnection();
      String sql = "INSERT INTO t_student(f_id, f_first,
            f_last) VALUES(?,?,?)";
      ps = conn.prepareStatement(sql);
      ps.setInt(1,1);
      ps.setString(2,"John");
      ps.setString(3,"Smith");
      ps.executeUpdate();
    } catch ( Exception e ) {
      System.out.println("Error:" + e );
    } finally {
      handleCleanup(conn,ps,null,null);
    }

}
```

This method starts out like the one before it. A connection is obtained and an
SQL is specified. Note, however, that this SQL includes question mark values.
These are parameters that will be added later by using the `set` methods of
the prepared statement.

If you use prepared statements, make sure that you've set the values of all
specified parameters. Otherwise, you'll get an error.

Submitting a query

A *query* is an SQL statement that returns data. The following code performs a
query:

```
public Collection query()
  throws RemoteException
{
  Connection conn = null;
  PreparedStatement ps = null;
  ResultSet rs = null;
  Collection result = new ArrayList();

  try {
    conn = getConnection();
    String sql = "SELECT f_id, f_first,f_last FROM
          t_student";
    ps = conn.prepareStatement(sql);
    rs = ps.executeQuery();

    while( rs.next() ) {
```

```
        result.add(rs.getString(3));

    }
} catch ( Exception e ) {
    System.out.println( e );
} finally {
    handleCleanup(conn,ps,rs,null);
}
return result;

}
```

This code uses `PreparedStatement` as well. A `select` statement retrieves all the data from the table. To move through the returned data, you use a result set named `ResultSet`. This result set allows you to access the rows and fields of the database being returned. The `next` method of `ResultSet` is used to move to the next row and also to verify that more data is coming. This method copies every last name into a collection of strings.

Monitoring JDBC

One problem with connection pools is that they may have too many requested connections to be effective. If you're not aware of the number of requested connections, you should monitor the current state of your connection pools.

You monitor only at the connection pool level. You can't monitor at the data source level.

To monitor your connection pool, follow these steps:

1. **Make sure that your connection pool and data source are set up and targeted to the correct server.**

2. **Make sure that your server is running, and then log on to Administrative Console.**

   For details on logging on, see the "Creating a Connection Pool" section.

3. **On the left side of the screen, click the following folders: Services, JDBC, Connection Pools, and then SchoolPool.**

4. **Click the Monitoring tab.**

   The screen shown in Figure 12-5 appears. From this screen, you can monitor the usage of your connection pool.

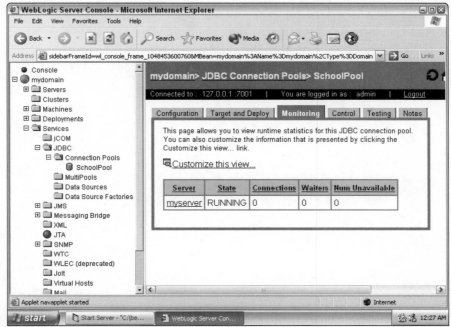

WebLogic Server Console - Microsoft Internet Explorer

File   Edit   View   Favorites   Tools   Help

Back ▾   Search   Favorites   Media

Address   sidebarFrameId=wl_console_frame_1048453600760&MBean=mydomain%3AName%3Dmydomain%2CType%3DDomain   Go   Links

Console
mydomain
  Servers
  Clusters
  Machines
  Deployments
  Services
    jCOM
    JDBC
      Connection Pools
        SchoolPool
      MultiPools
      Data Sources
      Data Source Factories
    JMS
    Messaging Bridge
    XML
    JTA
    SNMP
    WTC
    WLEC (deprecated)
    Jolt
    Virtual Hosts
    Mail

mydomain> JDBC Connection Pools> SchoolPool

Connected to : 127.0.0.1 :7001 | You are logged in as : admin | Logout

Configuration | Target and Deploy | Monitoring | Control | Testing | Notes

This page allows you to view runtime statistics for this JDBC connection pool. You can also customize the information that is presented by clicking the Customize this view... link.

Customize this view...

Server	State	Connections	Waiters	Num Unavailable
myserver	RUNNING	0	0	0

Applet navapplet started   Internet

start   Start Server - "C:\be...   WebLogic Server Con...   12:27 AM

Figure 12-5:
Monitoring
your con-
nection
pool.

Chapter 13

Finding EJBs with JNDI

● ●

In This Chapter

▶ Figuring out what JNDI is

▶ Listing an EJB in the JNDI phone book

▶ Finding an EJB in the JNDI phone book

● ●

Application servers, such as WebLogic, allow you to provide Enterprise Java Beans (EJBs) to client programs that are often running on computers other than the application server. These EJBs do the client programs no good if the client can't find them. In this chapter, I explain what you need to do so that your client programs can find the EJBs made available through WebLogic.

This is not a complex process. In fact, the process that a client program uses to find an EJB is similar to the process that you use to find the phone number to a pizza parlor: You look it up in a directory. Just as the phone book enables you to connect a pizza parlor's name with its phone number, JNDI (Java Naming and Directory Interface) enables your client programs to connect EJB names with the more technical and difficult-to-remember numbers that the program needs to find and use the EJBs.

In this chapter, you find out how to do two important tasks that enable your client application to find and use EJBs:

✔ Making resources available with JNDI

✔ Finding resources with JNDI

As a WebLogic administrator, you'll become pretty familiar with these two tasks. WebLogic also uses JNDI with JMS (Java Message Service), which is covered in Chapter 15.

Understanding JNDI

WebLogic administrators use JNDI to help others locate the EJBs stored on WebLogic Server. That is the main purpose of JNDI — to locate Internet resources, such as EJBs. Locating a resource based on its name is an important function of the Internet. Every time you use a browser to access a web site, you're using a network name resolution system. The host name of the server that you're trying to access must be translated from a human readable name (such as `www.yahoo.com`) to an IP address that the computer uses to access the web site.

JNDI is a specification that Sun created for Java to standardize network name resolution. Rather than having a variety of different interfaces for different name resolution systems, JNDI gives you one standard application programming interface (API) to program to. In this way, programmers don't have to waste time learning new interfaces to network name resolution software.

Many books about JNDI explain how to create your own JNDI-compatible interface for your applications. In this book, however, you find out how to use a JNDI interface, in particular the JNDI interface in WebLogic.

JNDI is more of a protocol than an actual program. Sun has defined a standard way for directories to work and any directory that adheres to this standard can be said to be JNDI compliant.

JNDI makes available two primary services:

- ✔ **Naming service.** Allows names to be used to locate and retrieve objects.

- ✔ **Directory service.** Allows attributes to be specified and a search to be performed.

To understand the differences between the two, it helps to think of how you use a phone book. The naming service is similar to the white pages, which you use to look up a person or business when you know the exact name. The directory service resembles the yellow pages, which you use when you know what sort of a business you're looking for but don't know the exact name. You look up a category, such as plumbing or picture framing, and then skim the yellow pages looking at the advertisements and find one that most closely matches that attributes that you're looking for.

Understanding JNDI names

You use a JNDI name to reference an EJB. A JNDI name has no preset format, but it does follow a few rules. The name must start with a letter. The rest of the name can contain periods, hyphens, numbers, and letters, for example, `MyEJBCollection.My1stEJB`. Now that you understand the format of a JNDI name, you're ready to begin using EJBs that have JNDI names.

Understanding naming services

JNDI provides a standard way to access name servers using Java. This means that if a Java program is written to be compatible with JNDI, this program is compatible with any other naming system that is also compatible with JNDI.

Name services are common on the Internet. You use a name service (DNS, or domain name service) every time you launch your browser and reach a web page.

If you open a browser and enter the URL www.dummies.com, for example, you are taken to the *For Dummies* home page. To find this page, you remembered a uniform resource location, or URL. This is just a fancy term for a name entry in a DNS. But this is not the actual site address that the computer uses. The actual address to this site is the IP address 208.215.179.139. DNS enables you to remember www.dummies.com rather than the much longer IP address. The naming service takes care of translating between the two.

JNDI as a universal naming service

DNS is only one of many naming services available on the Internet. The commands to use naming services vary greatly from one service to the next. There is already enough to learn without having to learn the idiosyncrasies of individual name services. This is where JNDI comes in to make life easier.

JNDI provides a common programming interface to access different name services. You have to understand only one programming interface to use many services. Table 13-1 summarizes some of the common services that JNDI gives you access to.

Table 13-1   Common Services Available Through JNDI

Abbreviation	Name	What It Does
COS	Common Object Services	Accesses CORBA resources, which are an alternative to EJBs. When using WebLogic, you usually use EJBs over CORBA resources.
DNS	Domain Name Service	Looks up the IP address for addresses, such as www.dummies.com.

(continued)

Table 13-1 *(continued)*

Abbreviation	Name	What It Does
LDAP	Lightweight Directory Access Protocol	Accesses named Internet resources. LDAP is an alternative to DNS developed by the University of Michigan and endorsed by more than 40 companies.
NIS	Network Information System	Accesses named Internet resources. NIS is an alternative naming service developed by Sun Microsystems.

Implementing JNDI Using WebLogic

WebLogic is fully compliant with the JNDI standard, which means that any Java program designed to work with JNDI can be used also with WebLogic. To be compliant with JNDI, WebLogic must:

✔ Allow client programs to access WebLogic name services

✔ Allow client programs to access WebLogic objects

By using the WebLogic implementation of JNDI, you can allow your WebLogic resources to be accessed from client programs running on other computers. As long as a client program knows the name that your WebLogic resource is listed under, the program can find the resource.

In this section, you find out how to configure WebLogic to make your objects available through JNDI. Then you find out how to access these objects from Java programs.

Making WebLogic resources available through JNDI

Before other programs can use your WebLogic objects, you must make those objects available. This step is similar to adding a person's name to a phone book. When you add a WebLogic object to the JNDI directory, you associate the name of the object with the object itself.

The objects that you make available through JNDI are called Enterprise Java Beans (EJBs). If you need more information on how to obtain or construct EJBs, refer to Chapter 6. This chapter assumes that you already have an EJB that you want to make available under a JNDI name.

EJBs are made up of regular Java classes and configuration files. Like any other Java class, the class files must be in the correct directory so that WebLogic (in this case) can find these files and allow your EJB to be used. You must place the class files to be used with an EJB in the WEB-INF/lib directory. (For more information on this directory, see Chapter 5.)

The WEB-INF/lib directory is hidden to Internet users accessing your server, so it's safe to place files such as an EJB file there. It would be a security risk if an Internet user were able to download your EJB file and examine it.

To add an EJB, you can use WebLogic Workshop, which is a development tool that can help set up EJBs Here's an overview of adding an EJB to WebLogic using WebLogic Workshop:

1. **Make sure that your EJB class files have been copied to** WEB-INF/lib.

2. **Start WebLogic Workshop.**

3. **Choose Add EJB from the Designer pull-down menu.**

4. **Enter the required information.**

5. **Restart WebLogic.**

Now that you know generally how to assign a JNDI name to an EJB, you're ready to dive in. Follow these steps:

1. **Place your EJB class files in the** WEB-INF/lib **directory.**

   On a Windows system with a typical installation of WebLogic, this directory is usually the following or something similar:

   ```
   c:\bea\weblogic81\samples\workshop\YourApplication
   ```

   In Figure 13-1, you can see the files that make up the EJBs that this instance of WebLogic Server is using. EJBs are usually distributed as Java archive files, which have the file extension .jar. You should place your .jar file in the lib directory.

2. **Start WebLogic Workshop.**

   WebLogic Workshop enables you to add an EJB to your application server. If you need help starting WebLogic Workshop, see Chapter 11.

3. **Choose Insert⇨Controls⇨Add EJB Control.**

   The screen shown in Figure 13-2 appears, providing many additional configuration options. Note that the Insert EJB Control dialog box is divided into three steps.

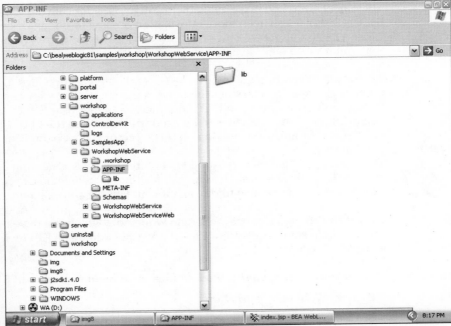

Figure 13-1:
WebLogic
directory
structure.

Figure 13-2:
The EJB
configu-
ration
window.

4. **In the Step 1 section, type a variable name to reference the EJB in WebLogic.**

   The name should describe your EJB and should be unique.

5. **In the Step 2 section, choose to use an EJB control or create an EJB control.**

   If you've already worked with this EJB and created a control file, specify the file that you would like to use. If you're using a new EJB, choose to create an EJB control.

6. **In the Step 3 section, type the JNDI name and the class names.**

   a. **In the jndi-name box, type the JNDI name that other applications use to access this EJB.**

      Use a name that is meaningful to your application and that is not duplicated by a similar resource. The name can contain periods, hyphens, numbers, and letters, but it must start with a letter.

   b. **In the home interface box, type the name of your EJB's home class. In the bean interface box, type the name of your EJB's bean class.**

      The home and bean interface boxes allow you to specify the exact classes used for this EJB. EJBs always have both a home and bean class. The documentation provided with your EJB should list the home and bean name for the EJB.

7. **Restart WebLogic Server.**

   You have to restart the server because you added a bean. After WebLogic Server has been restarted, your EJBs are available.

Congratulations! You've finished the first part of the process. In the next section, you delve into the second part.

Enabling JNDI to access WebLogic objects

When you create EJBs and make them available with WebLogic Server, other applications access the functionality of these objects. In this section, you find out how to use JNDI to access your WebLogic objects from other programs. The process is summarized as follows:

1. **Set up the** `InitialContext` **object.**

2. **Look up the required named object.**

3. **Use the remote object.**

4. **Complete the session.**

Set up InitialContext

First, you obtain an InitialContext object by providing information about the object you're seeking. This information is passed to the InitialContext object using a hash table. After this table has been constructed, it's passed to the constructor of the InitialContext object. Listing 13-1 shows this process.

Listing 13-1: **Obtaining an** InitialContext

```
Context context;
Hashtable hashTable = new Hashtable();

hashTable.put(
   Context.INITIAL_CONTEXT_FACTORY,
   "weblogic.jndi.WLInitialContextFactory");
hashTable.put(Context.PROVIDER_URL,
   "t3://localhost:7001");

try
{
   context = new InitialContext(ht);
}
catch (NamingException e)
{
   System.out.println("Error:" + e );
}
finally
{
   try
   {
      context.close();
   }
   catch (Exception e)
   {
      System.out.println("Error:" + e);
   }
}
```

A java.util.Hashtable object is used to organize a collection of name-value pairs. You can put any number of values into HashTable. Each value is located using a name. For example, in the preceding code, the name Context.INITIAL_CONTEXT_FACTORY is used to store the value "weblogic.jndi.WLInitialContextFactory". This allows JNDI to accept the following parameters to control its operation:

✔ javax.naming.Context.INITIAL_CONTEXT_FACTORY. **To access WebLogic, set this parameter to** weblogic.jndi.WLInitial ContextFactory.

> ✔ `javax.naming.Context.PROVIDER_URL`. This property specifies the URL of the WebLogic Server that provides the name service. The default for this property is `t3://localhost:7001`.

Note the `catch` statements in Listing 13-1. The `catch` statements contain blocks of code. If any error causes an exception to be raised, the program immediately executes the `catch` block.

Look up the named object

Now that you have a context object, you can attempt to look up the object that you need. Listing 13-2 shows a way to look up a named object.

Listing 13-2: Looking Up a Named Object

```
try
{
  ServiceBean bean =
          (ServiceBean)context.lookup("ejb.serviceBean");
}
catch (NameNotFoundException e)
{
  System.out.println("Error:" + e );
}
catch (NamingException e)
{
  System.out.println("Error:" + e );
}
```

An EJB named `ejb.serviceBean` is looked up. Two `catch` blocks handle two types of errors that can occur. The first, `NameNotFoundException`, occurs when an invalid EJB name has been specified. The second, `NamingException`, handles more generic errors that may occur during the lookup, such as an I/O error.

Use the remote object

You're now ready to instantiate an EJB based on the object that you requested, as shown in Listing 13-3. After you allocate this EJB, you can call the method provided by the bean.

Listing 13-3: Using the Remote Object

```
ServiceBean bean =
          ServiceBean.Home.create("ejb.ServiceBean");

bean.remoteMethod("some parm");
```

An EJB named `ejb.ServiceBean` is loaded, and then the `remoteMethod` method is called and passed a string. You're now free to use the bean as you would any other Java bean. When you're finished with this bean, you should close the connection.

This step is where you perform the work that you originally set out to do. Often this step includes many calls to the remote bean. Calling Java beans is similar to calling methods in regular classes.

One of the main features of beans is that they isolate you from what is going on. All you have to do is call your bean object, just like you'd access any other properly formatted object. A lot is going on in the background, as the request is routed from one computer to the next using EJB and RMI. Usually, you don't need to worry about the exact file formats.

Close the connection

When you're finished with the object, you need to close it. This frees up any resources that this object was using. This can be seen in Listing 13-4.

Listing 13-4:   Closing the Connection

```
finally
{
  try
  {
    context.close();
  }
  catch (Exception e)
  {
    System.out.println("Error: " + e );
  }
}
```

It's a good idea to put the context close inside a `finally` block. That way, you can be assured that the close was actually called.

If any exceptions are thrown by this operation, they're caught by `catch`. After a context has been closed, it should not be reused.

You should close the connection when you're finished with it. A common misconception is that Java does this for you. Although Java frees the memory associated with the bean, it doesn't free up any resources that have been allocated to the bean. This can lead to incomplete results because the bean was never given a chance to properly exit. Additionally, not calling the `close` method causes these resources to never be freed. If this practice continues, you eventually run out of resources and must restart your application server.

Chapter 14

Using Transactions with JTA

In This Chapter

▶ Understanding transactions and when to use them

▶ Finding out about bean-managed transactions

Transactions are a way to logically group database commands, so that all commands are processed as a group. If any single command in the transaction fails, all the other commands fail as well and the effects of those commands are "rolled back."

When a transaction is presented to WebLogic, one of two actions will occur: a commit or a roll back. When a transaction is *committed,* the changes to the database are made permanent. When a transaction is *rolled back,* the changes to the database are discarded. In this chapter, you discover the basics of using WebLogic transactions and find out when you should and shouldn't use them.

Understanding Transactions

Transactions, which are a fundamental feature of WebLogic, allow database changes to be completed accurately and reliably. These transactions are based on the ACID (atomicity, consistency, isolation, and durability) properties for high-performance transaction processing:

- ✔ **Atomicity.** Changes that a transaction makes to a database are made as a single unit. One failure results in the total failure of the transaction.

- ✔ **Consistency.** The database was valid before the transaction and will remain valid after the transaction. The database may never enter an invalid state.

- ✔ **Isolation.** As one operation performs a transaction, the transaction is visible to no other operations until the transaction completes successfully.

- ✔ **Durability.** A change to the database will survive future system or media failures.

ACID ensures that database updates are performed as intended: completely and accurately. To understand why this is important, consider a simple bank transfer, in which you move $100 from your checking account to your money market account. This transfer requires several database transactions:

1. Remove $100 from your checking account.

2. Add $100 to your money market account.

3. Add a line to the general ledger to reflect these transactions.

Each operation represents one or more separate database commands. Consider if Step 1 failed and the operation aborted with only Step 2 complete. The bank would have added $100 to your money market account, without having adjusted your checking account. The bank would lose $100.

Transactions allow all three steps to execute as a unit. If one step fails, they all fail. Additionally, no other operation can access the results of this change until all three steps are complete.

WebLogic's transaction implementation relies on Java Transaction Architecture (JTA), a standard developed by Sun Microsystems. JTA specifies standard Java interfaces between the transaction manager, the resource manager, the application server, and transactional applications.

Two-phase commit

WebLogic uses transactions to guarantee that a single database server maintains its integrity even if part of the transaction fails. A single database server, however, is not always the case.

Database servers can be clustered to allow more than one database server to function as a single logical database server. This arrangement has several advantages:

- ✔ **Scalability.** If one database server becomes overworked and impedes system performance, another database server can be added to the cluster.

- ✔ **Reliability.** If one database server crashes, the other database servers increase their load to account for the failed server.

- ✔ **Performance.** If your application runs at several geographic locations, each location can have a local server. This improves performance for read operations. Write operations synchronize among the databases.

To support distributed database access, WebLogic makes use of something called a two-phase commit. The *two-phase commit* allows data to be written to two or more databases while keeping both databases in sync.

Following are the participants of a two-phase commit:

- **Recoverable resource.** Provides permanent storage for data. The recoverable resource is almost always a relational database.

- **Resource manager.** Provides access to a collection of information and processes. The resource manager is almost always a transaction-aware JDBC driver.

- **Transaction manager.** Manages transactions for application programs. This is the role that WebLogic plays.

- **Transaction originator.** Uses the transaction services. The transaction originator can be an application, an Enterprise JavaBean, or a JMS client.

In the two-phase commit process, a transaction originator seeks to update a number of recoverable resources. As its name implies, the two-phase commit has two main steps:

- **Prepare phase.** During the prepare phase, the required updates are saved in a transaction log file. The resources must "vote" on whether to commit or roll back the changes.

- **Finalization phase.** The transaction manager evaluates the votes. If all resources have voted to commit the changes, the changes are committed. If even one resource votes not to commit the changes, they are rolled back to their previous state.

As you can see, the two-phase commit is essential when using multiple databases.

When to use transactions

Like any technology, transactions are not a silver bullet designed to be used in all cases. Knowing when to use transactions is just as important as knowing when not to use them. In this section, I describe a few examples that should use transactions.

Transactions across multiple databases

The first model where a transaction is likely appropriate is when the client application must perform operations on several objects stored in one or more databases. If any one command is unsuccessful, the entire transaction is rolled back.

For example, suppose that an insurance company has several branch offices, each of which has a database server. When a new policy is issued, this transaction is added to the database server at each branch office. If one of the database servers fails to update, the entire transaction fails.

Accumulation transaction

The second model where a transaction is likely appropriate is when the client application must communicate several times with a server object. The server object accumulates these transactions and updates the database at some point in the future, not on every communication with the client. Examples of this situation include the following:

- Data is stored in memory or written to a database each time the server method is called.

- Data is written to the database at the end of several exchanges with the client application.

- The server object needs to maintain the data from each invocation of its method and write the contents to a database at the end of the conversation.

- The client application needs a way to cancel all previous communication with the server object.

Each of these scenarios shares one similarity: committing the data to the database is the last event to happen. Each stage accumulates data, but doesn't actually apply the changes to the full database until the final commit.

An example of this model is a shipping application in which the server object is called several times to add items to the shipping list. The server method is called for each item that is added. If one item fails to be added to the list, the entire shipping list is rejected.

Multipart transaction

The third model where a transaction may be appropriate is when only a single call is made to the server object, but the server object must make several database calls to carry out the request. Because the transaction occurs in several calls, it's called a multipart transaction. If one of these database calls fails, the entire transaction fails.

An example of this was discussed earlier in this chapter. A user wants to move $100 from a checking account to a money market account. To be successful, this transaction must decrease the checking account by $100, increase the money market account by $100, and make an entry in the general ledger. If one of these steps fails, the entire transaction fails.

When not to use transactions

Perhaps the biggest problem with transactions is that they are all or nothing. You can't partially roll back a transaction. Your business application may represent a chain of events, where a failure will likely occur at some point. If you would like your data to be made permanent up to this point, a transaction is not a good choice for your application.

Consider a shopping cart program that uses the accumulation model. As items are added to the shopping cart, a failure may occur if an item is not recognized. This failure may be acceptable because the customer may be willing to accept a partial order.

Using Transactions

Using an EJB with transactions involves the following process:

1. **Import packages.**
2. **Use JNDI to return an object reference.**
3. **Update the database.**
4. **Start the transaction.**
5. **Complete the transaction.**

These same steps allow you to use your transaction connection also with an RMI application.

The example in this section uses the UserTransaction object for bean-managed transaction processing.

Importing packages

First, you must make sure that you import the correct classes. The following import statements must appear at the top of the class that will make use of transactions:

```
import javax.naming.*;
import javax.transaction.UserTransaction;
import javax.transaction.SystemException;
import javax.transaction.HeuristicMixedException;
import javax.transaction.HeuristicRollbackException;
import javax.transaction.NotSupportedException;
import javax.transaction.RollbackException;
import javax.transaction.IllegalStateException;
import javax.transaction.SecurityException;
```

And if any class itself requires other classes, be sure to import those as well.

Some of the previously listed `import` statements reference classes that are part of J2EE. Because of this, make sure that the J2EE JAR file is part of your `CLASSPATH`. For more information on setting up J2EE, refer to Chapter 2.

Using JNDI to return an object reference

After you import the correct classes, you're ready to use JNDI to obtain a `UserTransaction` object.

In this section, you use JNDI to return an object reference. First, you create a hash table that will contain the parameters used to create the object reference:

```
Context ctx = null;
Hashtable env = new Hashtable();
```

After you create `Hashtable`, you fill it with the appropriate configuration information. First you specify the class name for the context factory. You always specify this class when using transactions:

```
// Parameters for WebLogic Server
env.put(Context.INITIAL_CONTEXT_FACTORY,
  "weblogic.jndi.WLInitialContextFactory");
```

Next, you must specify the security provider, which is `t3://localhost:7001` when using WebLogic. You must also specify your user ID and password:

```
env.put(Context.PROVIDER_URL, "t3://localhost:7001");
env.put(Context.SECURITY_PRINCIPAL, "user");
env.put(Context.SECURITY_CREDENTIALS, "password");
```

After you've filled `Hashtable` with the required information, you're ready to create your `Context`:

```
ctx = new InitialContext(env);
UserTransaction tx = (UserTransaction)
  ctx.lookup("javax.transaction.UserTransaction");
```

The `javax.naming.Context` object allows you to access a JNDI name. At this point, you have access to a `UserTransaction` object, which will be used to work with your transactions.

Starting the transaction

Now that you have a `UserTransaction` object, you can start your transaction. The transaction begins by calling the `begin()` method of the User

Transaction object. Any database operation that occurs after the begin() method invocation and before the transaction completion is considered part of this transaction. The following lines of code begin the transaction:

```
UserTransaction tx = (UserTransaction)
  ctx.lookup("javax.transaction.UserTransaction");
tx.begin();
```

At this point, you may carry out the database commands that are considered part of the transaction. After you complete the necessary database transactions, you're ready to complete the transaction.

Updating the database

At the heart of a transaction is the database update. First, you need to obtain a database connection. This connection is a regular JDBC java.sql.Connection object:

```
Connection connection;
```

Next, you obtain the connection. Because it is possible for exceptions to be thrown during this process, you place this code in a try block:

```
try {

  Driver driver = (Driver)
  Class.forName("weblogic.jdbc.jts.Driver").newInstance();
```

This code obtains a JTS-capable driver from WebLogic. This driver will be used to access your Tx connection pool.

A connection is obtained by specifying the name of the Tx data source that you created earlier, which is the data source named MyTxPool:

```
connection = driver.connect("jdbc:weblogic:jts:MyTxPool");
```

You can now begin your transaction:

```
tx.begin();
```

Next, you build your SQL statement. The SQL statement shown here updates the database used in Chapter 12:

```
String sql = "INSERT INTO t_student(f_id, f_first, f_last)";
sql+=" VALUES(1,'John','Smith')";
```

Now that the SQL has been prepared, you assign a statement from your driver:

```
Statement statement = connection.createStatement();
```

The SQL is executed with a call to executeUpdate:

```
statement.executeUpdate(sql);
```

Next, you can close the statement and commit the transaction:

```
statement.close();
tx.commit();
```

Now you close the connection and handle any exceptions:

```
    connection.close();
}
catch( Exception e)
{
  e.printStackTrace();
}
```

In many languages, memory leaks and resource leaks are common problems. A *leak* occurs when a program allocates a memory or resource object and never returns it. Although Java will not leak memory, it can leak resources. Because of this, you should always close your database objects. Leaving them open can cause WebLogic to run out of database resources.

To properly close all database resources, it's often useful to implement a cleanup method and include that method in a finally clause. You can then close the database resources in the finally clause. Such a method is shown in Chapter 8.

After you update the database, you're ready to complete the transaction. The code just examined completed its transaction with a call to commit(). However, this is not the only way a transaction is completed, as covered in the next section.

Completing the transaction

When completing a transaction, you can either roll back or commit your transaction. When you roll back a transaction, no permanent changes are made to the database. To roll back a transaction, call the rollback() method of the UserTransaction object:

```
tx.rollback();
```

When you commit a transaction, all changes are written to the database. To commit a transaction, use the `commit()` method of the `UserTransaction` object:

```
tx.commit();
```

Both the `rollback()` and `commit()` methods may throw an exception during execution. If the `rollback()` method throws an exception, the data is not written to the database.

If an exception occurs while the `commit` method is called, the update does not occur. Exceptions can happen for many reasons. In a distributed database, all underlying databases must agree to the commit for it to be successful.

Chapter 15

Sending Messages Between Programs with JMS

. . . .

. . . .

Software components can use many different methods to communicate with each other. In this chapter, I show you a model for the exchange of information between software components. This system is Java Messaging Service, or JMS.

JMS clients connect to a JMS-compatible messaging server, such as WebLogic JMS (a component of WebLogic Server). A messaging server, such as WebLogic, provides facilities for sending and receiving messages. A JMS client can send messages to, and receive messages from, any other JMS client. You can think of the messaging service as the low-level infrastructure. The messaging service delivers a message from one program to another. The messaging service doesn't get involved in the contents of the message. It only facilities the message's transfer.

One of the main differences between JMS and other models that software components use to communicate is that JMS is asynchronous. In an *asynchronous* model, a component simply sends a message to a destination. The message recipient can then retrieve these messages from the destination. No direct communication exists between the sender and the receiver. The sender knows only that a destination exists to which it can send messages. Likewise, the receiver knows only that a destination exists from which it can receive messages. As long as both sender and receiver agree upon a common message format, the messaging system manages the message delivery.

Common concerns when working with asynchronous message systems are reliability and acknowledgement. If a message is sent from sender to receiver, with no required response, how can the sender know that the message was reliably sent? The specific level of reliability is typically configurable on a per-destination or per-client basis. However, messaging systems are capable of guaranteeing that a message is delivered — and delivered to each intended recipient exactly once.

WebLogic supports two styles of message-based communications:

- ✔ **Point-to-point messaging.** Point-to-point messaging is provided using JMS queues. A *queue* is a named resource configured in a JMS server. A JMS client exchanges messages with this queue.

  Point-to-point messages have a single consumer: the Java program that processes the messages. Multiple receivers may make use of the same queue as they listen for messages. However, after any receiver retrieves a message from the queue, that message is "consumed" and no longer available to other potential consumers.

  The message consumer must acknowledge receipt of every message it receives. This is because the messaging system continues attempting to resend a particular message until the message is retrieved. However, the sender does not resend the message indefinitely. The message is no longer sent after a predetermined number of retries.

- ✔ **Publish-and-subscribe messaging.** Publish-and-subscribe messaging is accomplished using JMS topics. A *topic* is a named resource configured in a JMS server. A JMS client publishes messages to a topic or subscribes to a topic. Published messages may have multiple subscribers. All current subscribers to a specific topic receive all messages published to that topic after the subscription becomes active.

Creating a WebLogic Message Service

Before you can create JMS senders and receivers, you must create a message service on your WebLogic Server. This process has a number of steps:

1. **Create a connection factory.**

   A connection factory is used to grant connections to your messaging service. The connection factory is identified by a JNDI name.

2. **Optionally define backing stores for your messages.**

   WebLogic needs to store incoming messages. You can store these messages using a JDBC database or disk-based files. (*Backing stores,* which allow incoming messages to be stored until processed, are discussed later in this section.)

3. **Optionally define destination keys.**

   Destination keys are a WebLogic extension to JMS that allows you to control the order in which messages are delivered.

4. **Optionally define templates.**

   Template keys are a WebLogic extension to JMS that allows you to group destinations. This gives you the ability to send messages to the group.

5. **Create a JMS server.**

   A JMS server contains your queues and topics. If you created an optional backing store, the JMS server routes your messages there as well.

6. **Create one or more queues or topics.**

   Queues or topics are mapped to your JMS server. Your clients, the senders and receivers, communicate with these queues and topics.

The following sections discuss how to set up a WebLogic message service using these steps.

Creating a connection factory

The first step in creating a message service is to create a connection factory. A *connection factory* is an object used to create connections. Client programs use the connection factory to access the JMS message service. Follow these steps:

1. **Log on to Administration Console.**

   This allows you to configure your transactions. Administration Console is typically at `http://localhost:7001/console`. For more information, see Chapter 4.

2. **On the left side of the screen, click the following folders: Services, JMS, and then Connection Factories.**

   The screen shown in Figure 15-1 appears. From here, you can see all current connection factories (if any) and create connection factories.

3. **Click the __Configure a new JMS Connection Factory__ link.**

   The screen shown in Figure 15-2 appears.

4. **Configure your connection factory.**

   To follow along with the example, set the name and the JNDI name as shown in Figure 15-2. Leave the other values as is. For a description of all connection factory settings, see Table 15-1.

5. **Click Create.**

   You now have a connection factory.

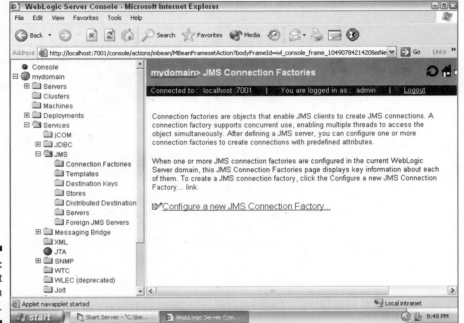

Figure 15-1:
All current
connection
factories.

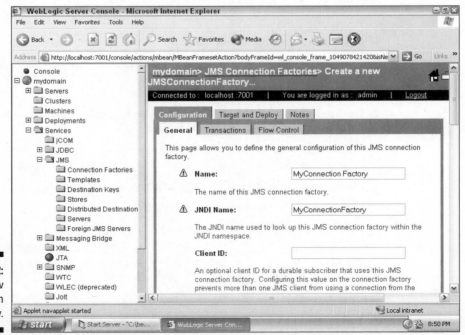

Figure 15-2:
A new
connection
factory.

Table 15-1	Connection Factory Settings
Setting	**What It Is or Does**
Name	Identifies this connection factory; not used outside Administration Console.
JNDI Name	The JNDI name for this connection factory.
Client ID	This field should be left blank unless you will be supporting durable subscribers. Messages for a durable subscriber will be held, even if the subscriber is not running.
Default Priority	Assigns a priority to messages that don't have a specified priority. This value should range between 0 and 9. This determines the order in which messages will be processed as they are received.
Default Time to Live	The amount of time, in milliseconds, that the message is retransmitted. If a message fails to reach its destination, the message is retransmitted until the time to live expires.
Default Time to Deliver	The amount of time, in milliseconds, that must pass before a message is delivered. The default value of 0 means instant.
Default Delivery Mode	The delivery mode, if no delivery mode is specified in the message. This value is either Persistent or Non-Persistent.
Default Redelivery Delay	The time, in milliseconds, before a recovered message is redelivered.
Maximum Messages	The maximum number of simultaneous messages supported. The default value is 10.
Overrun Policy	Specifies what WebLogic should do if the maximum number of messages is reached. This value is `KeepOld` or `KeepNew`. That is, is it better to keep older or newer messages? You must decide which one will affect the reliability of your applications the most.
Allow Close In OnMessage	Determines whether WebLogic allows a client to issue a close in the `OnMessage` method. This Boolean value is `True` or `False`.
Acknowledge Policy	Allows compatibility with a pervious specification of JMS. This value should always be set to `All`.
Load Balancing Enabled	Determines the degree to which load balancing is used in a cluster. If true, each message is load balanced. Load balancing refers to the process by which WebLogic chooses a server in the cluster to handle the request. For more information on clustering, see Chapter 16.
Server Affinity Enabled	Determines whether subsequent requests should be handled by the same machine when load balancing is enabled.

Defining a backing store

Now that you've created a connection factory, you can create a backing store. The use of a backing store is optional. The steps to create the backing store follow:

1. **On the left side of the Administration Console screen, click the following folders: Services, JMS, and then Stores.**

   The screen shown in Figure 15-3 appears. From here, you can see all current stores and create connection factories.

2. **Create a JDBC-based or file-based store.**

   To create a JDBC-based store, follow these steps:

   a. **Click the <u>Configure a new JMS JDBC Store</u> link.**

   b. **Type a name such as MyJMS JDBC Store.**

   c. **Select the connection pool to use, as shown in Figure 15-4.**

   For more information on connection pools, see Chapter 12.

   d. **If necessary, specify a prefix.**

   Some databases require a prefix. For example, SQL Server requires the *dbo* prefix for all table names.

   e. **Click Create.**

   To create a file-based store, follow these steps:

   a. **Click the <u>Configure a new JMS File Store</u> link.**

   b. **Type a name, such as MyJMS File Store.**

   c. **Select a directory to hold the files, as shown in Figure 15-5.**

   You have to scroll down to see the directory.

   d. **Leave all other settings as is, and then click Create.**

3. **Configure your backing store, as follows:**

   a. **Give your backing store a name.**

   You'll use this name later to refer to the store.

   b. **Choose Cache-Flush, the default, because it usually provides the best performance.**

   The synchronous write policy determines how WebLogic will handle concurrent writes to the store.

   c. **Choose a directory.**

   This directory should be on the local hard drive because that location will provide the fastest access.

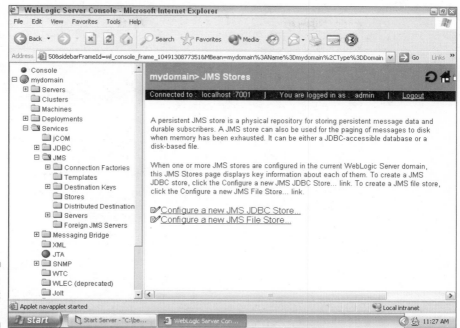

Figure 15-3:
All current
JMS stores.

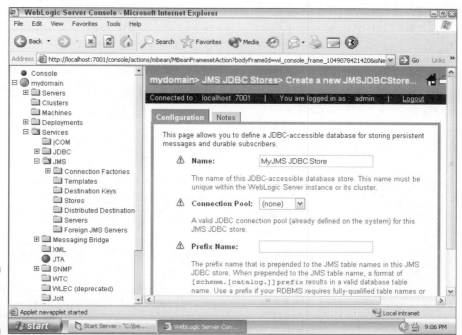

Figure 15-4:
A JDBC-
based store.

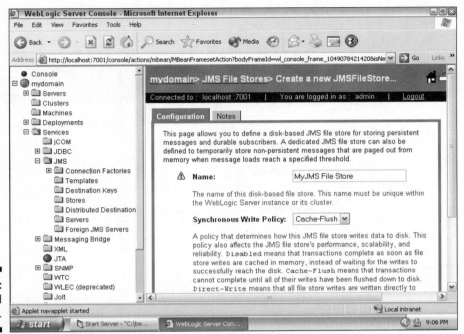

Figure 15-5:
A file-based
store.

Backing stores are used also for paging stores. If you'll be using a paging store, you have to go through the preceding steps twice to create an additional backing store for your paging store. Paging stores are discussed later in this section.

You may be wondering what tables are used by a JDBC-based store. The next time you restart WebLogic, several system tables are automatically created to hold the message store.

Defining destination keys

If you want, you can create destination keys to determine the order in which messages are delivered. Destination keys operate on the user-definable properties stored in a message. Follow these steps if you want to define a destination key:

1. **On the left side of the screen, click the following folders: Services, JMS, and then Destination Keys.**

   The screen shown in Figure 15-6 appears. From here, you can see all current destination keys (if any) and create destination keys.

2. **Click the <u>Configure a new JMS Destination Key</u> link.**

   The screen shown in Figure 15-7 appears.

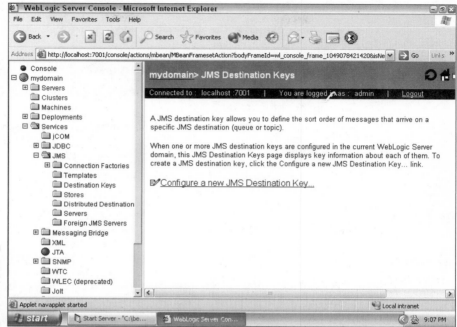

Figure 15-6:
All current destination keys.

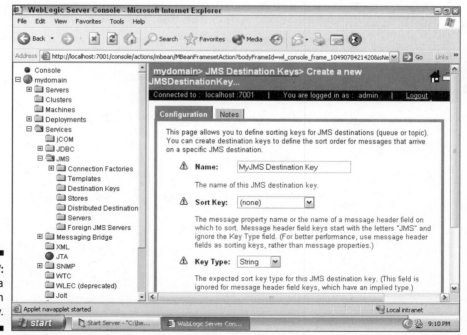

Figure 15-7:
Creating a destination key.

3. **Configure your destination key.**

   a. **Type a name for the destination key.**

      This is for your reference in Administration Console.

   b. **Type the name of the Sort Key to filter on.**

   c. **Using the Key Type field, select the type of data that you expect the Sort Key to be.**

   d. **Choose the direction in which you want sorting to take place.**

4. **Click Create.**

You now have a destination key that sorts messages as you've instructed.

Defining templates

If you have a number of destination keys that you want to apply to one or more JMS servers, queues, or topics, templates can make this process much easier. Creating a template is an optional step and makes sense only if you've defined quite a few destination keys.

To create a template, follow these steps:

1. **On the left side of the Administration Console screen, click the following folders: Services, JMS, and then Templates.**

   The screen shown in Figure 15-8 appears. From here, you can see all current templates (if any) and create templates.

2. **Click the <u>Configure a new JMS Template</u> link.**

3. **Type a name for your template.**

   To follow along with the example, type MYJMS Template.

4. **Click Create.**

5. **Add keys to your template.**

   Select a key, and click the right-facing arrow to move the keys from the Available list to the Chosen list. See Figure 15-9. Then click Apply.

You now have a template that allows you to easily group multiple destination keys.

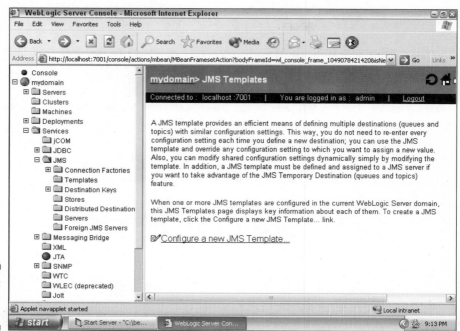

Figure 15-8:
Create a template.

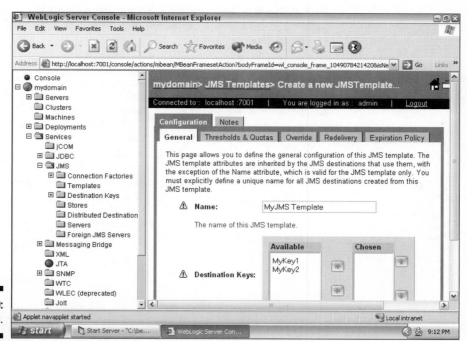

Figure 15-9:
Add Keys.

Creating a JMS server

Now you're ready to create your JMS server, tying together — in one server — many of the components you created previously. To create a JMS server, follow these steps:

1. **On the left side of the Administration Console screen, click the following folders: Services, JMS, and then Servers.**

   The screen shown in Figure 15-10 appears. From here, you can see all current servers (if any) and create servers.

2. **Click the <u>Configure a new JMSServer</u> link.**

3. **Configure your server as follows:**

   a. **Select a name for your JMS server, such as MyJMS Server (see Figure 15-11).**

   b. **Select a store.**

      This is the store that you created previously. Using a store is optional.

   c. **Select a paging store. (This step is optional.)**

      A paging store uses the same type of store as a backing store. If you choose to use a paging store, you should create two backing stores. (See the "Defining a backing store" section for more information.) This paging store holds messages as they come in and are waiting to be processed.

   d. **Specify a temporary template. (This step is optional.)**

      If you specify a value for a temporary template, it will be used to create temporary destinations, which are destinations created by Java programs, without Administration Console.

The paging store stores messages that can't fit into memory. This allows you to handle more simultaneous messages than your current memory allows.

Because of the heavy use that a paging store receives, always choose to make your paging store file based, rather than JDBC based.

After you've completed these steps, you have a JMS server ready for use. You're now ready to create queues or topics for this server.

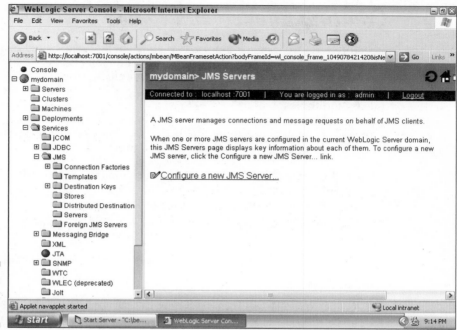

Figure 15-10:
All current
servers.

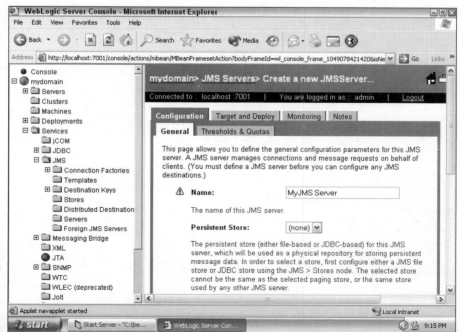

Figure 15-11:
Creating a
server.

Creating queues and topics

As mentioned, WebLogic supports two styles of message-based communications. You use a queue with point-to-point communications or a topic with publish-and-subscribe communications. Your client programs communicate directly with the JMS queue. In this section, you find out how to create both queues and topics.

Here you tie many of the components that you previously created together into one server. To create a JMS queue or a topic, follow these steps:

1. **On the left side of the Administration Console screen, click the following folders: Services, JMS, and Servers. Then click your server name, and finally click the Destinations folder.**

2. **Click the <u>Configure a new JMSQueue</u> or <u>Configure a new JMS Topic</u> link.**

   The screen shown in Figure 15-12 appears if you chose to configure a queue.

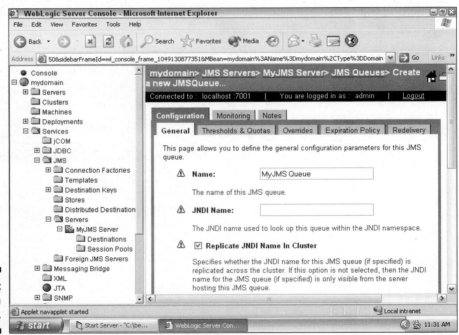

Figure 15-12: Creating a queue.

3. **Type the configuration information for the queue or topic as follows:**

   a. **Type a name for the queue or topic.**

   b. **Type a JNDI name that clients can use to locate this queue or topic.**

   c. **Click Apply to enable your store.**

   d. **Choose your template.**

   e. **Choose the destination keys.**

4. **Click Create.**

You've created a JMS message service with either a queue or a topic. Now you're ready to begin using this message store from client programs.

Accessing Your Message Service

In this section, you construct a Java application that can access the message service that you just created. To begin, review Table 15-2, which lists many of the classes used to construct a client program for JMS.

Table 15-2	JMS Classes
JMS Class	*What It Does*
Connection	Represents an open communication channel to the messaging system. The Connection object is used to create sessions.
ConnectionConsumer	Represents a consumer that retrieves server sessions to process messages concurrently.
ConnectionFactory	Encapsulates connection configuration information. A connection factory is your entry point into the JMS server, as the connection factory is used to create connections. You look up a connection factory using JNDI.
Destination	Identifies a queue or topic by its address.
Message	Holds the message being sent.
MessageProducer and MessageConsumer	Specifies the interface for sending and receiving messages. The MessageProducer class sends messages to a queue or topic; the MessageConsumer class receives messages from a queue or topic.

(continued)

Table 15-2 (continued)

JMS Class	What It Does
ServerSession1	Associates a thread with a JMS session.
ServerSession Pool1	Holds a pool of server sessions that can be used to process messages concurrently for connection consumers.
ServerSessionPool Factory	Encapsulates configuration information for a server-managed pool of message consumers. Used to create server session pools.
Session	Specifies a serial order for the messages produced and consumed.

The following sections describe these classes in greater detail. After that, you create a simple example that accesses a queue and a topic.

ConnectionFactory

The ConnectionFactory class is your entry into the JMS server. After you obtain ConnectionFactory, you can establish connections to the queues and topics of a JMS server. The ConnectionFactory class supports concurrent access, so you can use one ConnectionFactory object for multiple threads.

Connection factories are created by the systems administrator. All ConnectionFactory objects are identified using WebLogic JNDI names. A client program looks up ConnectionFactory using its unique JNDI name.

 By default, WebLogic JMS provides one connection factory. It can be accessed by using the JNDI name weblogic.jms.ConnectionFactory. You need to define a connection factory only if the default provided by WebLogic JMS is not suitable for your application.

Connection

You use the ConnectionFactory object to obtain a Connection object, which is an open communications channel between an application and the messaging system. From this Connection object, you create Session objects for producing and consuming messages. A connection creates both server-side and client-side objects that manage the messaging between the application and JMS. Like ConnectionFactory, Connection objects support concurrent use, enabling multiple threads to access the object simultaneously.

Connections require considerable resources. Because of this, most applications use one connection for all JMS processing.

Session

`Session` objects are obtained from `Connection` objects by calling the `createQueueSession` or `createTopicSession` method. A `Session` object defines the order that messages are produced and consumed. A `Session` object can create multiple message producers and message consumers.

Session objects should not be shared across threads. It's okay for the same thread to both produce and consume messages. However, if an application wants a separate thread for producing and consuming messages, the application should also create separate sessions for producing and consuming threads. Creating threads is illegal in EJBs.

Destination

A `Destination` object represents either a queue or topic. Destinations refer to destination keys, which you set up earlier using Administration Console. The `Destination` object allows the application program to communicate with the topic or queue.

A `Destination` object supports concurrent use. This allows multiple threads to access the object simultaneously.

MessageProducer and MessageConsumer

You use the `Session` object to create the `MessageProducer` and `Message Consumer` objects, which are attached to queues and topics. A `Message Producer` object sends messages to a queue or topic. A `MessageConsumer` object receives messages from a queue or topic.

The `MessageProducer` and `MessageConsumer` objects operate independently. The `MessageProducer` object sends messages regardless of whether a `MessageConsumer` object has been created and is waiting for a message and vice versa.

Message

The `Message` class holds the information to be exchanged by applications. Following are the three main components to a `Message` object:

✔ Standard header fields

✔ Application-defined properties

✔ The message body

The following sections examine the header fields and the message body .

Message header fields

JMS messages contain a standard set of header fields by default. Some of these fields can be modified by the sender. Table 15-3 describes the fields in a JMS message.

Table 15-3	Message Header Fields	
Field	*Defined By*	*What It Does*
JMSCorrelation ID	Application	Relates messages to each other. This field is often used to relate a reply message to the original request message.
JMSDelivery Mode	send() method	Specifies a PERSISTENT message, which is stored by JMS and is not considered successful until sent, or a NON-PERSISTENT message, which is simply transmitted and requires much less overhead.
JMSDeliveryTime	send() method	Specifies the time at which the message was sent. This field is used to sort messages.
JMSDestination	send() method	Stores the destination queue or topic to which this message is targeted.
JMSExpiration	send() method	Specifies the expiration time for the message. After the expiration time is reached, the message is no longer delivered.
JMSMessageID	send() method	Uniquely identifies this message.
JMSPriority	Message Consumer	Specifies the priority for this message. Priority levels range from 0 to 9, with 0 the lowest priority.
JMSRedelivered	WebLogic JMS	Specifies whether this message was redelivered due to non-receipt.
JMSReplyTo	Application	Specifies what message this message is a reply to, if it is a reply.

Field	Defined By	What It Does
JMSTimeStamp	Message Consumer	Contains the time at which the message was sent.
JMSType	Application	Specifies an application-defined type.

Message body

The body of a message contains the content that's being delivered. JMS supports a variety of content types, as shown in Table 15-4.

Table 15-4	JMS Message Types
Type	**What It Is**
javax.jms. BytesMessage	A stream of bytes. There is no implied meaning. Data in this form is accessed using stream-oriented readers and writers based on java.io.DataInputStream and java.io.DataOutputStream.
javax.jms. MapMessage	A set of name/value pairs in which the names are strings and the values are Java primitive types.
javax.jms. ObjectMessage	A single serializable Java object.
javax.jms. StreamMessage	A stream where only Java primitive types are written to or read from the stream.
javax.jms. TextMessage	A string message.
weblogic.jms. extensions. XMLMessage	XML content. Although XML can be stored in TextMessage, XMLMessage allows message filtering.

Creating a Point-to-Point JMS Client

In this section, you create a simple point-to-point (P2P) JMS client that sends text messages from one client to another. You can build on this simple example to create a more complex messaging system.

Creating the receiver

The receiver program, shown in Listing 15-1, waits for messages. The receiver is a regular Java application that you can run from the command line. Unlike an EJB, the receiver doesn't have to run in the context of WebLogic. In this example, both the sender and receiver are standalone Java applications that run outside WebLogic. WebLogic is only providing the infrastructure to pass the messages.

Listing 15-1:   P2P Receiver

```java
import javax.jms.*;
import javax.naming.*;
import java.util.*;


public class SampleQueueReceiver implements MessageListener {
   private boolean done = false;
   private Context ctx = null;
   private QueueConnectionFactory connectionFactory = null;
   private QueueConnection connection = null;
   private QueueSession session = null;
   private QueueReceiver receiver = null;
   private Queue queue = null;
   private Hashtable ht = null;

   public void init() {
     try {

       ht = new Hashtable();

       ht.put(Context.INITIAL_CONTEXT_FACTORY,
           "weblogic.jndi.WLInitialContextFactory");
       ht.put(Context.PROVIDER_URL, "t3://localhost:7001");

       ctx = new InitialContext(ht);
       connectionFactory =(QueueConnectionFactory)
         ctx.lookup("weblogic.jms.ConnectionFactory");
       connection = connectionFactory.createQueueConnection();
       session = connection.createQueueSession(
         false,
         javax.jms.QueueSession.AUTO_ACKNOWLEDGE);
       queue = (Queue) ctx.lookup("MyJMSQueue");
       receiver = session.createReceiver(queue);

       receiver.setMessageListener(this);

       connection.start();
     } catch ( Exception e ) {
       System.out.println(e);
     }
```

```
}

public void close() throws JMSException {

  try {
    receiver.close();
    session.close();
    connection.close();
  } catch ( Exception e ) {
    System.out.println(e);
  }
}

public void onMessage(Message message) {

  if ( message instanceof TextMessage ) {
    try {
      TextMessage textMessage = (TextMessage) message;
      String msg = textMessage.getText();

      System.out.println("Received message: " + msg);

      if ( msg.equals("exit") ) {
        synchronized (this) {
          done = true;
          this.notifyAll();
        }
      }
    } catch ( Exception e ) {
      System.out.println(e);
    }
  }

}

public static void main(String[] args) {

  try {
    SampleQueueReceiver sqr = new SampleQueueReceiver();

    sqr.init();
    System.out.println("Waiting for messages....");

    synchronized (sqr) {
      while ( !sqr.done ) {
        try {
          sqr.wait();
        } catch ( InterruptedException ie ) {
        }
      }
    }
```

(continued)

Listing 15-1 *(continued)*

```
      sqr.close();
    } catch ( Exception e ) {
      System.out.println(e);
    }
  }
}
```

The program begins execution at the `main` method, which instantiates an object of the sample receiver and begins waiting for messages. The class implements the `MessageListener` interface. This allows the class to receive messages. Implementing this interface requires that the `onMessage` method be provided by your class.

Next, the `init` method is called. The `init` method contains the code that registers this object to receive messages from the `MyJMSQueue` queue. The connection is retrieved from the connection factory and is started by calling the `start` method of the connection object.

When a message is received, the `onMessage` method is called. All message processing takes place inside this message. This program deals with only `Text Message` type messages. The program begins by examining the object sent to `onMessage` to determine whether it was `TextMessage`. If it was `TextMessage`, the message is displayed. If the message was not `TextMessage`, the message is ignored. After you execute the receiver, it begins waiting for messages.

Creating the sender

In this section, you create a sender that works with the receiver you created in the preceding section. The sender is shown in Listing 15-2.

Listing 15-2:   P2P Sender

```
import javax.jms.*;
import javax.naming.*;
import java.util.*;

public class SampleQueueSender {

  public static void main(String[] args) {

    Context ctx = null;
    Hashtable ht = new Hashtable();
    QueueConnectionFactory connectionFactory = null;
    QueueConnection connection = null;
    QueueSession session = null;
    QueueSender sender = null;
    Queue queue = null;
```

```
    TextMessage message = null;

    try {
      ht.put(Context.INITIAL_CONTEXT_FACTORY,
             "weblogic.jndi.WLInitialContextFactory");
      ht.put(Context.PROVIDER_URL, "t3://localhost:7001");

      ctx = new InitialContext(ht);
      connectionFactory =
      (QueueConnectionFactory)
          ctx.lookup("weblogic.jms.ConnectionFactory");
      connection = connectionFactory.createQueueConnection();
      session = connection.createQueueSession(false,
        javax.jms.QueueSession.AUTO_ACKNOWLEDGE);
      queue = (Queue) ctx.lookup("MyJMSQueue");
      sender = session.createSender(queue);

      System.out.println("Sending messages...");

      message = session.createTextMessage();

      for ( int i = 1; i <= 10; i++ ) {
        String str = "Message " + i;

        message.clearBody();
        message.setText(str);
        System.out.println("Sending message: " + str);
        sender.send(message);
      }

      message.clearBody();
      message.setText("exit");
      message.setIntProperty("severity", 0);
      System.out.println("Sending message: exit"););
      sender.send(message);
    } catch ( Exception e ) {
      e.printStackTrace();
    } finally {
      try {
        sender.close();
        session.close();
        connection.close();
      } catch ( Exception e ) {
        e.printStackTrace();
      }
    }
  }
}
```

The sender is somewhat simpler than the receiver, containing only one method, the `main` method. The sender simply opens a connection, sends some messages, and exits.

After the queue is located using JNDI and the connection is opened, the client program transmits ten messages. First a message is created:

```
message = session.createTextMessage();
```

This message is reused multiple times to send each message. The program loops through and sends the text message ten times:

```
for ( int i = 1; i <= 10; i++ ) {
  String str = "Message " + i;
```

The message is cleared, and then the text is defined. Then the message is sent using the send method of the sender:

```
    message.clearBody();
    message.setText(str);
    System.out.println("Sending message: " + str);
    sender.send(message);
}
```

The sender and receiver transmit ten messages, as shown in Figure 15-13. The P2P sender and receiver model works well when you want to send messages between two programs. You can also send a message from one sender to many receivers. You find out how to do this in the next section.

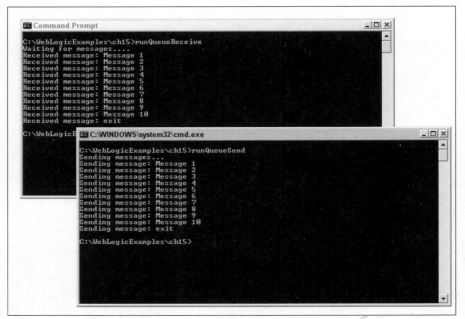

Figure 15-13:
A P2P
message.

Creating a Publish-and-Subscribe JMS Client

In this section, you use the publish-and-subscribe model. In this model, you have many subscribers and one publisher. (This is similar to a newspaper.) The same message is sent from the publisher to all the subscribers. You begin by constructing the subscriber.

Creating the subscriber

The subscriber for a publish-and-subscribe model is similar to the receiver discussed in the preceding section. The subscriber receives messages using a `MessageListener` interface. See Listing 15-3.

Listing 15-3: Subscriber

```
import javax.jms.*;
import javax.naming.*;
import java.util.*;


public class SampleTopicSubscriber implements MessageListener
        {
  private boolean done = false;
  private Context ctx = null;
  private Hashtable ht = null;
  private TopicConnectionFactory connectionFactory = null;
  private TopicConnection connection = null;
  private TopicSession session = null;
  private TopicSubscriber subscriber = null;
  private Topic topic = null;

  public void init() {

    try {
      ht = new Hashtable();

      ht.put(Context.INITIAL_CONTEXT_FACTORY,
            "weblogic.jndi.WLInitialContextFactory");
      ht.put(Context.PROVIDER_URL, "t3://localhost:7001");

      ctx = new InitialContext(ht);
      connectionFactory = (TopicConnectionFactory)

          ctx.lookup("weblogic.jms.ConnectionFactory");
```

(continued)

Listing 15-3 *(continued)*

```
      connection = connectionFactory.createTopicConnection();
      session = connection.createTopicSession(false,
        javax.jms.QueueSession.AUTO_ACKNOWLEDGE);
      topic = (Topic) ctx.lookup("MyJMSTopic");
      subscriber = session.createSubscriber(topic);
      subscriber.setMessageListener(this);

      connection.start();
    } catch ( Exception e ) {
      System.out.println(e);
    }
  }

  public void close() throws JMSException {

    try {
      subscriber.close();
      session.close();
      connection.close();
    } catch ( Exception e ) {
      e.printStackTrace();
    }
  }

  public void onMessage(Message message) {

    if ( message instanceof TextMessage ) {
      try {
        TextMessage textMessage = (TextMessage) message;

        String msg = textMessage.getText();

        System.out.println("Received message: " + msg);

        if ( msg.equals("exit") ) {
          synchronized (this) {
            done = true;

            this.notifyAll();
          }
        }
      } catch ( Exception e ) {
        e.printStackTrace();
      }
    }
  }

  public static void main(String[] args) {
```

```
    try {
      SampleTopicSubscriber ts = new SampleTopicSubscriber();

      ts.init();
      System.out.println("Waiting for messages....");

      synchronized (ts) {
        while ( !ts.done ) {
          try {
            ts.wait();
          } catch ( InterruptedException ie ) {
          }
        }
      }

      ts.close();
    } catch ( Exception e ) {
      e.printStackTrace();
    }
  }
}
```

The program is nearly the same as the receiver in Listing 15-1. The main difference is that the other program connects to a queue, and this program connects to a topic. By connecting to a topic, you establish a nonexclusive relationship to the publisher. After the connection is established, you receive messages in the same way as any other subscribers.

Creating the publisher

The publisher for a publish-and-subscribe model is similar to the sender in the preceding section. The publisher sends messages, except these messages can be sent to many subscribers. Listing 15-4 shows a publisher.

Listing 15-4:   Publisher

```
import javax.jms.*;
import javax.naming.*;
import java.util.*;

public class SampleTopicPublisher {

  public static void main(String[] args) {

    Context ctx = null;
    Hashtable ht = new Hashtable();
    TopicConnectionFactory connectionFactory = null;
```

(continued)

Listing 15-4 *(continued)*

```
    TopicConnection connection = null;
    TopicSession session = null;
    TopicPublisher publisher = null;
    Topic topic = null;
    TextMessage message = null;


    try {
      ht.put(Context.INITIAL_CONTEXT_FACTORY,
             "weblogic.jndi.WLInitialContextFactory");
      ht.put(Context.PROVIDER_URL, "t3://localhost:7001");

      ctx = new InitialContext(ht);
      connectionFactory = (TopicConnectionFactory)
        ctx.lookup("weblogic.jms.ConnectionFactory");
      connection = connectionFactory.createTopicConnection();
      session = connection.createTopicSession(
        false,
        javax.jms.TopicSession.AUTO_ACKNOWLEDGE);

      topic = (Topic) ctx.lookup("MyJMSTopic");
      publisher = session.createPublisher(topic);

      System.out.println("Publishing messages...");

      message = session.createTextMessage();

      for ( int i = 1; i <= 10; i++ ) {
        String str = "Message " + i;

        message.clearBody();
        message.setText(str);
        System.out.println("Publishing message: " + str);
        publisher.publish(message);
      }

    } catch ( Exception e ) {
      System.out.println(e);
    } finally {
      try {
        publisher.close();
        session.close();
        connection.close();
      } catch ( Exception e ) {
        System.out.println(e);
      }
    }
  }
}
```

The program is nearly the same as the sender in Listing 15-2. The main difference is that the other program connects to a queue whereas this program connects to a topic. By connecting to a topic as a publisher, you can send your messages to many clients. You receive messages the same way as any other subscribers does.

The sender and receiver transmit ten messages, as shown in Figure 15-14. As you can see from the figure, one publisher is sending messages to two subscribers.

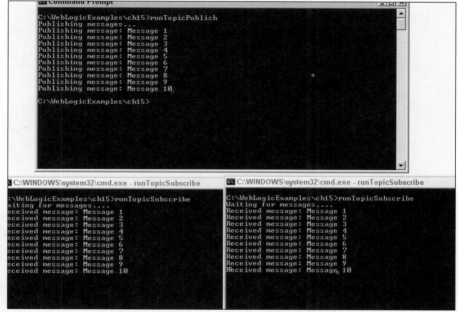

Figure 15-14:
A publish/
subscribe
message.

As you've found in this chapter, you can easily use WebLogic as the infrastructure to send messages between programs. You can do this using either a point-to-point or a publish-and-subscribe model.

Part V

Big-Time, Heavy-Duty Server Configuration

The 5th Wave   By Rich Tennant

"I'm not saying I believe in anything. All I know is since it's been there our server is running 50% faster."

In this part . . .

Here is where you find out about more advanced configuration options. For example, WebLogic allows you to combine individual servers into one large virtual server. This feature, called clustering, enables you to expand your system by adding hardware rather than by completely replacing your existing system.

Security is very important to any web application. In this part, you find out about the WebLogic features that allow you to secure data exchanged with your system and control how users access your system. You also find out how to tune your system for maximum performance.

Chapter 16

Working with Server Clusters

*T*he old saying that there's strength in numbers applies to computers as well as to humans. You can achieve considerable advantages by using many computers together to run WebLogic. These groups of computers are called *clusters*. These clusters can appear as a single server, which delegates tasks to the appropriate computer in the cluster.

In this chapter, you discover the advantages and disadvantages of using clustering. You uncover the components that make up a cluster, and then you set up a cluster.

Understanding Clustering

A *cluster* is a group of computers that collectively perform the same task. In the case of a WebLogic cluster, the tasks performed by the cluster include all the tasks that you might assign to one WebLogic Server. These tasks are covered throughout this book.

The two main reasons why you might want to create a WebLogic cluster are performance and reliability The disadvantages to setting up a cluster have to do with the costs of hardware, software, and administration:

✔ **Hardware cost.** A cluster contains at least twice the amount of computer hardware that you would have with a single computer system. You also have additional repair costs to keep these computers up and running.

✔ **Software cost.** You need a cluster license for WebLogic. This increases the amount of money that it costs to purchase your server software. In addition to WebLogic, other third-party software that you're using may require additional license fees when used with a cluster.

✔ **Administration cost.** Every network administrator knows that more computers means more support time. It takes time to install the required software to the additional computer systems in your cluster.

Even if your system easily fits on one machine, you should still be aware of how clustering works. There may come a point when your application has grown large enough that clustering will be needed. If you know how clustering works, you can construct your application so that it can support clustering when it's needed.

Performance through clustering

Clustering can increase performance because you have additional computers to handle requests, rather than just one computer. However, clustering doesn't necessarily result in an increase in speed. The amount of performance gain from clustering is determined by the type of application you're running.

When clustering can't improve performance

Consider a system that calculates economic forecasts when given current market conditions. This program must access a large amount of historical data to produce its output. This program is hosted on WebLogic Server. Only a few users will access this program throughout the day. The response time is slow, in that the program takes a while to generate the forecast.

A cluster would not likely increase the speed of this application. Clusters improve performance primarily when they serve a large number of concurrent requests. In this example, a lengthy process is executed by just a few users. If an additional computer were added to the system to form a cluster, the second computer would sit idle while the first performed the forecast. A server cluster is not capable of splitting a single request among the cluster members. The only case where the cluster would speed up this process is if several users where submitting requests at the same time.

To speed up the forecast application, you'd need to buy a larger, faster server or rewrite the application to be more efficient.

When clustering can improve performance

Now consider a system that allows users to look up information about any of the products that their company produces. This program allows the user to view sales reports on each item. This system is accessed by users throughout the company. Additionally, many automated programs access the system through EJB calls to obtain sales information.

The system has been giving unacceptably bad response times, especially during peak usage. Additionally, the server sometimes goes off-line from excessive use.

A cluster would improve the performance of this application. By having more than one server available to process the requests, no individual server would be overworked. This would result in faster responses, and the system wouldn't go off-line due to one overloaded server.

 Perhaps the most important thing to keep in mind when deciding whether to use a cluster to improve performance is that a cluster will only allow the system to handle more requests faster. It will not often speed up requests when these requests come in one at a time. A cluster is used to increase the performance for many concurrent accesses.

Reliability through clustering

Performance is not the only reason to consider clustering. Reliability is another factor. A cluster can increase reliability because several computer systems handle the requests sent to the server. If one computer in the cluster crashes, the cluster remains operational.

 Reliability, unlike performance, is always improved by clustering. Therefore, whether or not to run a cluster to increase reliability boils down to a question of cost.

Components of WebLogic Clustering

Unfortunately, clustering is not something that you can set up by changing a simple configuration setting. Many related systems are used to set up a cluster:

- ✔ Node Manager
- ✔ Clustered domain
- ✔ Clustered JDBC
- ✔ Load balancing
- ✔ Connection proxy

In this section, I explain each of these systems and how they fit together to allow you to create a cluster of WebLogic servers.

Node Manager

Node Manager is a standalone Java application that allows you to manage the servers that make up your cluster. There are two immediate benefits to this. You can

✔ Manage the cluster from one computer
✔ Automatically restart crashed cluster computers

When you create a cluster, it will be made up of several computers. This can be somewhat difficult to manage because you will need to start and stop server instances on each machine. Additionally, you now have log files on each machine. Node Manager allows you to work with the computers in the cluster as though they were a single unit. You can quickly restart individual cluster computers or obtain information about any machine in the cluster.

You may choose to use Node Manager after your system is up and running. Node Manager is more beneficial when your system has settled into a routine. When you're first setting up your system, it's better to directly control the computers that make up the cluster.

Clustered domain

In other chapters, you work with WebLogic domains. In this chapter, you're introduced to the concept of a clustered domain. The clustered domain combines the computers of the domain into one virtual computer. This makes the fact that you're using a cluster nearly invisible to a client program accessing your server. To the client program, your cluster looks like one very fast single-server system.

Clustered domains are configured in much the same way as non-clustered domains. You can set up both using WebLogic Domain Wizard.

Clustered JDBC

Clustered JDBC allows you to use JDBC resources across the cluster. WebLogic manages the concurrent access to the connection pools on each managed server. Clustered JDBC is set up just like regular JDBC, except the JDBC resources are assigned to a cluster rather than to individual servers.

Load balancing

Load balancing allows WebLogic to send requests to servers that aren't working as hard as other servers. This prevents one overworked server from becoming a bottleneck. As RMI and EJB requests come in, the load-balancing algorithm determines which managed server will handle the request.

WebLogic provides several algorithms for load balancing. You use Administration Console to choose the one you want. These methods are discussed later in this chapter.

Connection proxy

Clustering is not just for RMI and EJB requests. You may also choose to cluster your JSP and servlet requests. WebLogic provides for a connection proxy that routes servlet and JSP requests to a managed server that's not overloaded.

The connection proxy feature of WebLogic is extendable. You may choose to write your own, buy a third-party proxy, or use the connection proxy built into WebLogic.

Configuring WebLogic Clustering

Now that you understand the components that make up a WebLogic cluster, it's time to see the steps required to install one. These steps are summarized as follows:

1. **Install WebLogic Server.**

2. **Create a clustered domain.**

3. **Start the WebLogic Server cluster.**

4. **Configure Node Manager (optional).**

5. **Configure load balancing.**

6. **Configure proxy plug-ins (optional).**

7. **Configure clustered JDBC.**

In the following sections, you examine each step in detail.

Installing WebLogic Server

You must install WebLogic Server on each machine that you want to run it on. You must use the same version of WebLogic on each machine and pay for the necessary WebLogic licenses.

Although not required, try to make the environment of each cluster machine as close to identical as possible. The directory structure and location of WebLogic and your application should be the same on each system.

The machines that make up the cluster don't need to be identical, but they must meet the following minimum requirements:

- **Static IP address.** A managed server must have permanently assigned, static IP addresses. Dynamically assigned IP addresses are not allowed in a cluster environment.

- **Client accessible.** The server computers must be accessible to clients. You may not place server computers behind a firewall and clients in front of the firewall. This is because each server instance must have a public IP address that can be reached by the clients.

- **Multicast accessible.** The managed servers must be located on the same local area network (LAN) and must be reachable by IP multicast. This means that the IP address configured for each server machine must have the same submit mask.

You shouldn't use a shared file system to run multiple WebLogic Server instances on separate machines. This creates a bottleneck because all server instances must compete to access this area. Additionally, concurrent access to the log files may cause some logging information to become unreliable. Always install a separate copy of WebLogic for each server, preferably on the server's local hard drive.

Creating a clustered domain

After your software is installed, you're ready to create a clustered domain. In other chapters, you create a domain for a single-computer WebLogic installation. Here, you create a domain that works with a clustered environment.

A number of steps are involved in setting up a clustered domain. Here's an overview:

A. **Configure your Administration Server.** Each domain must have one server that you configure as your Administration Server. (See Step 4 in the next numbered list.)

B. Configure your managed servers (optional). You can add managed servers or change existing ones. (See Step 6 in the next list.)

C. Assign servers to clusters (optional). You can group your managed servers into clusters or change existing groupings of servers. (See Step 10.) If you choose this option, you must first configure your cluster. (See Step 8.)

D. Associate servers to machines (optional). You can assign your servers and clusters to machines or change existing assignments. (See Step 14.) If you choose this option, you must first configure the machine. (See Step 12.)

You begin creating a clustered domain in Domain Configuration Wizard, as follows:

1. **Start Configuration Wizard.**

   Choose Start➪Programs➪BEA WebLogic Platform➪Domain Configuration Wizard.

2. **Select the <u>Create a new WebLogic configuration</u> link, and then click Next.**

   The screen shown in Figure 16-1 appears.

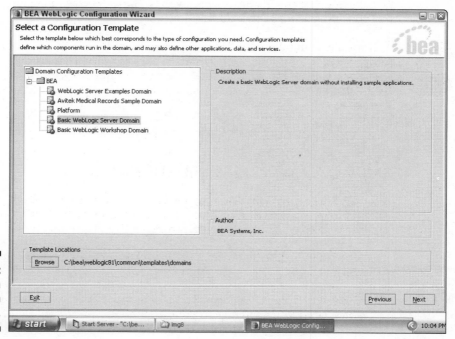

Figure 16-1:
Choose a domain type.

3. **Choose a type of domain, and then click Next.**

   To follow along with the example, click Basic WebLogic Server Domain.

4. **Choose Customized Configuration, and then click Next.**

   The screen shown in Figure 16-2 appears.

5. **Configure your Administration Server as follows:**

   a. **For the Name box, type a unique name for your server.**

   b. **Leave the ListenAddress box blank, unless your computer has multiple IP addresses.**

   c. **Leave the ListenPort at 7001 and the SSL Listen Port at 7002.**

   d. **If you will be using SSL, click the SSL Enabled box.**

   For more information about SSL, see Chapter 17.

   e. **Click Next.**

   The screen shown in Figure 16-3 appears.

6. **Click Yes to begin configuring your managed server, and then click Next.**

   The screen shown in Figure 16-4 appears.

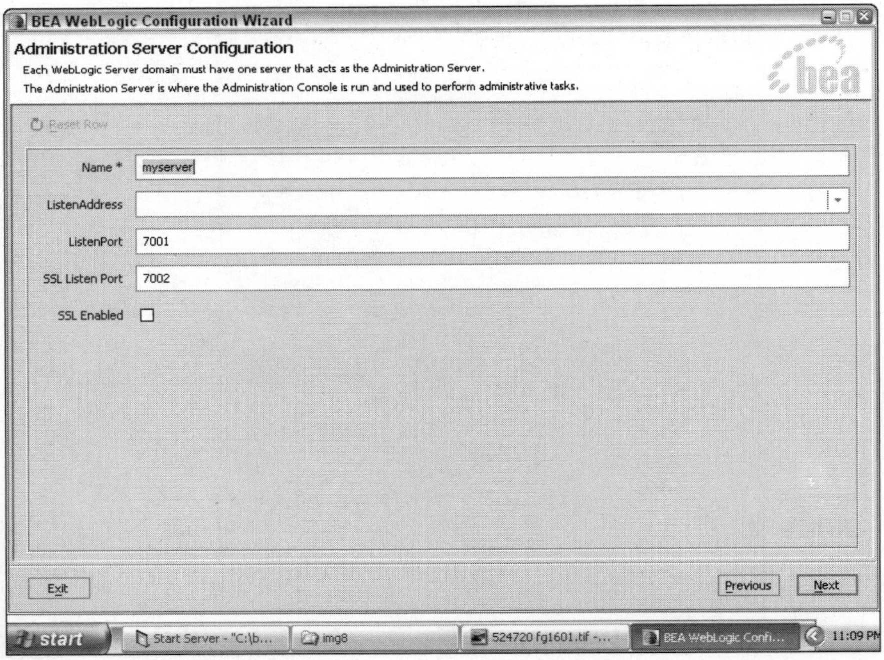

Figure 16-2:
Configure
your server.

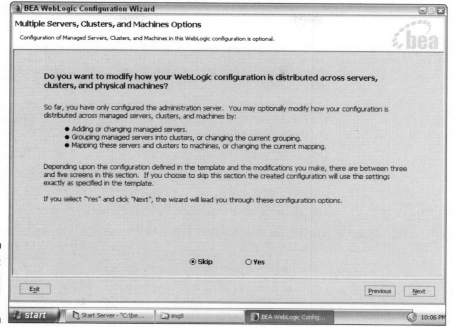

Figure 16-3: Choosing a managed server.

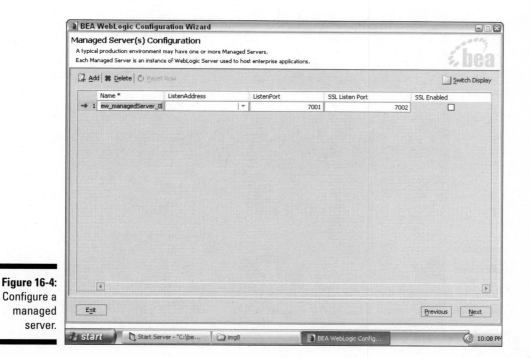

Figure 16-4: Configure a managed server.

7. For *each* managed server that you want to add, do the following:

   a. Click Add.

   b. Under Name, type a unique name for your server.

   c. Under Listen Address, use the IP address of the server that's being added.

      This should be the unique IP address that you assigned to the server when you installed the operating system and networking support on the server.

   d. Under Listen Port, use the port that the computer listens over.

      The range of allowable values is 1 to 65,535. You should accept the default value.

   e. Under SSL Listen Port, use the port that the computer listens over.

      The range of allowable values is 1 to 65,535. You should accept the default value.

8. When you have finished adding servers, click Next.

   The screen shown in Figure 16-5 appears.

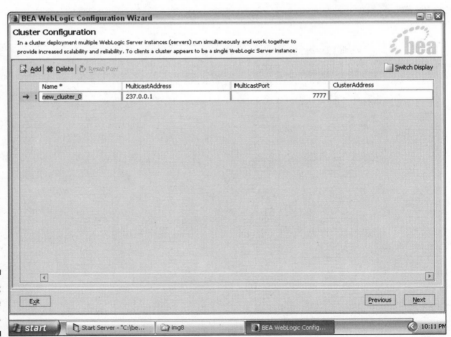

Figure 16-5: Configure the cluster.

9. **Configure your cluster as follows:**

   a. **Click Add.**

   b. **Under Name, type a unique name for your cluster.**

   c. **MulticastAddress should specify the IP addresses of your managed machines.**

   MulticastAddress contains a range of IP addresses that the managed machines are located on. A multicast address is a special IP address that broadcasts to all IP addresses on its network. Your network administrator will be able to give you the cluster address and multicast addresses for your server.

   d. **Leave MulticastPort at its default value of 7777.**

   The cluster address contains the address and ports for each server instance.

10. **When you have finished configuring your cluster, click Next.**

    The screen shown in Figure 16-6 appears.

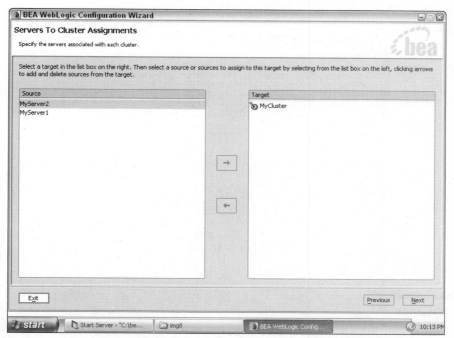

Figure 16-6:
Assign servers to clusters.

11. For *each* server that you want to assign to a cluster, do the following:

    a. On the left, click the server that you want to assign.

    b. On the right, click the cluster that you want to assign the server to.

    c. Click the right arrow to make the assignment.

12. When you've finished assigning servers to clusters, click Next.

    The screen shown in Figure 16-7 appears.

13. For each machine that you want to configure, do the following:

    a. Click Add.

    b. Under name, type a unique name for your machine.

    c. Under ListenAddress, type the IP address of the machine you are adding.

    d. Under ListenPort, accept the default.

14. When you've finished configuring machines, click Next.

    The screen shown in Figure 16-8 appears.

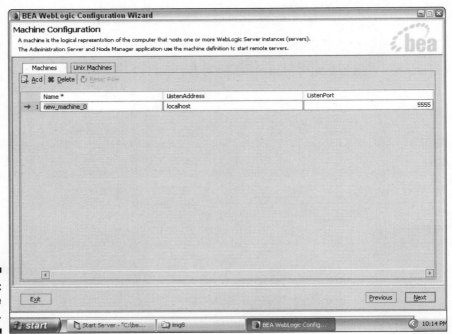

Figure 16-7: Configure machines.

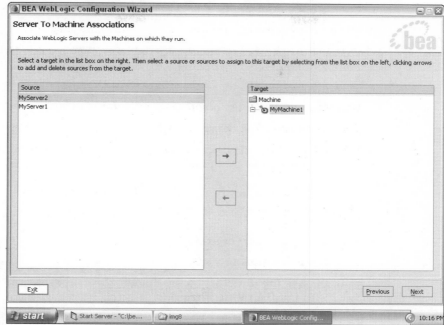

Figure 16-8:
Assign
servers to
machines.

15. For *each* server that you want to assign to a machine, do the following:

   a. On the left side of the screen, click the server you want to assign.

   b. On the right side, click the machine you wish to assign the server to.

   c. Click the right arrow to make the assignment.

16. When you have finished assigning servers to machines, click Next.

Now that you've set up your distributed domain, you're ready to start your cluster. This is discussed in the next section.

Starting the WebLogic Server cluster

To start a cluster, you first start Administration Server for the cluster, and then start each of the managed servers in the cluster. Each server instance is started with a command that you execute in a separate command shell. (For a comprehensive discussion of procedures for starting and stopping server instances, see Chapter 3.)

Follow these steps:

1. **Open a command shell.**

2. **Move to the domain directory.**

   Change the directory to the domain directory that you created with Configuration Wizard by issuing the following command:

   ```
   cd \bea\user_projects\mycluster
   ```

   where *mycluster* is the name of your cluster.

3. **Start Administration Server by typing** StartWebLogic **at the command prompt.**

4. **Type the user name and password.**

5. **Observe the Administration Server startup.**

   The command shell displays messages that report the status of the startup process.

6. **Start a managed server as follows:**

   a. **Open a command shell.**

   b. **Change the directory to the domain directory that you created with Configuration Wizard.**

   c. **Type the following command:**

   StartManagedWebLogic *server_name address:port*

   Replace *server_name* with the name of your managed server, and replace *address:port* with the address and port of Administration Server.

   d. **To start another server instance in the cluster, return to Step 6c.**

   If you have no additional managed servers to start, your startup is now complete.

You may run one managed server on the same computer as Administration Server. Because Administration Server doesn't require much processing power, this allows you to take full advantage of the computer.

Configuring Node Manager

As you saw in the preceding section, the process of starting your cluster involves starting up managed servers on all machines in the cluster. This can be tedious and time consuming. Node Manager alleviates this tedium.

Node Manager, which is covered in Chapter 3, is a standalone Java program that you can use to start managed servers on remote machines. Node Manager can also restart managed servers that may have crashed. You're not required to use Node Manager to set up a cluster.

Configuring load balancing

Load balancing allows WebLogic to better allocate the machines in the server cluster. This prevents machines from becoming overloaded with tasks. One of the biggest tasks for these machines is servicing requests to EJB and RMI objects. In this section, you find out how to load balance the machine to handle EJB and RMI requests.

WebLogic uses the following three methods to load balance EJB and RMI requests:

- **Weight-based load balancing.** New requests are sent to the server that's currently processing the least.
- **Random load balancing.** The next incoming request is sent to a server chosen at random.
- **Round-robin load balancing.** The incoming request is given to the next server in line. Round-robin load balancing is the default balancing algorithm.

WebLogic uses the round-robin load-balancing method by default. To use a different method, you must explicitly configure WebLogic as follows:

1. **Start Administration Console.**

   For more information on this task, refer to Chapter 4.

2. **Select your cluster.**

   On the left side of the screen, click the Clusters folder, and then click your cluster name.

3. **Select a load algorithm in the drop-down Default Load Algorithm list.**

4. **Click Apply to save your changes.**

Configuring proxy plug-ins

In addition to load balancing EJB and RMI requests, you may also want to load balance servlet and JSP requests. This is accomplished by using a proxy plug-in. A proxy plug-in sends, or *proxies,* requests from a web server to WebLogic Server instances in a cluster. In the process, the plug-in provides load balancing and failover for the proxied HTTP requests. This allows your JSP pages and servlets to be handled by multiple machines in your cluster.

You can choose from two categories of proxy plug-ins:

- The WebLogic HttpClusterServlet plug-in
- A third-party proxy plug-in

You set up HttpClusterServlet in this chapter. For third-party plug-ins, refer to their documentation.

To use a proxy with your web application, you must first set up the proxy. The steps to set up HttpClusterServlet are summarized as follows:

1. **Create a web application that includes HttpClusterServlet.**

2. **Create a deployment descriptor file.**

3. **Create a web.xml file.**

4. **Configure your application.**

For information on creating a web application, see Chapter 5. The deployment descriptor file must contain the elements described in this section, specifically the `servlet-mapping` and `servlet` tags. For more on creating descriptors, see Chapter 8.

Step 3, creating a web.xml file that's designed to use the proxy, is covered next. Information on configuring web applications is in Chapter 4.

To make use of the HttpClusterServlet proxy plug-in, you must add it to the `<servlet>` element of web.xml. The following code segment shows how to do this:

```
<servlet-name>
HttpClusterServlet
</servlet-name>

<servlet-class>
weblogic.servlet.proxy.HttpClusterServlet
</servlet-class>
```

Now you must map URLs to the proxy based on the file extension. This allows you to configure the proxy to handle *.jsp or *.html.

If you set `<url-pattern>` to /, you'll divert all requests that are not covered by another handler to the proxy. The following shows how to do this:

```
<servlet-mapping>
   <servlet-name>HttpClusterServlet</servlet-name>
   <url-pattern>/</url-pattern>
</servlet-mapping>

<servlet-mapping>
   <servlet-name>HttpClusterServlet</servlet-name>
   <url-pattern>*.jsp</url-pattern>
</servlet-mapping>
```

```
<servlet-mapping>
  <servlet-name>HttpClusterServlet</servlet-name>
  <url-pattern>*.htm</url-pattern>
</servlet-mapping>

<servlet-mapping>
  <servlet-name>HttpClusterServlet</servlet-name>
  <url-pattern>*.html</url-pattern>
</servlet-mapping>
```

Listing 16-1 incorporates this configuration into a complete web.xml file for proxy support.

Listing 16-1: Sample web.xml for Proxy Support

```
<!DOCTYPE web-app PUBLIC "-//Sun Microsystems, Inc. //DTD Web
        Application 2.2//EN"
        "http://java.sun.com/j2ee/dtds/web-app_2_2.dtd">
<web-app>

<servlet>

  <servlet-name>HttpClusterServlet</servlet-name>
  <servlet-
        class>weblogic.servlet.proxy.HttpClusterServlet</s
        ervlet-class>
  <init-param>

<param-name>WebLogicCluster</param-name>

<param-value>
        myserver1:7736:7737|myserver2:7736:7737|myserver:7
        736:7737
</param-value>

</init-param>

  <init-param>
<param-name>DebugConfigInfo</param-name>
<param-value>ON</param-value>    </init-param>
</servlet>

<servlet-mapping>
<servlet-name>HttpClusterServlet</servlet-name>
<url-pattern>/</url-pattern>
</servlet-mapping>

<servlet-mapping>
<servlet-name>HttpClusterServlet</servlet-name>
```

(continued)

Listing 16-1 *(continued)*

```
<url-pattern>*.jsp</url-pattern>
</servlet-mapping>

<servlet-mapping>
<servlet-name>HttpClusterServlet</servlet-name>
<url-pattern>*.htm</url-pattern>
</servlet-mapping>

<servlet-mapping>
<servlet-name>HttpClusterServlet</servlet-name>
<url-pattern>*.html</url-pattern>
</servlet-mapping>

</web-app>
```

 You can use Listing 16-1 as a starting point for your own web.xml file. Listing 16-1 supports JSP, HTM, and HTML files. You could add support for additional files simply by adding servlet mappings with the `<servlet-mapping>` tag.

Configuring clustered JDBC

Data access is usually a significant part of any WebLogic-based application. Because of this, you must properly cluster your data-related resources when clustering your server. In this section, you find out what you must do to keep your database connections compatible with your cluster.

Two JDBC resources are commonly assigned to clusters: connection pools and data sources. When you create a connection pool or a data source, you assign it to a server, as discussed in Chapter 12. To use these resources with clustering, you simply assign them to a cluster rather than to a server.

To use a connection pool or a data source with clustering, follow these basic steps:

1. **Create a connection pool.**

2. **Assign the connection pool to the cluster.**

3. **Create the data source.**

4. **Assign the data source to the cluster.**

After you set up your connection, you're ready to use distributed JDBC. Clustered JDBC is accessed the same way as regular JDBC through WebLogic. The fact that you're using clustering is transparent to your application.

Chapter 17

Tuning WebLogic Server

*P*erformance is an important consideration in any enterprise application. For your enterprise application to be successful, it must respond to user requests in a reasonable amount of time. Your application must hold up to even demanding heavy-use situations.

You can increase the performance of your application in two primary ways: through the use of hardware and software. Using hardware to increase performance is covered in Chapter 16. In this chapter, you find out how you can use your existing hardware to increase performance by adjusting performance settings in WebLogic Server.

WebLogic Server Performance Packs

Java uses a virtual machine to execute its code, so Java code can execute on a variety of hardware platforms. The price for platform independence, however, is performance. To overcome this limitation in Java, you can use performance packs.

WebLogic performance packs contain native code for specific hardware systems. *Native code* refers to low-level instructions unique to a given platform. Native code has been crafted to pull the most performance possible out of a platform.

Most benchmarks provided by BEA show that you can reap major performance improvements by using native performance packs on machines that host WebLogic Server instances. These packs use a platform-optimized, native-socket multiplexor to improve server performance. However, if you use a performance pack, you're no longer working in a "pure Java" environment. This isn't usually an issue, unless you want to execute WebLogic on a platform that doesn't have a native performance pack.

In nearly all cases, you'll want to use a performance pack if one is available for your platform. Performance packs result in one of the easiest performance gains.

Follow these steps to use a native performance pack:

1. **Make sure that your server is running.**

   The server that you want to configure must be running. For a refresher on starting your server, see Chapter 3.

2. **Log on to Administration Console.**

   Administration Console is usually at `http://localhost:7001/console`. For more information on Administration Console, see Chapter 4.

3. **Select your server.**

   On the left side of the screen, click the Servers folder and then click your server. Your server's configuration page appears.

4. **Click the Tuning tab.**

   The screen shown in Figure 17-1 appears.

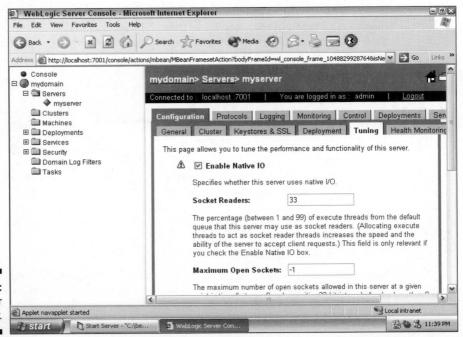

Figure 17-1:
Tuning your
server.

5. **Make sure that the Enable Native IO option is selected, and then click Apply.**

6. **Restart your server.**

   These changes take effect when your server is restarted.

Thread Settings

Threads are an important aspect of WebLogic. Many performance settings are related to threads. In this section, you work with some of the thread settings that you can use to improve WebLogic Server's performance.

Setting thread count

Requests to WebLogic are processed through *execute queues*. When you first install your server, you are given two execute queues named __weblogic_ admin_html_queue and __weblogic_admin_rmi_queue. These queues are reserved for communicating with Administration Console. If you don't configure additional execute queues, all web applications and RMI objects use the default queues.

The size of the default execute queue is set to 15 threads. You can change this value if needed, but be careful. If you set this value too high, WebLogic spends most of its time switching between threads rather than performing real work. If you set the value too low, WebLogic may not be able to respond to requests in a timely manner.

The value of the ThreadCount attribute of an ExecuteQueue element in the config.xml file equals the number of simultaneous operations that can be performed by applications that use the execute queue. As work enters an instance of WebLogic Server, it's placed in an execute queue. This work is then assigned to a thread. Threads consume resources, so handle the ThreadCount attribute with care — you can degrade performance by increasing the value unnecessarily.

 If native performance packs are not being used for your platform, you may need to change the default number of execute queue threads and the percentage of threads that act as socket readers to achieve optimal performance.

Thread count considerations

Before you modify the thread count, you should consider several things. Simply adding threads to the queue will not necessarily increase performance. Although threads allow a program to do more than one thing at time, you're still ultimately limited by the processing power of your computer.

Two types of applications that often require more threads are

- Thin client applications that perform much of their processing on the application server.

- Applications in which the calls to the application server may take a long time to execute. This is because the calls are usually waiting on an external event, such as a database query.

Determining an optimal thread count

To determine the optimal thread count for an execute queue, monitor the queue's throughput while all applications in the queue are operating at maximum load. Now increase the number of threads in the queue. At some point, you reach the optimal throughput for the queue.

To monitor the throughput or change the number of threads, follow these steps:

1. **Make sure your server is running, and log on to Administration Console.**

2. **Select your server.**

   On the left side of the screen, click the Servers folder and then click your server. You now see your server's configuration page.

3. **Display the execute queues that can be modified.**

   Click the Monitoring tab, which is shown in Figure 17-2. Then click the Monitor all Active Queues link. The screen shown in Figure 17-3 appears.

4. **Create and modify a queue as follows:**

   a. **Click the Configuration tab.**

   b. **Click the Configure a new Execute Queue link.**

   This will allow you to create a new execute queue. From this screen you can specify the maximum and minimum number of threads. How to choose these values will be discussed next.

   c. **Click Create.**

   The screen shown in Figure 17-4 appears.

   d. **Modify any of the parameters shown.**

5. **Scroll down and click Apply to apply your changes.**

6. **Restart your server.**

   These changes take effect when your server is restarted.

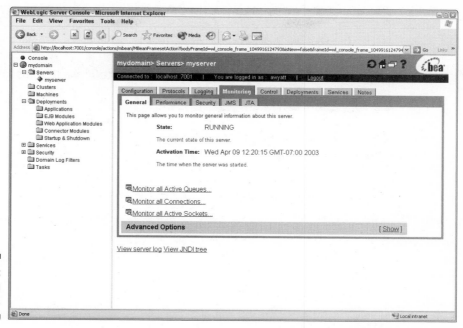

Figure 17-2:
Monitoring
your server.

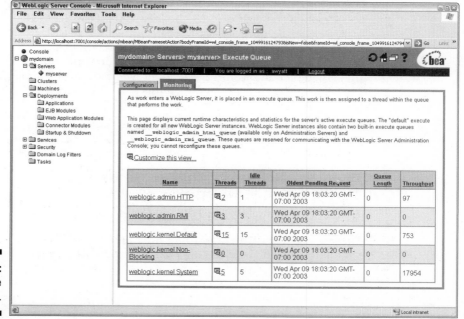

Figure 17-3:
Active
queues.

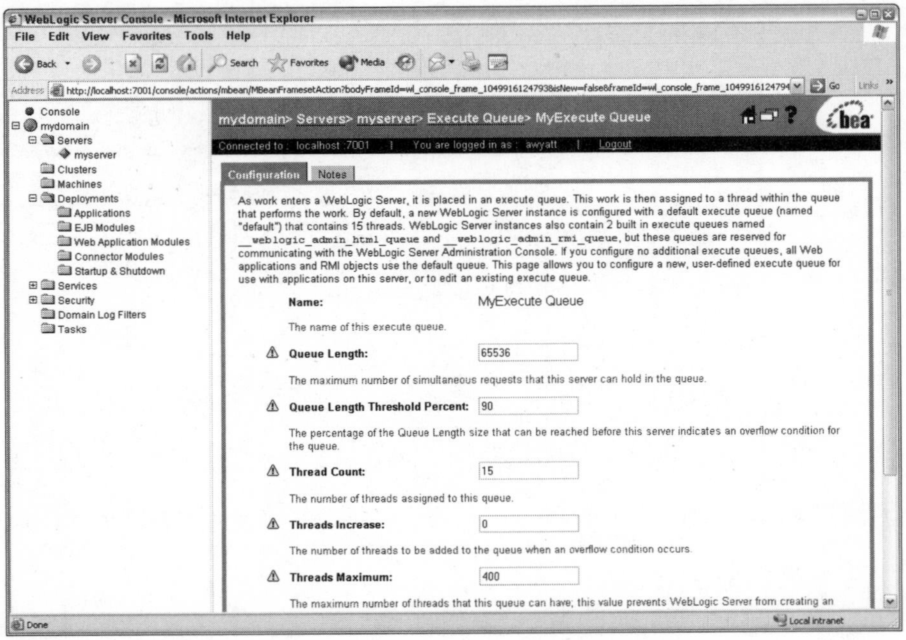

Figure 17-4:
The execute
queue
attributes.

The number of CPUs in your system has a big effect on the number of threads that you should be using. Consider the following CPU scenarios:

- **Thread count less than the number of CPUs.** Your thread count may be too low. This is true if the CPU is waiting to do work, but there is work that could be done. Your thread count is too low also if you never reach 100 percent CPU utilization rate. If this is the case, increase your thread count and compare performance results.

- **Thread count equal to the number of CPUs.** In theory, this is the ideal situation. It's most likely, however, that each CPU is underutilized. Increase the thread count and compare performance results.

- **Thread count moderately larger than the number of CPUs.** This could be an ideal setup if there is a moderate amount of thread switching and a high CPU utilization rate. If this is the case, tune the moderate number of threads and compare performance results.

- **Thread count greatly larger than the number of CPUs.** An excess amount of thread switching is probably taking place, adding overhead to the system. Decrease the number of threads and compare performance results.

Detecting stuck threads

Occasionally, a thread becomes *stuck* — that is, it no longer executes additional tasks. When a thread is stuck, it's wasting system resources. The server can continue as long as all threads have not entered a stuck state.

A thread can become stuck for many reasons. WebLogic Server automatically detects when a thread in an execute queue becomes stuck and gives the stuck threads a certain amount of time to continue. If the thread exceeds this amount of time, the thread is restarted.

To configure WebLogic Server thread detection behavior, follow these steps:

1. **Make sure that your server is running, and then log on to Administration Console.**

2. **Select your server.**

   On the left side of the screen, click the Servers folder, and then click your server. You now see your server's configuration page.

3. **Click the Tuning tab.**

   This tab was shown in Figure 17-1.

4. **Set the stuck thread properties.**

   In the Stuck Thread Max Time box, type the maximum amount of time before the thread is restarted. In the Stuck Thread Timer Interval box, type the time between the thread scans.

5. **Restart your server.**

   These changes take effect when your server is restarted.

JDBC Performance Settings

Most enterprise applications use the database and JDBC for their data access. Because of this, you can achieve great performance gains by simply setting up the JDBC performance settings properly.

JDBC connection pools

You should always use JDBC connection pools when accessing databases from server components such as EJBs. It's easy to set up connection pools using Administration Console. For more information on setting up a JDBC connection pool, see Chapter 12.

For each connection to a database, a certain amount of overhead is incurred. This can add up considerably if many connections are opened to the same database. A connection pool opens up multiple connections to a database, and the EJBs share this access.

You have the option of setting how many connections a pool allows. The pool can grow and shrink between the configured minimum and maximum values. In general, the best performance occurs when the connection pool has as many connections as there are concurrent client sessions.

Connection pool initial capacity

Connection pools have a defined initial capacity. This value represents the smallest number of connections that the pool can have.

If you set the connection pool initial capacity too high and WebLogic can't initialize that number of connections, the connection pool fails to start.

During development, you may want to set the pool initial capacity lower so that the server starts faster.

Pool maximum capacity

The pool maximum capacity specifies the maximum size that a connection pool can reach.

In production systems, the pool maximum capacity and the initial capacity are often set to the same number. This causes the server to create all connection objects immediately.

Caching prepared statements

The prepared statement object allows you to define SQL with parameter values. In this way, JDBC can compile the SQL statement once and use the object to execute the statement over and over. However, it's not always the same statement, because of the parameters you can specify. To create a prepared statement, you use the `PreparedStatement` class.

WebLogic caches these prepared statements so that they don't have to be recreated each time they're used. You can define the size of this cache of prepared statements. If you set the value too low, prepared statements are not cached. If you set the value too high, the system is processing needless overhead.

EJB Performance Settings

EJBs are a major component of WebLogic, and you can set many performance options for them. These settings are stored in the weblogic-ejb-jar.xml deployment file, which contains information specific to WebLogic Server. It contains also the descriptors that map available WebLogic Server resources to EJBs. WebLogic Server resources include security role names and data sources such as JDBC pools, JMS connection factories, and other deployed EJBs.

Like any other XML file, the weblogic-ejb-jar.xml file can be loaded with a regular text editor. To change parameters in the file, you use the editor, save the file, and then restart WebLogic Server.

Setting EJB pool size

For every stateless session bean class, WebLogic keeps a free pool for EJBs. The `max-beans-in-free-pool` element of the weblogic-ejb-jar.xml file specifies the size of this pool. The default is no limit, which means the pool is limited only by available memory.

You shouldn't change the value of the `max-beans-in-free-pool` parameter unless your program frequently creates session beans and then discards them. If this is the case, enlarge the free pool by 25 to 50 percent and see whether performance improves. If object creation represents a small fraction of your workload, increasing this parameter will not significantly improve performance. For database-intensive EJBs, do not change the value of this parameter.

Tuning `max-beans-in-free-pool` too high uses extra memory. Tuning it too low causes unnecessary object creation. If in doubt, leave it unchanged.

Allocating pool size for session and message beans

When an EJB is created, the session bean is given an identity. When the client program removes this bean, it's placed back in the free bean pool. When subsequent beans of the same type are created, the original bean is used, thus saving the overhead of recreating the bean. The `max-beans-in-free-pool` element, which controls the size of this pool, can improve performance if the same EJBs are frequently created and removed.

EJB instances are created as needed by the container for message processing. The `max-beans-in-pool` element establishes an absolute limit on the number of these instances created. WebLogic may override this setting according to available runtime resources.

In general, for the best performance when using stateless session and message beans, you should use the default setting for the `max-beans-in-free-pool` element. The default is optimized to allow you to run beans in parallel, using as many threads as possible. The only reason you would change this setting is to limit the number of beans running in parallel.

Allocating pool size for anonymous entity beans

Anonymous entity beans are beans without a primary key assigned to them. The `max-beans-in-free-pool` element controls the size of not only the free bean pool but also the pool of anonymous entity beans. If you're running many finders or home methods or creating lots of beans, you may want to tune the `max-beans-in-free-pool` element so that enough beans are available for use in the pool.

Tuning initial beans in the free pool

The `initial-beans-in-free-pool` element of the weblogic-ejb-jar.xml file specifies the number of stateless session bean instances in the free pool at startup. If you specify a value for `initial-beans-in-free-pool`, WebLogic Server populates the free pool with the specified number of bean instances. Populating the free pool ahead of time is a way to improve initial response time for the EJB, because initial requests for the bean can be satisfied without generating a new instance.

Setting EJB caching size

WebLogic Server allows you to set the number of active beans present in the EJB cache. The `max-beans-in-cache` element of the weblogic-ejb-jar.xml file specifies the maximum number of objects of this class that are allowed in memory. The value of this element sets the cache size for both stateful session and entity beans.

Starting WebLogic Server with Performance Options

WebLogic requires that you specify certain Java parameters when it starts. For simple startups, you can specify these parameters on the command line. However, WebLogic usually requires many parameters, so using a script makes more sense. (For more information about starting WebLogic, see Chapter 3.)

Two startup scripts are automatically provided when you install WebLogic. The Administration Server scripts are startWLS.sh (UNIX) and startWLS.cmd (Windows). These two scripts are in the WebLogic bin directory.

You can modify some of the default Java values in these scripts to fit your environment and applications. The important performance-tuning parameters in these files are the JAVA_HOME parameter and the Java heap size. Change the value of the JAVA_HOME variable to the location of your JDK. For example:

```
JAVA_HOME=C:\bea\jdk131_03
```

For even higher performance throughput, set the minimum Java heap size equal to the maximum heap size. For example:

```
"%JAVA_HOME%\bin\java" -hotspot -Xms512m -Xmx512m -classpath
        %CLASSPATH% -
```

Setting Your Java Compiler

JSP pages and servlets must be compiled on-the-fly, as they're needed by a WebLogic process. By default, the standard Java compiler is used. You can improve performance significantly by setting your server's Java compiler to one that's faster than Sun's javac. One common replacement is IBM's jikes:

```
http://oss.ibm.com/developerworks/opensource/jikes
```

Follow these steps to change your compiler:

1. **Make sure that your server is running, and log on to Administration Console.**

2. **Select your server.**

    Click the Servers folder, and then click your server.

 3. **Click the Compilers tab.**

 4. **In the Java Compiler box, type the full path to your compiler.**

 5. **Specify the library location.**

    In the Append to Classpath box, type the full path to the JRE `rt.jar` library. This allows you to access the runtime library from Java.

 6. **Click Apply.**

 7. **Restart your server.**

Now you know some of the software items that you can configure to make your application run faster. In addition to the software changes that you can make, you've seen how you can tune WebLogic at the server level.

Chapter 18

Implementing Security

● ●

● ●

Security is an important part of any web application. You've probably read some of the highly publicized cases of corporate computer systems compromised by hackers. Many more go unreported. In this chapter, you find out how to use some of the many features in WebLogic that help you enhance the security of your application.

Understanding WebLogic Security

WebLogic has many built-in features to enhance security, but you must be aware of them to properly defend your system. Many of these security features must be customized to suit your particular application. Security is not automatic; you must take steps to ensure that your system is secure.

WebLogic's security architecture is open and flexible. It delivers advantages to all levels of users and provides an advanced security design for application servers.

In this chapter, you examine some of the common security features of WebLogic. For information on features not covered here, refer to the online help included with WebLogic.

Secure Sockets Layer (SSL)

Secure Socket Layer (SSL) is one of the most common forms of web security. SSL is usually used through Hyper Text Transfer Protocol Secure (HTTPS). If you log on to almost any financial web site to check your account, for example, you'll see the URL change to one that begins with *https*. HTTPS and SSL provide the following advantages:

- ✓ Host verification
- ✓ Data encryption

HTTPS allows you to be sure that you're connecting to the intended host. If you enter the URL `https://www.weblogic.com`, for example, SSL ensures that you're using that site. A domain name such as `http://www.weblogic.com` is mapped to an IP address by domain name service (DNS). If a hacker tampers with the DNS, you could be taken to an IP address other than the one you were expecting. SSL ensures you're accessing the correct IP address, which ensures that you're accessing the correct server.

Data encryption is another valuable feature provided by SSL. If you log on to your bank's web site to view your account, for example, you must enter your user ID and password. Without SSL, this user ID and password would be transmitted, unencrypted, across the Internet. Your password and ID could be intercepted by a malicious user. SSL encrypts your password and user ID so that they're not visible to someone monitoring the packets between the user and web server.

Setting up SSL on WebLogic Server involves a number of steps. These steps are summarized here and explained in more detail in the next sections:

1. **Obtain an identity and a trust.**

   An *identity* is a private key and a digital certificate. The *trust* is a certificate issued to you by a trusted certificate authority (CA). Digital certificates, private keys, and trusted CA certificates can be obtained from the WebLogic Server kit, the Cert Gen utility, Sun Microsystem's keytool utility, or a reputable certificate authority such as Entrust or Verisign.

2. **Store the keys and certificates.**

   You must store the private keys, digital certificates, and trusted CA certificates in a location accessible by WebLogic. Digital certificates are stored in a file in the domain directory of WebLogic Server. Private keys and trusted CA certificates are stored in a keystore.

3. **Enable SSL on your server.**

   You must set SSL attributes for the server's identity and trust locations in WebLogic Server's Administration Console or in a server start script. The SSL attributes define the location of the private key, digital certificate, and trusted CA certificates.

Obtaining an identity

The first step in setting up SSL on WebLogic Server is obtaining a certificate from a certificate authority. This CA certificate, which contains your key, is used to ensure web visitors that you really are who you say you are. WebLogic includes a tool to help you generate a request form that can be used to obtain a certificate from a CA. To use this tool, follow these steps:

1. **Make sure that your server is running.**

   The server that you want to configure must be running. For a refresher on starting your server, refer to Chapter 3.

2. **Log on to Certificate Generator.**

   Certificate Generator is usually at `http://localhost:7001/ certificate`. You have to enter the administrator user ID and password. The screen shown in Figure 18-1 appears.

3. **Enter the required information.**

   Scroll down so that you can see the form for entering information about your web site. Figure 18-2 shows how I filled out the form for my web site.

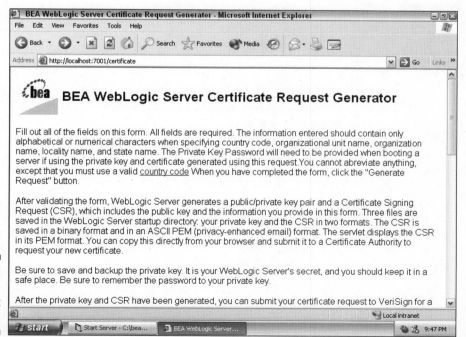

Figure 18-1:
Certificate
request
generator.

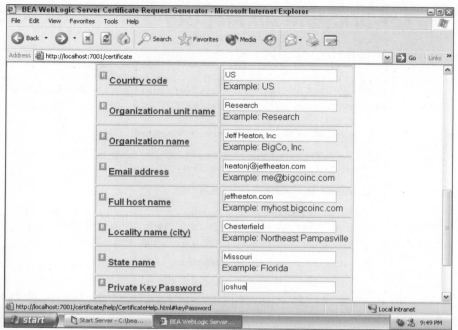

Figure 18-2:
Certificate
request
generator.

4. Click Generate to generate a certificate.

The screen shown in Figure 18-3 appears. This is the request certificate that you send to a certificate authority, such as Verisign.

After you obtain your certificate, you must store it into the keystore. This is explained in the next section.

Storing keys and certificates

Certificates must be stored in a *keystore*. The keystore is managed using the Java `keytool` command. If you've added the WebLogic `bin` directory to your path, you can access the `keytool` command from the command prompt. Some of the common tasks that you can perform with the `keytool` command are described next.

Figure 18-3:
Output
from the
certificate
request
generator.

Creating a keystore

The first thing you should do is create a new keystore for WebLogic's use. You need to do this only once. To create the keystore, use the following command:

```
keytool -genkey -keystore keystorename -storepass
        keystorepassword
```

Replace *keystorename* with the path and file name of the file you want to use as the keystore. The keystore also needs to have a password, which you should use in place of *keystorepassword*. You'll use that password to access the keystore.

Loading a private key

When you ran the certificate generator in the preceding section, one result was that a private key was generated in a file whose name ends in the .pem extension. This file should be added to the keystore using the following command line:

```
keytool -alias aliasforprivatekey -import -file
        privatekeyfile.pem -keypass privatekeypassword -
        keystore keystorename -storepass keystorepassword
```

To add the private key, you need to know the file name of the keystore (`keystorename`) and its password (`keystorepassword`). You also need the name of the file containing the private key (`privatekeyfile.pem`) and the password for that file (`privatekeypassword`). You also specify an alias (`aliasforprivatekey`) by which this private key will be known in the keystore.

When you're finished adding a private key to your keystore, copy the .pem file to a backup device (such as a floppy disk) and store it someplace safe. You'll need this file if your keystore becomes damaged.

Loading a trusted CA certificate

When a certificate is granted to you by a certificate authority, you need to load that certificate into the keystore. To do so, use this command line:

```
keytool -alias aliasfortrustedca -trustcacerts -import -file
        trustedcafilename.pem -keystore keystorename -
        storepass keystorepassword
```

Again, you use `keystorename` and `keystorepassword` to specify the key-store's location and password, respectively. You also need to specify an alias by which the certificate will be known in the keystore (`aliasfortrustedca`) and the path and file name of the certificate file (`trustedcafilename.pem`).

Displaying keystore contents

To display the complete contents of the keystore, use the following command:

```
keytool -list -keystore keystorename
```

Deleting a key

To delete a private key that you no longer need, use the following command. You delete a key by referring to its alias:

```
keytool -keystore keystorename -storepass keystorepassword -
        delete -alias aliasforprivatekey
```

You can't undo a delete operation. If you decide you still want to use the private key, you must add it to the keystore again. (This is one reason why you should store the .pem file for the private key on a floppy disk and put it in a safe place.)

Displaying help

If you need a short refresher on how to use keytool, use the following command:

```
keytool -help
```

Enabling SSL on your server

Now that you have obtained the needed certificates, you can enable SSL in WebLogic. Follow these steps:

1. **Make sure that your server is running.**

   The server that you would like to configure must be running. For a refresher on starting your server, refer to Chapter 3.

2. **Log on to Administration Console.**

   Administration Console is usually at `http://localhost:7001/console`. If you need a refresher on getting into the administration console, refer to Chapter 4.

3. **Select your server.**

   Click the Servers folder, and then click your server's name.

4. **Configure SSL.**

   Click the Keystores & SSL tab. The screen shown in Figure 18-4 appears. Provide the alias that you used for your certificate when you added it to your keystore.

5. **Change your keystore.**

   WebLogic uses a demo keystore by default. When you want to specify your own keystore, click the Change link in Figure 18-4 and configure the keystore.

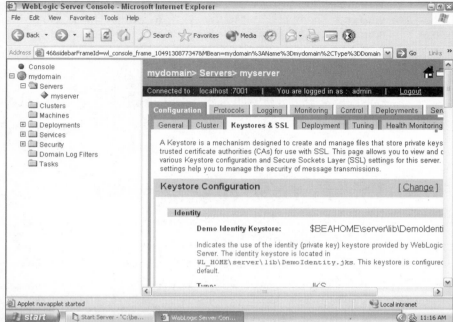

Figure 18-4:
Configure
SSL.

Introduction to Security Realms

WebLogic allows you to lock down certain resources of WebLogic called security realms. You can create users, groups, and roles to manage access to the following security realms:

- ✔ Administrative resources such as the WebLogic Server Administration Console
- ✔ Enterprise applications
- ✔ Component Object Model (COM) resources
- ✔ Enterprise Information System (EIS) resources
- ✔ Enterprise JavaBean (EJB) resources
- ✔ Java DataBase Connectivity (JDBC) resources
- ✔ Java Naming and Directory Interface (JNDI) resources
- ✔ Java Message Service (JMS) resources
- ✔ MBean resources

✔ Server resources related to WebLogic Server instances, or servers

✔ URL resources related to web applications

✔ Web services resources

You can control access to each of these resources by using Administration Console. You discover how to secure these resources later in the chapter. Next, you find out how to create the different entities that inhabit security realms.

Users

Users are the most basic type of entity that can be authenticated in a security realm. A user is not necessarily a person. User are typically one of the following:

✔ A developer or an administrator

✔ An application end user

✔ A client application

✔ Other instances of WebLogic Server

When a user wants to access a specific resource, the user must be authenticated in one of two ways:

✔ Using a password

✔ Using a digital certificate

Just like groups, users must have unique names. Further, a user and a group may not have the same name.

Follow these steps to create a user:

1. **Make sure that your server is running, and log on to Administration Console.**

2. **Select the Users folder.**

   Click the following folders: mydomain, Security, Realms, myrealm, and then Users. The screen shown in Figure 18-5 appears, listing all current users.

3. **Click the <u>Configure a new User</u> link.**

   The screen shown in Figure 18-6 appears.

Figure 18-5:
Realm users.

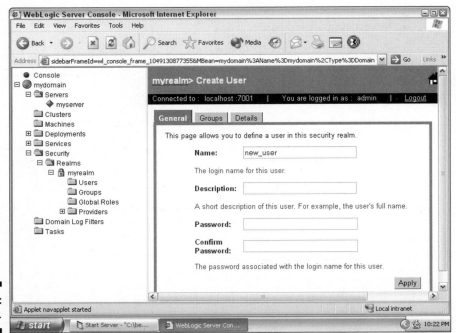

Figure 18-6:
A new user.

4. **Create the user.**

   Type a name and password for the user. (You must type the password twice: once in the Password box and once in the Confirm Password box.) Then click Apply.

5. **Assign the user to one or more groups.**

   Click the Groups tab. The screen shown Figure 18-7 appears. Assign the user to whatever groups you want. Then click Apply.

Groups

A group is another entity used in a domain. A *group* is made up of users that have something in common. These users usually share a common level of access. This allows the WebLogic administrator to quickly assign users to the correct groups. It's much more efficient to manage a large number of users through the use of a group.

Just like users, a group must have a unique name. Further, a user and a group can't have the same name.

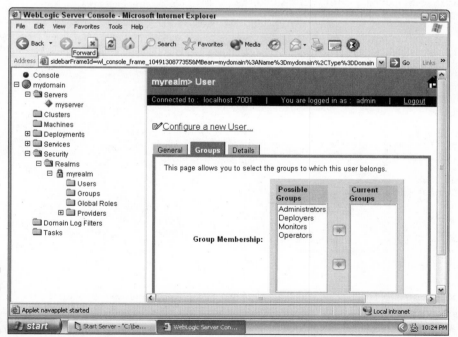

Figure 18-7:
Assign
groups.

Groups enable you to quickly configure settings for many users.

To create a new group, follow these steps:

1. **Make sure that your server is running, and log on to Administration Console.**

2. **Select the Groups folder.**

   Click the following folders: mydomain, Security, Realms, myrealm, and then Groups. The screen shown in Figure 18-8 appears, listing all current groups.

3. **Click the <u>Configure a new Group</u> link.**

   The screen shown in Figure 18-9 appears.

4. **Create a group.**

   Type a name for the group, and then click Apply.

5. **Assign other groups to the group.**

   Click the Membership tab. The screen shown in Figure 18-10 appears. Assign another group or groups to this group. For example, if you want everyone in this group to be an administrator, assign the Administrators group to the Current Groups list.

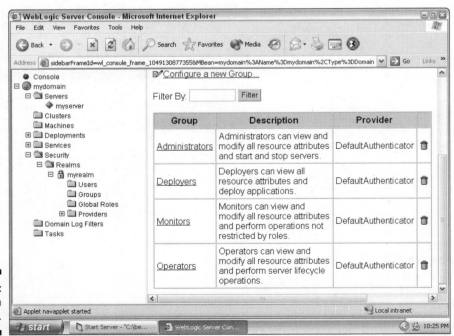

Figure 18-8: Realm groups.

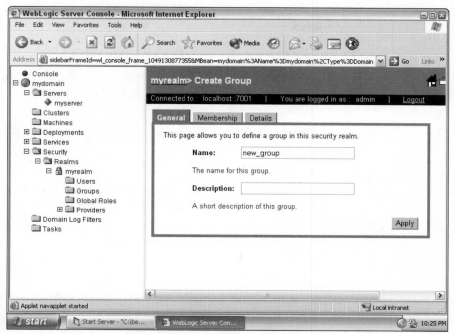

Figure 18-9:
A new
group.

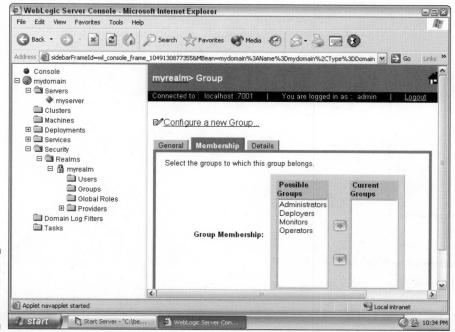

Figure 18-10:
Assigning
users to the
groups.

Security roles

Security roles grant privileges to users and groups based on specific conditions. Like groups, security roles allow users to be grouped. Unlike groups, however, security roles are calculated dynamically, as the server runs.

To create a security role, follow these steps:

1. **Make sure that your server is running, and log on to Administration Console.**

2. **Select the Global Roles folder.**

   Click the following folders: mydomain, Security, Realms, myrealm, and then Global Roles. The screen shown in Figure 18-11 appears, displaying all current roles.

3. **Click the <u>Configure a new Global Role</u> link.**

   The screen shown in Figure 18-12 appears.

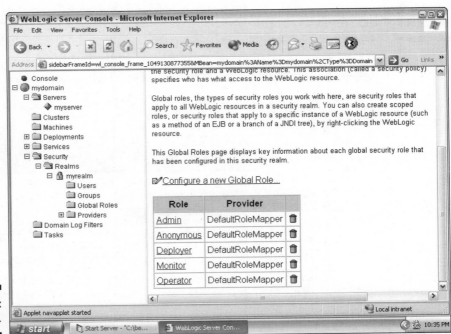

Figure 18-11:
Realm roles.

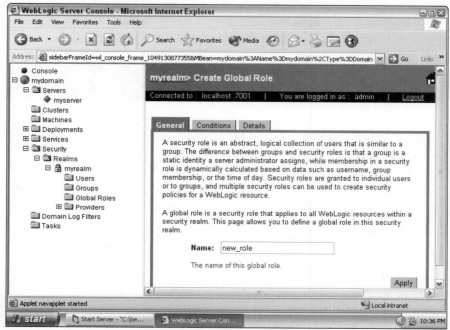

4. Create a role.

Type a name for the role, and then click Apply.

5. Create conditions.

Click the Conditions tab. The screen shown in Figure 18-13 appears. Assign any of the following conditions, and then click Add:

- **User name of the caller.** You can require that the user's name is a certain value. If you select this option, you're prompted for the user name that you want to compare against.

- **Caller is a member of the group.** You can require that the user be a member of a certain group. If you select this option, you're prompted for the group name that you want to compare against.

- **Hours of access are between.** You can specify a range of time during which the system can be accessed. If you select this option, you're prompted for the time range.

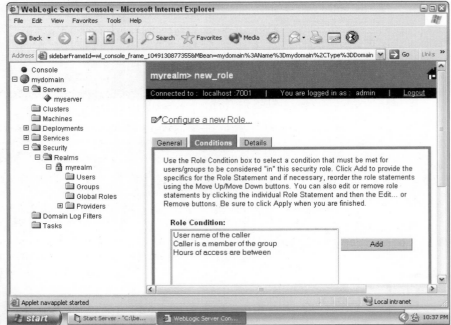

Figure 18-13:
Conditions.

Security policies

Security policies are the connection between WebLogic resources and users, roles, and groups. Using security policies, you can define which resources are available to which users, and under what conditions.

Security policies, introduced in WebLogic Server 7.0, replaced access control lists (ACLs), a feature in WebLogic Server 6.x.

Security policies are not configured from one central location in Administration Console. Rather, you can right-click nearly any resource in the Administration Console tree and set up a policy for it.

To create a security policy, follow these steps:

1. **Make sure that your server is running, and log on to Administration Console.**

2. **Select the resource for which you want to set a policy.**

   To follow along with the example, select the EJB Modules folder. To do so, click the following folders: mydomain, Deployments, and then EJB Modules.

3. Define a policy.

Right-click EJB Modules, and choose Define Security Policy. The screen shown in Figure 18-14 appears. Choose one or more of the following policies and then click the Add button:

- **User name of the caller.** Allows you to require that the user's name is a certain value. If you select this option, you're prompted for the user name that you want to compare against.

- **Caller is a member of the group.** Allows you to require that the user be a member of a certain group. If you select this option, you're prompted for the group name that you want to compare against.

- **Caller is granted the role.** Allows you to specify a role that the caller must match to be able to access the specified resource. If you select this option, you're prompted for the role that you want to compare against.

- **Hours of access are between.** Allows you to specify a range of time that the system can be accessed. If you select this option, you're prompted for the time range during which this resource will function.

For the user to be able to access the resource, all specified conditions must be met.

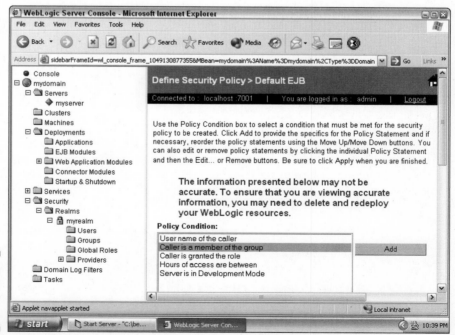

Figure 18-14: Define a security role.

You've examined how to define a policy for a web resource. You can also modify the policy of nearly every folder in the Deployments folder.

As you can see from this chapter, WebLogic provides a number of security features. You saw how SSL can make transmissions to and from the server more secure. You also saw how realms can control how WebLogic resources are accessed.

Part VI
The Part of Tens

The 5th Wave   By Rich Tennant

Now maybe these folks have a decent disaster recovery plan and maybe they don't...

DANGER
WILD RHINOCEROS

In this part . . .

*O*ver time, you'll discover many techniques pertaining to WebLogic and programming in general. Here, I pass along some of these techniques that I've found while working with WebLogic. I provide ten suggestions for developers and administrators as well as ten suggestions to follow before going live with your application.

Chapter 19

Ten Best Practices for Developers

As a WebLogic developer, it's important to know how to structure your applications and development environment. You must also know how to reach out to the WebLogic community when you run into problems. In this chapter, I discuss these recommendations and other information that has helped me over the years as a developer.

Keep Adequate Documentation

Documentation is an important part of any application. As a developer, you should do your part to ensure that your application is properly documented. Documentation falls into several categories:

✓ **Program code documentation.** The most obvious form of documentation consists of the comments in the source code. Javadoc is a good way to provide this documentation.

✔ **Developer handbook.** A basic but often overlooked use for documentation is bringing new programmers up to speed. On mature applications, developers' computers often contain a mix of files used as the application was developed. This environment can be difficult for a new developer to recreate. The developer's handbook describes the process needed to set up the development environment on a new machine.

✔ **Program specification.** Changes to the specifications of your application must be communicated to all who are involved in these changes.

✔ **End user documentation.** This is the documentation that your users refer to for information on how to use your system. As features are added to the system and existing features changed, make sure that you update the user documentation.

By keeping all forms of documentation properly maintained, developers and users can stay current with the application.

Use Usenet

One of the greatest benefits of the Internet is the sense of global community. And no single portion of the Internet embodies this more than Usenet, which consists of a large collection of messages posted by Internet users on a variety of topics.

You can access Usenet in several ways. You can install client programs that download and filter Usenet postings for you. You can also use web-based portals. One of the most common web portals is Google, at `http://groups.google.com`.

Don't Over-Engineer

WebLogic provides you with a wealth of technologies. EJBs allow you to distribute your processing tasks and skip writing database caching code. Web services allow you to make your application available over a standard SOAP interface. XML allows you to design standard content structures for your data.

However, you should avoid the temptation to use a technology just because WebLogic makes it available. For example, web services have a specific purpose. They enable you to expose your application to other applications that must use it across the Internet. In general, web services shouldn't be used internally by your application. I came across an application that used web services for all communication between the back-end EJB components and the front-end JSP pages. This resulted in many web service calls for each displayed page, a slow process that led to bottlenecks and an overall poor site.

Set Up Development Environments

WebLogic allows you to create multiple servers that run from the same machine. This provides a convenient way to provide several development environments, such as the following:

- ✔ **Development.** The development environment is where developers test their code. This allows developers to test their code in a controlled environment. Stable versions on the development server are usually rolled over to the test server.

- ✔ **Test.** Your project team will likely consist of quality assurance (QA) people who test the software and report new bugs. QA people shouldn't be testing from your development server because the server is too volatile. Rather, you should roll out a stable version from your development server to the test server. This version can then be tested by your QA staff.

- ✔ **Demo.** You'll have to demo your software, either to clients to show the progress of the system you're creating, or to internal users who will soon be using your system. If you don't create a demo server and a developer destabilizes your development server, your demo is shot.

- ✔ **Documentation.** It's likely that a group of people will be creating the documentation for your application. They'll be logging on to the server and taking screen shots and performing other activities related to the end-user documentation. It is important to give your tech writers a stable environment from which to develop their documentation.

- ✔ **Beta.** When you think that your application is ready for production, have your end users test the software one final time before it's rolled out to production. This process is called *end user acceptance testing*. It's a good idea to perform this testing from a special beta server.

- ✔ **Production.** The production version of your program is the one that's used by end users. It's up to your server administrators to make sure that the production server stays available to them. This will be the last stop that any version of your software is rolled to.

It's not necessary to set up all these environments on different machines. Several of these environments can be combined on a single machine.

Know What You're Developing

As a developer, you should understand the problem you're trying to solve. This may seem obvious, but developers on large applications can easily lose sight of the goal for several reasons:

- ✔ Unclear program specifications
- ✔ Developers who are aware of only their own local areas of the program
- ✔ Poor access to business users who understand the specifications

Understand the Tools

Many tools are available to make the developer's life easier. Unfortunately, you can spend a lot of time learning to use these tools before you realize any gain in programming time. In effect, your time to learn a tool is an investment. A developer should at least have the following tools:

- ✔ A text file editor
- ✔ An integrated development environment (IDE) that supports debugging
- ✔ A build tool, such as ANT
- ✔ A source code beautifier
- ✔ WebLogic Resource Workshop
- ✔ Version control

Create Modular, Decoupled Systems

A large application will have many classes and intertwined systems. Creating a system comprised of many modules has several advantages:

- ✔ Common modules can be reused.
- ✔ The program is easier to understand because large problems are broken into many smaller problems.
- ✔ Different programmers can be working on different modules without interfering with each other.

As the system grows, specific modules will move from active development to maintenance mode. Make sure that these modules are constructed in such a way that ongoing development doesn't cause errors to occur in previously working code. Such errors are called regression errors.

Be Mindful of Security

The media is filled with reports of people exploiting security faults in software. As you design and implement your application, you must be mindful of security. Security faults can creep into your system in many ways:

- ✔ Taking advantage of unvalidated parameters
- ✔ URL tampering
- ✔ Buffer overruns
- ✔ Injecting commands into parameters that may make their way to SQL
- ✔ Exploiting known security flaws in the operating system or server software

To cover all of these is beyond the scope of this chapter. However, one common security issue for web applications is tampering with the URL. Consider a program that allows users to view information about their bank accounts. As soon as users log on, they're shown a list of all their accounts. They can then click one account and get detailed information about it. The program was implemented to redirect the user to a page named display-account.jsp?number=201, which displays account 201. But what if the user doesn't own account 201? You may think that you're safe because the system provides hyperlinks only to accounts that the user owns. However, the user could just edit the URL line to display, for example, account number 202. If the web application doesn't check ownership on the account, someone else's account information would now be available to the unauthorized user. This same type of exploit can be used against hidden form variables.

Tools can scan for various security deficiencies in a web server. For example, an open source scanner called Web Scarab can automate such checking. You can get this tool from the Open Web Application Security Project at http://www.owasp.org.

Many security flaws are the result of not having the latest patches for your operating system or server software. Make sure that you have the most current patches.

Test Your Software

As a developer, you should always test your modules as well as you can before they're integrated with the other modules. This is called *unit testing*. When you first create a module, you should do all unit testing by hand.

When you're satisfied with the results of the unit test, you're ready to integrate your module with those developed by others. This process is called *integration testing*. Integration testing involves teamwork with other developers as your components are put together for the first time.

In addition to testing performed by the developers, there will be testing performed by QA people and end users. As these users test your software, they'll find bugs. If you have a number of QA people and developers, a bug-tracking tool can be handy. In addition, bug-tracking tools allow notes to be attached to individual bugs. When developers or users find a bug, they can document the resolution. This is important because not all bugs are a result of programming errors.

When the system is almost ready to be run from the production server, you should perform *end user acceptance testing*. This gives end users one final chance to test the system before it is rolled into production.

Manage Your Build Process

The build process is one of the most important aspects of software development. The build process is what creates compiled files that will be run by WebLogic Server. The most common build method is to use operating system scripts to execute the commands necessary to build your application.

Most new Java projects, including WebLogic, use Apache Ant, a tool that allows you to create XML script files that control how your application is built. Ant provides many features, including the following:

- Compiles Java files
- Creates and removes directories
- Copies files
- Converts text files between UNIX and Windows formats
- Archives files into JARs

Another big advantage to ANT is that WebLogic uses it for many command-line utilities, such as those that create the files necessary for web services. Because of this, it's a great advantage to be able to call these WebLogic utilities from your own ANT build script.

Chapter 20

Ten Tips for Administrators

A WebLogic administrator's job has many facets. And as you administer systems, you gain experience of what works and what doesn't work. In this chapter, I provide some tips for WebLogic administration that I've found useful.

Document Procedures

As a WebLogic administrator, you'll follow many procedures, including tasks such as

- ✔ Restarting the server
- ✔ Shutting down the server for routine maintenance
- ✔ Deploying new versions of WebLogic
- ✔ Backing up the server
- ✔ Installing the latest patches
- ✔ Creating WebLogic resources such as data sources

You should have written instructions for each of these procedures. This enables you to follow the same procedure each time, ensuring consistency.

Written procedures also enable your company to perform these operations when you're away. In addition, if you take a new position in the company or with a new firm, having written procedures enables you to fulfill your responsibility to transfer knowledge to the new administrator.

Define a Service Level Agreement

A service level agreement (SLA) helps to define what end users expect from your server in terms of reliability. Most users expect that a system will be up and running 24 hours a day, 7 days a week. Such a schedule is simply not possible. Many events will cause your system to be down for a period of time. For example:

- Dealing with hardware failures
- Routine updates
- Installing new versions of WebLogic or patches to the existing version
- Monitoring for acceptable performance
- Rebooting your server

The service level agreement is the contract between you and the users that your system supports. This contract should specify the amount of time that your system will be allowed to be down through the year.

In addition to defining maintenance periods, a properly written service level agreement should also specify the following:

- When maintenance will be performed
- How many minutes of unexpected outage are allowed per year
- How soon the system must return after an unexpected outage
- How often backups will be performed
- The overall percent of time that the server should be up

Set Up On-Call Procedures

At some point, the system will go down unexpectedly. When an unexpected outage occurs, you and your staff must be ready to deal with it. The outage might be something that the administrator can handle or something related to the software. If the outage is caused by a software error, a developer will need to get involved in the solution. Additionally, these outages may occur outside regular business hours. This is especially true if you work for a multi-national corporation.

Plan for Growth

When your system is first deployed, you may not be thinking about growth. But you should have a plan when your current system is outgrown. In general, you have two choices when your system can no longer handle the amount of processing required:

- Upgrade your server to a faster machine.
- Add additional servers to your cluster.

Perhaps one of the simplest ways to handle more requests is to upgrade to a faster machine. This may mean the purchase of a new server or simply adding another processor to your current server. When you upgrade to a faster machine, you must make sure that your server is properly copied across the network to the new machine. All configuration settings and installed packages should be copied to the new machine.

If you're running a cluster of servers, you can simply add another server. If you're not running a cluster of servers and your request volume is becoming too high, you should consider using a cluster of servers. Adding another server to the cluster causes WebLogic to have another server that can share some of the workload. This allows the application as a whole to be able to accept more connections.

Monitor Your Servers

Monitoring your sever is an important task that every WebLogic administrator must deal with. You'll monitor whether your server is up as well as the server load.

Monitoring server availability makes sure that your server is up and properly responding. You can choose from many software packages for monitoring servers. When the software detects that your server is no longer accessible, an e-mail message is sent to the administrator.

WebLogic gives you many tools to monitor the load placed on a server. These tools are accessible from Administrative Console. For more information on using the monitoring tools in Administrative Console, refer to Chapter 4.

Back Up Your Servers

Backing up data is an important part of any administrator's job. In this section, I describe backing up WebLogic. You will need to back up the part of your web application that changes. This is the SQL database. If this data is already being backed up by a database administrator, you don't need to worry about backing up application data.

If you lose the hard drive on your WebLogic server, you'll be expected to reinstall everything and get the server running again. If your application was packaged as a WAR file, you can quickly get your application back up by redeploying the WAR file.

Keep Your Systems Secure

Security has become an increasingly important topic. As an administrator, you must keep your system secure. This is accomplished through passwords, firewalls, and other measures.

When you create your server, you are allowed to create an administrative user. You should ensure that you enter a hard-to-guess password for your user. Never set the password to the same value as the user ID. The administrative user's password allows you to access Administrative Console, from which a person can perform any administrative task. Because of this, keep your password secure.

Passwords should never be words contained in the dictionary. If your password does exist in the dictionary, your account is vulnerable to a number of cracking systems. A good method for choosing passwords is to use a dictionary word with a few digits on the end.

You should make sure that your database server and application server are behind a firewall. You then expose port 80 of your web server to the outside world. Hackers will be able to access the database only through the vulnerabilities of the application on the web server — they won't be able to connect directly to the database.

Understand Log Files

When something does go wrong, the log files should be one of the first places that you check. Log files should contain the full stack trace for any exceptions thrown, so you can quickly determine which module caused the exception.

When you do find an error in a log file, you can often find a solution at `groups.google.com`. Simply paste the error message in the input box.

Log files contain a large amount of information, such as

- Exceptions that were thrown
- Beans that failed to deploy
- Other resources that failed to deploy

These errors can be tracked down by a developer. Copy the log information that contains the exception and send it to the developer. Make sure that you include the stack trace, which can help the developer. A *stack trace* looks like this:

```
at weblogic.jdbc.common.internal.JdbcInfo.validateConnectionPool
(JdbcInfo.java:127)
at weblogic.jdbc.common.internal.JdbcInfo.startDataSource(JdbcInfo.java:260)
at weblogic.jdbc.common.internal.JDBCService.addDeployment
(JDBCService.java:293)
at weblogic.jdbc.common.internal.JDBCService.addDeployment
(JDBCService.java:270)
at weblogic.management.mbeans.custom.DeploymentTarget.addDeployment
(DeploymentTarget.java:375)
at weblogic.management.mbeans.custom.DeploymentTarget.addDeployment
(DeploymentTarget.java:154)
```

Test with Clusters

If your system was developed on a single machine, it may not function with a cluster. Clustering has issues that don't exist with a single machine applications. Clustering is discussed in Chapter 16.

If you think you'll be using a cluster to improve access, you should be developing with two machines. Clusters provide many benefits, such as

- **Performance.** You'll have more than one server that can handle a request.
- **Reliability.** If one server fails, other servers can pick up for that server.

If you'd like to ensure that your system stays compatible with clustering, test using at least two computers.

Keep WebLogic Up-to-Date

You should be aware of any patches as well as the current version of WebLogic. Patches correct errors and security issues that occur between major releases of WebLogic. You should download and install patches for WebLogic as well as other system components. This is particularly true of the Windows operating system, which has many security patches available.

When the security of a system is compromised, it's often because the administrator didn't have the most up-to-date patch installed.

Upgrading to the current version of WebLogic is much less critical than applying operating system and WebLogic patches. Sometimes it takes a redesign of the source code to get the current version to work properly. After the initial release of a new version, many companies prefer to wait until the release has been proven. When you decide to upgrade to the latest version of WebLogic, you should do so on a test server. Then, after you verify that the test server is performing well, you can put the new version onto your production system.

Chapter 21

Ten Tasks Before Going Live

Sooner or later, you'll determine that your system is ready to enter production. The process by which you take your system into production is referred to as *going live*. This process can be stressful to users, administrators, and programmers alike. To help minimize that stress, follow the ten tips in this chapter before you go live.

Test Your System

It may sound obvious, but you should test your system before it rolls into production. By *testing*, I don't mean that the developers haven't seen the system crash in awhile. I mean real solid testing that mimics how your application will be used.

Because you can't test for everything, you must provide a way for problems to be resolved. Ask yourself the following:

➜ Have you provided a support e-mail for users to report bugs?

➜ Are errors and exceptions logged and dealt with?

➜ What do you do with reported bugs? Are they tracked?

➜ Are you monitoring your system? How quickly would you know about a problem?

Ask your QA people to produce a test script for your system. A test-scripting program also allows you to retest the entire system quickly. This can be useful when a programmer submits a change and you need to analyze the change's effect on the system.

Conduct a Stress Test

A system that's going live will face many stresses that a development system never encountered. For example, when your system was being developed, WebLogic Server probably handled requests from only the developers. When the system goes live, large numbers of users may access the system. These additional users will place stress on WebLogic Server.

Every system has a breaking point, where it can handle no more users. If your site's initial users push the server beyond its limits, it will go down. The first step in conducting a stress test is to try to estimate how many users your system will likely have at a time. If the system is a replacement, you can use statistics from the previous system. If this is a new system, you'll have to estimate as best you can.

After you estimate the amount of traffic that your site will likely see, test that your site is up to the challenge. Testing tools simulate the load of many simultaneous users and tell you the breaking point of your server. Here are a few examples:

➜ WebStone at `www.mindcraft.com/webstone/`

➜ Paessler at `www.paessler.com/`

➜ Web Performance at `www.webperformanceinc.com/`

Don't conduct a stress test just to prove that your current system can handle the expected amount of traffic. Stress tests should determine the breaking point of your server. After you know this breaking point, you can plan accordingly as you approach that point.

Set Up a Parallel Environment

Give your users a way back as you roll out the new production system. The most common way of doing this is a parallel system deployment. That is, you keep the old system up for some specific amount of time, while the users adjust to the new system — and while bugs are fixed. A parallel rollout gives you the following benefits:

- ✔ Minimizes interruption to business processes
- ✔ Allows you time to fix initial bugs in the new system
- ✔ Uses the old system to verify the results of the new system

You should specify the amount of time that you will leave the old system up. If that amount of time is too long, users might delay adopting the new system.

Perform Fault Testing

Most likely, your new server has been designed to withstand some degree of hardware failure. Such systems include the following:

- ✔ A battery backup power supply in the event of a power failure
- ✔ A generator in the event of an extended power failure
- ✔ Redundant web, application, and database servers
- ✔ Co-location in the event of failure of the entire main facility
- ✔ Redundant Internet connections

You should have documented procedures that test the performance of each system. Whichever of these systems you have in place, make sure that they're functioning. You don't want to test such systems when the first hardware or power outage occurs.

Excessive testing on some uninterruptible power supply (UPS) systems can greatly shorten the battery life — and replacement batteries can be expensive. Check with your vendor to determine the recommended frequency of testing.

Set Up a Bug Tracking System

No system is perfect. Your system will have bugs, and you should have a procedure for tracking them. Many bug-tracking systems are available, such as the following:

✔ Bug Collector Pro at `www.nesbitt.com`

✔ FogBugz at `www.fogcreek.com/FogBUGZ/`

✔ Aardvark at `www.red-gate.com/bug_tracking.htm`

These systems often manage the entire life of a bug, as follows:

1. The bug is reported.
2. The bug is assigned to a developer.
3. The developer corrects the bug.
4. The bug is QA tested.
5. The bug issue is closed.

Another important consideration when tracking bugs is to separate issues into two categories: true bugs and suggestions for improvement. A *bug* occurs when the program does not perform as it was designed. A suggestion for improvement, also known as a feature request, is something beyond the original scope of the program.

Programmers find it daunting when they have to treat everything as a bug, which implies that they did something wrong. Additional features, although perhaps just as pressing as bugs, should be recognized as a shortcoming in the requirement-gathering phase.

Some bug-collection packages offer Web access, which allows your users to report bugs from a simple browser. This can be a big help because most bug-collection packages require users to be on the same network.

Formulate a Disaster Recovery Plan

Any number of issues can affect your main data center, such as a backed-up sewer that floods your computer room or a nearby transformer that explodes and leaves you without power for nearly a day. Disaster recovery means that your application could continue, even after a total loss of your main facility. You should assume that all computer systems and data from that site are gone. You should also assume that you won't be able to reach employees from the main site for some time.

The most common solution to disaster recovery is *co-location,* whereby you set up a separate data center. Often, a vendor company will lease computer equipment to get your system up and running from a remote location.

Disaster recovery must be tested just like any other business process. You don't want to wait until your first disaster to discover that your disaster recovery plan doesn't work.

Choose Your Date

You should choose a go-live date well in advance. Those who will be using the system should know this date, so that they can plan accordingly. Try not to schedule the go-live date at a busy time of the year. Coordinate the go-live date so that it occurs on the first day of a quarter or the first day of the month, depending on how your company does its accounting.

Keep the Lines of Communication Open

After your system goes live, keep in contact with the users of your system. Being able to quickly contact someone who is knowledgeable about the new program will make users feel much better about the new system. And being in contact with users will give you valuable feedback about the program and what can be improved.

Be Ready for Anything

Be ready for long hours during the first few weeks when you go live. Never forget Murphy's law: Whatever can go wrong, will go wrong — and at the worst possible time. Although you can't anticipate every problem that can occur after you go live, you should have procedures in place for dealing with most problems.

Be Ready with Support

You will never be totally ready to go live. There is always more testing or more preparation to do. Eventually, however, the go-live date will arrive and users will begin using your system. Now is the time to provide support to the users. Collect and correct bugs. Explain features of the system that users don't understand — many times, users mistake unknown functions as bugs.

Index

• X •

FOR DUMMIES®

The easy way to get more done and have more fun

PERSONAL FINANCE

0-7645-5231-7

0-7645-2431-3

0-7645-5331-3

Also available:

Estate Planning For Dummies
(0-7645-5501-4)
401(k)s For Dummies
(0-7645-5468-9)
Frugal Living For Dummies
(0-7645-5403-4)
Microsoft Money "X" For
Dummies
(0-7645-1689-2)
Mutual Funds For Dummies
(0-7645-5329-1)

Personal Bankruptcy For
Dummies
(0-7645-5498-0)
Quicken "X" For Dummies
(0-7645-1666-3)
Stock Investing For Dummies
(0-7645-5411-5)
Taxes For Dummies 2003
(0-7645-5475-1)

BUSINESS & CAREERS

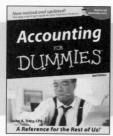

0-7645-5314-3

0-7645-5307-0

0-7645-5471-9

Also available:

Business Plans Kit For
Dummies
(0-7645-5365-8)
Consulting For Dummies
(0-7645-5034-9)
Cool Careers For Dummies
(0-7645-5345-3)
Human Resources Kit For
Dummies
(0-7645-5131-0)
Managing For Dummies
(1-5688-4858-7)

QuickBooks All-in-One Desk
Reference For Dummies
(0-7645-1963-8)
Selling For Dummies
(0-7645-5363-1)
Small Business Kit For
Dummies
(0-7645-5093-4)
Starting an eBay Business For
Dummies
(0-7645-1547-0)

HEALTH, SPORTS & FITNESS

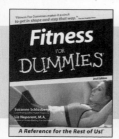

0-7645-5167-1

0-7645-5146-9

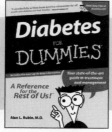

0-7645-5154-X

Also available:

Controlling Cholesterol For
Dummies
(0-7645-5440-9)
Dieting For Dummies
(0-7645-5126-4)
High Blood Pressure For
Dummies
(0-7645-5424-7)
Martial Arts For Dummies
(0-7645-5358-5)
Menopause For Dummies
(0-7645-5458-1)

Nutrition For Dummies
(0-7645-5180-9)
Power Yoga For Dummies
(0-7645-5342-9)
Thyroid For Dummies
(0-7645-5385-2)
Weight Training For Dummies
(0-7645-5168-X)
Yoga For Dummies
(0-7645-5117-5)

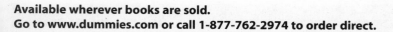

FOR DUMMIES®

A world of resources to help you grow

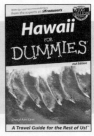

FOR DUMMIES

Plain-English solutions for everyday challenges

COMPUTER BASICS

0-7645-0838-5

0-7645-1663-9

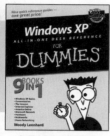
0-7645-1548-9

Also available:

PCs All-in-One Desk Reference For Dummies (0-7645-0791-5)

Pocket PC For Dummies (0-7645-1640-X)

Treo and Visor For Dummies (0-7645-1673-6)

Troubleshooting Your PC For Dummies (0-7645-1669-8)

Upgrading & Fixing PCs For Dummies (0-7645-1665-5)

Windows XP For Dummies (0-7645-0893-8)

Windows XP For Dummies Quick Reference (0-7645-0897-0)

BUSINESS SOFTWARE

0-7645-0822-9

0-7645-0839-3

0-7645-0819-9

Also available:

Excel Data Analysis For Dummies (0-7645-1661-2)

Excel 2002 All-in-One Desk Reference For Dummies (0-7645-1794-5)

Excel 2002 For Dummies Quick Reference (0-7645-0829-6)

GoldMine "X" For Dummies (0-7645-0845-8)

Microsoft CRM For Dummies (0-7645-1698-1)

Microsoft Project 2002 For Dummies (0-7645-1628-0)

Office XP For Dummies (0-7645-0830-X)

Outlook 2002 For Dummies (0-7645-0828-8)

Get smart! Visit www.dummies.com

- **Find listings of even more *For Dummies* titles**
- **Browse online articles**
- **Sign up for Dummies eTips™**
- **Check out *For Dummies* fitness videos and other products**
- **Order from our online bookstore**

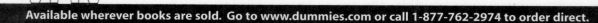

Available wherever books are sold. Go to www.dummies.com or call 1-877-762-2974 to order direct.

FOR DUMMIES®

Helping you expand your horizons and realize your potential

INTERNET

0-7645-0894-6

0-7645-1659-0

0-7645-1642-6

DIGITAL MEDIA

0-7645-1664-7

0-7645-1675-2

0-7645-0806-7

GRAPHICS

0-7645-0817-2

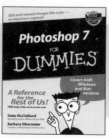

0-7645-1651-5

0-7645-0895-4

FOR DUMMIES®

The advice and explanations you need to succeed

SELF-HELP, SPIRITUALITY & RELIGION

Sex FOR DUMMIES
0-7645-5302-X

Parenting FOR DUMMIES
0-7645-5418-2

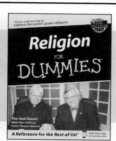
Religion FOR DUMMIES
0-7645-5264-3

Also available:

The Bible For Dummies
(0-7645-5296-1)

Buddhism For Dummies
(0-7645-5359-3)

Christian Prayer For Dummies
(0-7645-5500-6)

Dating For Dummies
(0-7645-5072-1)

Judaism For Dummies
(0-7645-5299-6)

Potty Training For Dummies
(0-7645-5417-4)

Pregnancy For Dummies
(0-7645-5074-8)

Rekindling Romance For Dummies
(0-7645-5303-8)

Spirituality For Dummies
(0-7645-5298-8)

Weddings For Dummies
(0-7645-5055-1)

PETS

Puppies FOR DUMMIES
0-7645-5255-4

Dog Training FOR DUMMIES
0-7645-5286-4

Cats FOR DUMMIES
0-7645-5275-9

Also available:

Labrador Retrievers For Dummies
(0-7645-5281-3)

Aquariums For Dummies
(0-7645-5156-6)

Birds For Dummies
(0-7645-5139-6)

Dogs For Dummies
(0-7645-5274-0)

Ferrets For Dummies
(0-7645-5259-7)

German Shepherds For Dummies
(0-7645-5280-5)

Golden Retrievers For Dummies
(0-7645-5267-8)

Horses For Dummies
(0-7645-5138-8)

Jack Russell Terriers For Dummies
(0-7645-5268-6)

Puppies Raising & Training Diary For Dummies
(0-7645-0876-8)

EDUCATION & TEST PREPARATION

Spanish FOR DUMMIES
0-7645-5194-9

Algebra FOR DUMMIES
0-7645-5325-9

The ACT FOR DUMMIES
0-7645-5210-4

Also available:

Chemistry For Dummies
(0-7645-5430-1)

English Grammar For Dummies
(0-7645-5322-4)

French For Dummies
(0-7645-5193-0)

The GMAT For Dummies
(0-7645-5251-1)

Inglés Para Dummies
(0-7645-5427-1)

Italian For Dummies
(0-7645-5196-5)

Research Papers For Dummies
(0-7645-5426-3)

The SAT I For Dummies
(0-7645-5472-7)

U.S. History For Dummies
(0-7645-5249-X)

World History For Dummies
(0-7645-5242-2)

FOR DUMMIES®

We take the mystery out of complicated subjects

WEB DEVELOPMENT

0-7645-1643-4

0-7645-0723-0

Dreamweaver MX

0-7645-1630-2

PROGRAMMING & DATABASES

0-7645-0746-X

0-7645-1657-4

0-7645-0818-0

LINUX, NETWORKING & CERTIFICATION

0-7645-1545-4

0-7645-0772-9

0-7645-0812-1